madel

DRINK OF THE STREAM

DRINK OF THE STREAM

STREAM

Prayers of Carmelites

Compiled by Penny Hickey, O.C.D.S.

IGNATIUS PRESS   SAN FRANCISCO

Nihil obstat: Harrisburg, Pennsylvania, January 25, 2001,
Reverend Edward C. Malesic, J.C.L., Censor Librorum

Imprimatur: Harrisburg, Pennsylvania, January 25, 2001,
+ Nicholas C. Dattilo, Bishop of Harrisburg

Cover illustrations (clockwise from top left):
John of the Cross, Cyril of the Mother of God,
Teresa of Jesus of the Andes, Edith Stein, Elijah, Thérèse of Lisieux

Cover design by Riz Boncan Marsella

© 2002 Ignatius Press, San Francisco
All rights reserved
ISBN 978-0-89870-852-3
Library of Congress Control Number 2001094792
Printed in the United States of America ∞

A Carmelite . . . is a soul who has *gazed on the Crucified*, who has seen Him offering Himself to His Father as a Victim for souls, and, recollecting herself in this great vision of the charity of Christ, has understood the passionate love of His soul, and has wanted to give herself as He did! . . . And on the mountain of Carmel, in silence, in solitude, in prayer that never ends, for it continues through everything, the Carmelite already lives as if in Heaven: "*by God alone*". The same one who will one day be her beatitude and will fully satisfy her in glory is already giving Himself to her. He never leaves her, He dwells within her soul; more than that, the two of them *are but one*. So she *hungers for silence* that she may always listen, penetrate ever deeper into His Infinite Being. She is identified with Him whom she loves, she finds Him everywhere; she sees Him shining through all things! Is this not Heaven on earth!

— Saint Elizabeth of the Trinity
CWET 2 Letter 133

CONTENTS

FOREWORD

As you take this book and begin to read, you soon become aware that the content requires much more than a mere quick reading. These prayers of Carmelite saints do not favor those of us who like to skim; rather they take hold and plunge us into deep abysses, enabling us to catch glimpses of the jewels of God's mysteries. They overwhelm with their power and theological depth. How true it is that God who is Love is only attained through love. In the words of John, "Love is of God; everyone who loves is begotten of God and has knowledge of God" (1 Jn 4:7).

These prophets, saints, Doctors, and mystics, then, are like prisms revealing the divine light but in a marvelous variety of colors. They become for us splendid instruments for delving into the divine mysteries and coming to know the profundities of Christ's love, "which surpasses all knowledge" (Eph 19:3). Indeed, the simplest prayer of all, "Jesus, I love you," is a master key that opens the door to all God's mysteries. The gift of love is the most elevated of the Holy Spirit's gifts, but here on earth inseparable from faith and hope. In their prayers, in the depths of their union with God, these Carmelite saints spread before us a remarkably rich fare for our theological reflections and our spiritual meditations. Their prayers are not simply for recitation. When read slowly and reflectively, these devout outpourings have the power to snatch us up as well into the sublime intimacy of knowledge and love that our saints experienced in the divine mysteries. With this help from God's saints, the Holy Spirit will want to make us sharers in that blessed communion.

When saints embrace the mystery of God with the totality of their being, and love the Lord with all their hearts, they embrace as well their neighbor. The practice of the love of the Lord in prayer will weaken and become effete without the practice of the love of neighbor. The Holy Spirit brings the two together in beautiful counterpoint: love of our neighbor, who is visible; love of God, who is invisible. And it was this divine love aflame in the hearts of these Carmelite saints that made their reading of Sacred Scripture always more luminous. Before these saints spoke they listened. Love burns away all the impurities that prevent individuals from hearing and relishing the language of God. Saint John of the Cross says the Samaritan woman forgot the water and the water jar for the sweetness of God's words. She was eager to listen.

I for one want to express my gratitude to Penny Hickey for gathering these prayers of the Carmelite saints into one volume. Now we can have them always at hand, pick up this book, read from almost any page, and go away enriched. We have a new "stream from which to drink".

Kieran Kavanaugh, O.C.D.

ACKNOWLEDGMENTS

Thank you from the bottom of my heart to all those who so graciously assisted me in this endeavor. I only hope that I do not fail to mention anyone who helped me. First on my list is my dear husband, John, who has supported me all the way. I am especially grateful to Father Theodore N. Centala, O.C.D., who encouraged me, provided his own books as a resource, and helped me to use the Carmelitana Library on Lincoln Road. I must thank Brother Antonine, O.C.D., for the wonderful dinner he provided while I was doing my research. The warm welcome at the Whitefriars Carmelitana Library from Father Patrick McMahon, O.Carm., and Patricia O'Callahan made the research so simple and pleasant. Thank you to Father Stephen Payne, O.C.D., for directing me to the wonderful collection at the Whitefriars Library. Thank you, Father John Sullivan, O.C.D., for helping with some translation. Merci beaucoup, Sister Christiane, O.C.D., de Luxembourg, et Père Philippe Hugele, O.C.D., vice-postulator pour Père Jacques. I am most grateful to Father Francis Murphy for directing me to the nuns in Luxembourg for the works of Père Jacques. Thank you to Father Kieran Kavanaugh, O.C.D., for his inviting foreword and his editorial suggestions. Many Carmelites throughout the world have given their gracious permissions and kind words of blessing. I extend my thanks to all.

Batzdorff, Susanne. *An Edith Stein Daybook*. Springfield, Ill.: Templegate Publishers, 1994.

Benedictine of Stanbrook. *Just for Today*. Springfield, Ill.: Templegate Publishers, 1988.

Bush, William. *To Quell the Terror*. Washington, D.C.: ICS Publications, 1999.

Buzy, D. *The Thoughts of Sister Mary of Jesus Crucified*. Jerusalem, 1974.

Carmel of Flemington. *God Alone and I: Carmelite Meditations*. Flemington, N.J.: Carmel of Flemington, 1965.

Carmelite Institute, International Center. *Carmel in the World*. Periodical published in Rome.

Elizabeth of the Trinity. *The Complete Works*, vol. 1. Translated by Sr. Aletheia Kane, O.C.D. Washington, D.C.: ICS Publications, 1984. *I Have Found God*, *Complete Works*, vol. 2: *Letters from Carmel*. Translated by Anne Englund Nash. Washington, D.C.: ICS Publications, 1995. *Light, Love, Life*. Edited by Conrad de Meester, O.C.D., and the Carmel of Dijon. Translated by Sr. Aletheia Kane. Washington, D.C.: ICS Publications, 1987.

Gabriel of St. Mary Magdalen, O.C.D. *Divine Intimacy*. Translated from the sixteenth Italian edition, Carmelite Monastery of Pittsford, N.Y. 4 vols. San Francisco: Ignatius Press, 1987. Reprinted with permission of Dimension Books.

Gonzalez, Marcelo, D.D. *The Power of the Priesthood*. San Antonio, Tex.: Society of St. Teresa of Jesus, 1971.

Griffin, Michael, O.C.D. *God the Joy of My Life: Blessed Teresa of the Andes.* Washington, D.C.: Teresian Charism Press, 1989.

Institutum Carmelitanum. *Proper of the Liturgy of the Hours.* Rome: Carmelite Institute, International Center, 1993.

John of the Cross, St. *The Collected Works.* Translated by Otilio Rodriguez, O.C.D., and Kieran Kavanaugh, O.C.D. Washington, D.C.: ICS Publications, 1979.

Lawrence, Brother. *The Practice of the Presence of God with Spiritual Maxims.* Westwood, N.J.: Fleming Revell Co., 1967.

Mary Magdalen de'Pazzi. *The Complete Works of St. Mary Magdalen de'Pazzi.* Translated by Gabriel Pausback, O.Carm. Darien, Ill.: Carmelite Province of the Most Pure Heart of Mary, 1969–1975.

Molins, Victoria. *Henry de Osso, Priest and Teacher.* Translated by Odette Daigle. Edited by Judy Roxborough. Covington, La.: Society of St. Teresa of Jesus, 1993.

Murphy, Francis. *Père Jacques: Resplendent in Victory.* Washington, D.C.: ICS Publications, 1998.

O'Donnell, Christopher. *Love in the Heart of the Church.* Dublin: Veritas, 1997.

Praskiewicz, Szczepan, O.C.D. *Saint Raphael Kalinowski.* Translated by Thomas Coonan, Michael Griffin, and Lawrence Sullivan. Washington, D.C.: ICS Publications, 1998.

Rodriguez, Gloria. *Experiencia espiritual de Enrique de Osso,* Barcelona: Ediciones STJ, 1995.

Teresa Benedicta of the Cross. *Edith Stein: Selected Writings.* Edited by Susanne Batzdorff. Springfield, Ill.: Templegate Publishers, 1990.

Teresa of Avila, St. *The Collected Works.* Translated by Otilio Rodriguez, O.C.D., and Kieran Kavanaugh, O.C.D. 3 vols. Washington, D.C.: ICS Publications, 1976-1985.

Thérèse of Lisieux, St. *General Correspondence.* Translated by

John Clarke, O.C.D. Vol. 1: 1877-1890. Washington, D.C.: ICS Publications, 1982.

Thérèse of Lisieux, St. *The Poetry of Saint Thérèse of Lisieux*. Translated by Donald Kinney, O.C.D. Washington, D.C.: ICS Publications, 1996.

Thérèse of Lisieux, St. *The Prayers of Saint Thérèse of Lisieux*. Translated by Aletheia Kane, O.C.D. Washington, D.C.: ICS Publications, 1973.

Thérèse of Lisieux, St. *Story of a Soul*. Translated by John Clarke, O.C.D. Washington, D.C.: ICS Publications, 1976.

Valabek, Redemptus, O.Carm. *Beatification of Father Titus Brandsma*. Rome: Carmelite Institute, International Center, 1986.

Valabek, Redemptus, O.Carm. *Mary, Mother of Carmel*. 2 vols. Rome: Carmelite Institute, International Center, 1988.

Valabek, Redemptus, O.Carm. *Prayer Life in Carmel*. Rome: Carmelite Institute, International Center, 1982.

Slight alterations in the original text were occasionally made in some of the secondary sources quoted. These have been retained in the present compilation.

ABBREVIATIONS

A	John of the Cross, *The Ascent of Mount Carmel*. In *CWJC*.
CD	Discalced Carmelite Nuns of Milwaukee. *Carmelite Devotions*. Milwaukee: Carmelite Nuns, 1956.
CIW	*Carmel in the World*, 1985, 1986.
CP	Institutum Carmelitanum. *Proper of the Liturgy of the Hours*. Rome: Carmelite Institute, International Center, 1993.
CWET	*Elizabeth of the Trinity: I Have Found God. The Complete Works*. Washington, D.C.: ICS Publications, 1984– .
CWJC	*The Collected Works of Saint John of the Cross*. Translated by Kieran Kavanaugh, O.C.D., and Otilio Rodriguez, O.C.D. Washington, D.C.: ICS Publications, 1979.
CWMM	*The Complete Works of St. Mary Magdalen de'Pazzi*. Translated by Gabriel Pausback. O.Carm. 5 vols. Darien, Ill.: Carmelite Province of the Most Pure Heart of Mary, 1969-1975.
CWT	*The Collected Works of Saint Teresa of Avila*. Translated by Kieran Kavanaugh, O.C.D., and Otilio Rodriguez, O.C.D. 3 vols. Washington, D.C.: ICS Publications, 1976-1985.
DCC	Carmelite Nuns of Salford, England. *Del Carmela*

	al Calvario: The Three Martyred Carmelites of Guada-lahara. Rome: General Postulation, 1986.
DI	Gabriel of St. Mary Magdalen, O.C.D., ed. *Divine Intimacy.* 4 vols. San Francisco: Ignatius Press, 1987.
DN	John of the Cross. *The Dark Night.* In *CWJC.*
EE	Gloria Rodriguez, S.T.J. *Esperiencia espiritual de Enrique de Osso.* Barcelona: Ediciones STJ, 1995.
ESD	Susanne Batzdorff. *An Edith Stein Daybook.* Springfield, Ill.: Templegate Publishers, 1994.
F	Teresa of Jesus. *The Foundations.* In *CWT* 3.
FSH	Gabriel of St. Mary Magdalen, O.C.D. *From the Sacred Heart to the Trinity.* Kansas City, Mo.: Chapel of St. Theresa Margaret Discalced Carmelite Nuns, 1965.
FP	Carmelite Missionaries. *Francisco Palau.* Rome: Carmelite Missionaries, General House, 1988.
FPP	Patricio Sciadini, O.C.D. *Francisco Palau: Profeta de Esperanca.* Sao Paolo: Edicoes Loyola, 1990.
FRK	Czeslaus Gil, O.C.D. *Father Raphael Kalinowski.* Krakow: Karmel/TowBosych,1978.
GA	Flemington Carmel. *God Alone and I: Carmelite Meditations.* Flemington, N.J.: Flemington Carmel, 1965.
GIL	Sr. Teresa Margaret, D.C., *God Is Love: St. Teresa Margaret—Her Life.* Milwaukee: Spiritual Life Press, 1964.
GJ	Michael Griffin, O.C.D. *God the Joy of My Life: Blessed Teresa of the Andes.* Washington, D.C.: Teresian Charism Press, 1989.
HDO	Victoria Molins, *Henry de Osso, Priest and Teacher.*

Translated by Odette Daigle. Edited by Judy Rox-borough. Covington, La.: Society of St. Teresa of Jesus, 1993.

IC   Teresa of Jesus. *The Interior Castle*. In *CWT* 2.

IJOP   The Infant Jesus of Prague. Website http:// www.karmel.at/prag-jesu/.

JFT   Benedictine of Stanbrook. *Just for Today*. Spring-field, Ill.: Templegate Publishers, 1988.

L   Teresa of Jesus. *The Book of Her Life*. In *CWT* 1.

LC   Thérèse of Lisieux. *St. Thérèse of Lisieux: Her Last Conversations*. Translated by John Clarke, O.C.D. Washington, D.C.: ICS Publications, 1977.

LCJ   Hilary Doran, O.C.D. *Living in Christ Jesus: Blessed Mary of Jesus, O.C.D.* Darlington, Eng. Carmel of Darlington.

LF   John of the Cross, *The Living Flame of Love*. In *CWJC*.

LHC   Christopher O'Donnell. *Love in the Heart of the Church*. Dublin: Veritas, 1997.

LLL   Elizabeth of the Trinity. *Light, Love, Life*. Edited by Conrad de Meester, O.C.D. Translated by Sr. Aletheia Kane. Washington, D.C.: ICS Publica-tions, 1987.

M   Teresa of Jesus. *Meditations on the Song of Songs*. In *CWT* 2.

MC   John of the Cross. *Maxims and Counsels*. In *CWJC*.

MLA   Amedee Brunot, S.C.J. *Mariam the Little Arab: Sr. Mary of Jesus Crucified*. Eugene, Ore.: Carmel of Maria Regina, 1984.

MMC Redemptus Valabek, O.Carm. *Mary, Mother of*

Carmel. 2 vols. Rome: Carmelite Institute, International Center, 1988.

PJ   Michel Carrouges. *Père Jacques.* Translated by Salvator Attanasio. New York: McMillan, 1961.

PLC   Redemptus Valabek, O.Carm. *Prayer Life in Carmel.* Rome: Carmelite Institute, International Center, 1982.

PP   Marcelo Gonzalez, D.D. *The Power of the Priesthood.* San Antonio, Tex.: Society of St. Teresa of Jesus, 1971.

PPG   Brother Lawrence, *The Practice of the Presence of God with Spiritual Maxims.* Westwood, N.J.: Fleming Revell Co., 1967.

PST   Thérèse of Lisieux. *Prayers of St. Thérèse of Lisieux.* Translated by Sr. Aletheia Kane. Washington, D.C.: ICS Publications, 1973.

PSTL   Thérèse of Lisieux. *The Poetry of Saint Thérèse of Lisieux.* Translated by Donald Kinney, O.C.D. Washington, D.C.: ICS Publications, 1996.

SA   La Comtesse D. de Beaurepaire de Louvangy, *Saint Albert de Messine de l'Ordre des Carmes.* Paris: Ancienne Maison Ch. Douniol, 1895.

SAA   Sr. Mary Minima, O.Carm., *Seraph among Angels.* Carmelite Press, 1958.

SC   John of the Cross. *The Spiritual Canticle.* In *CWJC.*

SL   John of the Cross. *Sayings of Light and Love.* In *CWJC.*

SR   Victor de la Vierge, O.C.D. *Spiritual Realism of St. Thérèse of Lisieux.* Milwaukee: Bruce Publishing Co., 1961.

SRK   Szczepan Praskiewicz, O.C.D. *Saint Raphael Kali-nowski: An Introduction to His Life and Spirituality.* Washington, D.C.: ICS Publications, 1998.

SS   Thérèse of Lisieux, *Story of a Soul.* Translated by John Clarke, O.C.D. Washington, D.C.: ICS Publications, 1976.

ST   Teresa of Jesus. *Spiritual Testimonies.* In *CWT* 1.

STM   Joseph Bardi. *Sister Theresa Margaret.* Derby, N.Y.: Daughters of Saint Paul, 1939.

SW   Teresa Benedicta of the Cross. *Edith Stein, Selected Writings.* Edited by Susanne Batzdorff. Springfield, Ill.: Templegate Publishers, 1990.

TGC   Thérèse of Lisieux, *General Correspondence.* Translated by John Clarke, O.C.D. 2 vols. Washington, D.C.: ICS Publications, 1982-1988.

TQT   William Bush, *To Quell the Terror.* Washington, D.C.: ICS Publications, 1999.

TSM   D. Buzy, S.C.I. *The Thoughts of Sister Mary of Jesus Crucified.* Jerusalem, 1974.

WP   Teresa of Jesus, *The Way of Perfection.* In *CWT* 2.

INTRODUCTION

Carmelite history and prayer begin with Elijah on Mount Carmel. He heard the voice of the Lord calling: " 'Leave here, go east and hide in the Wadi Cherith, east of the Jordan. You shall drink of the stream. . . .' He went east and drank from the stream" (1 Kings 17).

From Elijah has descended a long line of hermits who have heard the voice of the Lord calling them to leave everything behind and come and drink from the stream. Although Elijah physically went to the heights of Mount Carmel, where great expanses of breathtaking vistas abound and silence permeates the air, Carmelites of the future would find this beauty and the rare vistas in the deep stillness of their souls. There they would meet their Beloved; and there they would speak in these prayers that follow.

The prayers in this book were compiled to help the reader listen to the saints of Carmel throughout the ages. In these prayers are stories of particular times, places, longings, sometimes suffering, and at other times ecstatic joy. In looking at these prayers one enters into the most intimate depths of the souls of the saints. Carmelites are called to contemplative prayer. It is a time reserved for communion with God. How better to learn than from the masters themselves.

In recent years there has been much interest in the works of Saint Thérèse of Lisieux, Saint John of the Cross, and Saint Teresa of Avila—and this is understandable. This book has been undertaken to try to include as many of the Carmelite saints' prayers as possible—not just the more notable ones. A careful search has been made, with the help of those who have been recognized in the acknowledgments. There are many Carmelite saints, but not all of them have written down their prayers. Some must remain in the heart.

These works are presented in chronological order with a brief word about each saint, so the reader will understand the context of the prayers. Since it is not intended to be a biographical study, the information about each of the saints is greatly abbreviated.

May the journey into the abyss of these beautiful souls be fruitful for all readers in increasing their love for the One who calls them to prayer and communion with Him. May they drink deeply from the stream, a stream that has surged on in time and has become a vast river.

DRINK OF THE STREAM

Elijah listens to the Lord's word:
"Go and drink of the stream" (1 Kings 17:3–4)

I

Elijah the Prophet

(850 B.C.)

Elijah the prophet originated from Tishbe in Transjordania. He lived in the ninth century before Christ. Elijah heard the voice of the Lord telling him to go and hide himself and drink of the stream and that ravens would feed him there. He did as he was told; and thus he was chosen by God to lead the people back to Him. Some had been worshipping the god Baal, while the rest followed Yahweh. The Kingdom was divided. In the accomplishment of his mission, there was a test on Mount Carmel. The prophets of Baal cried out from morning until evening invoking him, but to no avail. The prophet of Yahweh, Elijah, rebuilt the altar of the Lord with twelve stones (representing the twelve tribes of Israel). Elijah prepared a holocaust and surrounded it with water (in the midst of a drought), and the Lord consumed it with fire. The truth had been shown in a dramatic way. The drought ended, and Elijah was recognized as a prophet of the true God. The cult of Baal survived, and Elijah faced many challenges and humiliations but remained steadfast in his faith. The prophet listened for the Lord to pass by and found Him, not in an earthquake or fire, but in a gentle breeze. Elijah's prayers are direct and clear. He is confident in the power of the one true God.

PRAYERS

O Lord, my God, will you afflict even the widow with whom I am staying by killing her son? (1 Kings 17:20)

O Lord, my God, let the life breath return to the body of this child. (1 Kings 17:21)

Lord, God of Abraham, Isaac, and Israel, let it be known this day that you are God in Israel and that I am your servant and have done all these things by your command. Answer me, Lord! Answer me, that this people may know that you, Lord, are God and that you have brought them back to their senses. (1 Kings 18:36–37)

This is enough, O Lord! Take my life, for I am no better than my fathers. (1 Kings 19:4)

I have been most zealous for the Lord, the God of hosts. But the Israelites have forsaken your covenant, torn down your altars, and put your prophets to the sword. I alone am left, and they seek to take my life. (1 Kings 19:14)

The Spring of Elijah

II

Elisha the Prophet

(850 B.C.)

Elisha also lived on Mount Carmel at the time of Elijah. He was known as a man of prayer, and people seemed to come to him for intercession. Elijah had been told by the Lord to anoint Elisha as his successor. As he was following Elijah to where he would be taken up to heaven, he asked for a double portion of Elijah's spirit. Elijah told him that if he saw him taken up, he would have his wish granted. He was the successor of Elijah, as we see in 2 Kings 2:1–18. He saw Elijah taken up into heaven in a chariot in a fiery whirlwind. Seeing this he took his own mantle and rent it in two. He took Elijah's mantle, struck the water, divided it in two, and crossed over. Those who observed this bowed down and recognized him as Elijah's successor. His work was to continue to bring the truth of Yahweh to those still following Baal. His recorded prayers are few and simple; they express a confidence that is seen in the prayers of Elijah.

PRAYERS

Where is the LORD, the God of Elijah? (2 Kings 2:14)

Thus says the LORD: "I have purified this water. Never again shall death or miscarriage spring from it." (2 Kings 2:21)

O LORD, open his eyes, that he may see. (2 Kings 6:17)

Strike this people blind, I pray you. (2 Kings 6:18)

O LORD, open their eyes that they may see. (2 Kings 6:20)

*Elijah being carried into heaven
as Elisha receives his mantle*

Our Lady giving her scapular to Saint Simon Stock

III

Saint Simon Stock

(A.D. 1200S)

Little is known of Saint Simon Stock, except that he was an Englishman who lived in the thirteenth century. He was the prior general of the Carmelite Order at Aylesford in Kent, England.

On the night of July 15, 1251, he had a vision in which our Lady appeared to him. She told Saint Simon that "this shall be to thee and all Carmelites a privilege, that whosoever dies clothed in this shall never suffer eternal fire." He was given the brown Scapular at that moment; and Carmelites have worn the Scapular ever since.

Saint Simon Stock has been venerated by the Carmelites for his personal holiness and his devotion to our Lady. Simon Stock died at Bordeaux in the mid-thirteenth century.

PRAYER

Flos Carmeli

Flower of Carmel,
Tall vine blossom laden;
Splendor of heaven,
Child-bearing, yet maiden.
None equals thee.

Mother so tender,
Whom no man did know,
On Carmel's children
Thy favors bestow.
   Star of the Sea.

Strong stem of Jesse,
Who bore one bright flower,
Be ever near us
And guard us each hour,
   Who serve thee here.

Purest of lilies,
That flowers among thorns,
Bring help to the true heart
That in weakness turns
   And trusts in thee.

Strongest of armor,
We trust in thy might:
Under thy mantle,
Hard press'd in the fight,
   We call to thee.

Our way uncertain,
Surrounded by foes,
Unfailing counsel
You give to those
   Who turn to thee.

O gentle Mother
Who in Carmel reigns,
Share with your servants
That gladness you gained
   And now enjoy.

Hail, Gate of Heaven,
With glory now crowned,
Bring us to safety
Where thy Son is found,
　　True joy to see.

(*CP*)

(This prayer has been attributed to Saint Simon Stock,
but the origin is uncertain.)

*The Blessed Virgin places the Child Jesus
in the arms of Saint Albert*

IV

Saint Albert of Trápani

(D. 1307)

Albert degli Abbati was born in Trápani in Sicily in the thirteenth century. Having joined the Carmelites and been ordained a priest, he soon became famous for his preaching and miracles. At Messina he was able to bring about the end of a famine through prayer. He was permitted a visit by the Queen of Heaven with her divine Son in which he was allowed to hold Infant Jesus. During that same apparition he was told when he would die. This he revealed to his fellow religious in his monastery. He was provincial in Sicily in 1296 and died at Messina, probably in 1307, with a reputation for purity and prayer.   (*CP*)

PRAYERS

[*In a famine in Messina, he prayed for and received deliverance.*]

O King of kings, Sovereign God and Father of all mankind, You who refuse none of those who implore You. Look down from the heights of heaven on Your repentant people. They have confidence in Your mercy; do not turn away from their prayers, and answer from the abundance of Your blessings. You see these men, these women, these children! They are hungry! They ask You to give them their daily bread. Give it to them, O You who, in the desert, have fed the numerous multitudes. Extend to them the power of Your saving arm. The city trembles with fright, reassure them. It is nearly lifeless; revive it. Without Your aid, it cannot hope to survive; nothing can pull it out of this disaster. The unfortunate ones! They cannot depend on the number of fighters, on the force of the armies, they have not been called to the aid of men, they have no hope in the power of Your name. They are going to die; come to their help, so they do not succumb to despair and that Satan does not triumph over the loss of these souls!

(SA)

O my God! Was it not said that by You and Your ineffable power You have created mankind? Is it not as a the result of Your clemency that You call us to partake of Your glory and the happiness of eternal life? When original sin condemned us to suffer death, did it not please Your goodness to repurchase us through the blood of Your Son, to unite us to You through our faith and Your great mercy? You have repurchased us from the shame of original sin; You have covered our dishonor with a fragment of Your glory. And now here is this difficult work built by You, this work with which You soften the limbs and joints, with which You have ennobled the destiny of the immortal soul with sublime beauty, and Satan's attacks! the father of hatred, pride, with the introduction of his jealousy, in order to wound this body which You have created. Deign therefore, Lord, to rebuild Your work! Deign to cure this blindness, so that Your power may be glorified and that the malice of the enemy may be confounded. [The Saint repeated this prayer three times. When the unhappy mother returned home, she found that her son had been healed and was hurrying toward her!]

(SA)

V

Blessed Nuno Alvares Pereira

(1360–1431)

Nuno Alvares Pereira was born in 1360 and for many years pursued a military career, becoming the champion of Portuguese independence. He became the constable of Portugal and the head of the army. He experienced the awesome power of God at Fatima when his outnumbered army won a victory on the Vigil of the Assumption. He had prayed to our Lady, Queen of Portugal. After the death of his wife, he joined the Order as a brother in 1423 at the monastery in Lisbon, which he had founded himself, and took the name Nuno of Saint Mary. There he lived until he died in 1431. He was noted for his prayer, his practice of penance, and his filial devotion to the Mother of God.

PRAYER

Mother of Mount Carmel, I kiss your Holy Scapular and thank you for this precious gift. Help and guide me always. I place my confidence in your intercession. Never has it been known, dearest Lady and Mother, that anyone who fled to your protection was left unaided. (*GA*)

Blessed Nuno prays at Fatima following his battle

VI

Blessed Baptist Spagnoli of Mantua

(1447–1516)

On April 17, 1447, a scholar, poet, and true lover of our Lady was born in Mantua. The world would come to know him for his many works of poetry inspired by his great depth of prayer. He wrote more than 55,000 lines of poetry in his lifetime. He entered the Carmelite Order at a young age and served as vicar general six times. In 1513 he was elected prior general of the whole Order. Father Baptist was even invited to preach to the pope and his court. This renowned poet died on March 20, 1516, in Mantua, but his writings live on.

PRAYERS

[Referring to the presentation of the Child Jesus in the Temple.]

Implacable weakness, O Virgin,
and sorrow will grip you with immense force,
deeply wounding you in your sorrowing heart.
You will lament over your Son more than the
    daughters of the Sun
wept over their brother . . .
but bear with it all, support it with a strong will.
Heaven is won at this price—with such a breeze
the eternal harbor and the shores of life are reached.

God Himself will lavish His strength on you.
  He will raise you up
when you fall, in any case He will go with you as a
  companion,
and in the end, tears will be transformed into
  laughter, mourning
into delightful joy; you will be venerated throughout
  the world.
You will be called Queen of earth and of highest
  Heaven.
When your Child will have washed His disciples
in the saving streams, and called every race of ours to
  Himself,
earth's dwellers will celebrate rites to you.   (*MMC* 1)

Mary and Carmel

For a long time Carmel had been planning
  widespread honors
for you, and in its happy caves it trains sons
who in white cloaks will witness to perpetual
  chastity
for you and will bind your name with the name of
  this Mount
in everlasting covenant. You are purer than gold.
You are whiter than snow. You are brighter than the
  star of Venus.
Your virginity was not vitiated by child-bearing, nor
  can
your brightness be darkened by any stain.
You certainly were not bound to this legitimate
custom, and in all justice you could have renounced
  these gifts.

Time will come when a future age will remember us
and on this solemn day will offer you honor on the
  altars,
and will carry candles in long procession of a well-
  celebrated liturgy.
Then your priest, processing in golden vestments,
will chant your hymns and will send forth a sweet-
  smelling cloud
throughout the Church and the breeze will
  spread the pleasant scent far and wide,
and because our paths cross at his point,
posterity will call this day *Hypante*,
in the Greek language, and it will be lit up with
  numberless torches.   (*MMC* 1)

Supplication to the Most Blessed Virgin Mary

Glory of the world, Queen of heaven, Mother
of the Almighty, harbor for mankind, soothing breeze
  in adversity,
As in my memory I call my sins to mind,
I am ashamed to open my lips in your sight.
For you lack any stain. You are brighter than gold,
which the smith submitted to the crackling fire ten
  times.
However I am sacrificed by the consuming waves of
  the nether world,
and my members are besmirched by the mud of hell.
But as often as I call to mind your heart of mercy
that shame of mine haunts me just a little less.
Hope gives me a pledge that you will prove to be
  benign and gentle
and it promises your help to us.

Thus, do not be disgusted by my uncleanness, always
grant me your favor before your Son.
Subdue my senses which seek pleasure in earthly
   goods
which poison the mind and rush to wrong doing.
Make heavenly nourishment give taste to our lips,
make love of God pierce my heart.
Make me look down on the earth; make me conquer
   hell,
While anger seizes the evil spirits.
Be my guide at the critical moments of my life,
nor let any hand attack me in body.
Under your care, may I be allowed to return to the
   kingdom of heaven,
and with shattered yoke to submit my vows to you.
May your Child, at your intercession, govern
me and my house in every adversity.   (*MMC* 1)

VII

Saint Teresa of Jesus of Avila

(1515–1582)

Teresa de Cepeda y Ahumada was born in Avila, Spain, in 1515. She came from a well-to-do family and enjoyed the social life that went with her station in life. She lived in a time of castles and knights and kings. Her entrance into Carmel (the monastery of the Incarnation) was in 1535. She actually turned away from prayer for about two years, 1542–1544, out of a false sense of humility. Following a conversion experience, Teresa returned to prayer and began to experience the living presence of God in her soul. Previously Martin Luther had broken away from the Church and begun his own reform. The pain this caused Teresa is very evident in her writings. There was much laxity in her Carmel, and Teresa was well aware of the harm this was causing the life of silence and contemplation for the nuns.

She began the Reform of Carmel in 1562 by founding the monastery of Saint Joseph in Avila. At first her efforts met with great opposition, but gradually the nuns saw the benefit of her Reform. She met John of the Cross in 1567 and found that he shared her zeal for the Reform. He began the reform of the friars at the same time. Teresa, although cloistered, managed to travel throughout Spain making foundations of the Reform.

She was a true contemplative, receiving the highest mystical graces. She was a teacher, and her prolific writings continue to be a source of inspiration. They are without equal, and she has been named a Doctor of the Church. The *Book*

Transverberation of Saint Teresa of Avila

of Her Life is her autobiography. *The Way of Perfection* was written as a guide for her nuns, to teach them to pray. *The Meditation on the Song of Songs* was boldly written at a time when it was not considered proper for women to have free access to Sacred Scripture. A later confessor to the saint actually ordered her to burn her commentary, which she promptly did, but fortunately other copies of it remained unharmed. She lived in the time of the Inquisition, and all her writings were suspect. These writings and the *Soliloquies* express her burning love for God and her yearning to be wholly consumed by Him. The *Soliloquies* were her Post-Communion prayers. *The Foundations* speak of her humility in face of such an enormous task and her need for the One who alone could help her. *The Interior Castle* is a lesson on prayer. She used the image of a castle to describe the soul because at that time it would have been readily understood. In this day it takes a little imagination but is easily translated into the current vernacular of perhaps a mansion with a guard-house. Unlike the prayers of the previous saints mentioned, Teresa's sometimes seem to ramble and become diverted, but that is because other thoughts were mingled with her prayer. Everything is brought to her Beloved, and prayer is part of all things. She died October 4, 1582. The Church celebrates her feast day on October 15.

PRAYERS

THE BOOK OF HER LIFE

O my Lord, since it seems You have determined to save me, I beseech Your Majesty that it may be so. And since You have granted me as many favors as You have, don't You think it would be good (not for my gain, but for Your honor) if the inn where You have so continually to dwell were not to get so dirty? It wearies me, Lord, even to say this, for I know that the whole fault was mine. It doesn't seem to me that there was anything more for You to do in order that from this age I would be all Yours. *(L 1:8)*

O blindness of the world! You would have been served, Lord, if I had been most ungrateful to all that world and not the least bit ungrateful to You! But it has been just the reverse because of my sins.

May He be blessed forever. May it please His Majesty that I die rather than ever cease to love Him. *(L 5:4,11)*

May You be blessed forever! Although I abandoned You, You did not abandon me so completely as not to turn to raise me up by always holding out Your hand to me. And often times, Lord, I did not want it; nor did I desire to understand how often You called me again, as I shall now tell. *(L 6:9)*

As the sins increased I began to lose joy in virtuous things and my taste for them. I saw very clearly, my Lord, that these were failing me because I was failing You. *(L 7:1)*

Oh, the greatness of God! With how much care and pity You were warning me in every way, and how little it benefited me! *(L 7:8)*

O Lord of my soul! How can I extol the favors You gave me during these years! And how at the time when I offended You most, You quickly prepared me with an extraordinary repentance to taste Your favors and gifts! Indeed, my King, You, as One who well knew what to me would be most distressing, chose as a means the most delicate and painful punishment. With wonderful gifts You punished my sins.

(*L* 7:19)

O infinite goodness of my God, for it seems to me I see that such is the way You are and the way I am! O delight of angels, when I see this I desire to be completely consumed in loving You! How certainly You do suffer the one who suffers to be with You! Oh, what a good friend You make, my Lord! How You proceed by favoring and enduring. You wait for the other to adapt to Your nature, and in the meanwhile You put up with his! You take into account, my Lord, the times when he loves You, and in one instant of repentance You forget their offenses.

I have seen this clearly myself. I do not know, my Creator, why it is that every one does not strive to reach You through this special friendship, and why those who are wicked, who are not conformed to Your will, do not, in order that You make them good, allow You to be with them at least two hours each day, even though they may not be with You, but with a thousand disturbances from worldly cares and thoughts. . . . Through this effort they make to remain in such good company (for You see that in the beginning they cannot do more, nor afterward, sometimes), You, Lord, force the devils not to attack them, so that each day the devils' strength against them lessens; and You give them the victory over the devils. Yes, for You do not kill—life of all lives!—any of those

who trust in You and desire You for friend. But You sustain
the life of the body with more health, and You give life to the
soul.   (L 8:6)

O Lord of my soul and my good! When a soul is determined to love You by doing what it can to leave all and
occupy itself better in this divine love, why don't You desire
that it enjoy soon the ascent to the possession of perfect love?
                                                          (L 11:1)

My Lord, what do You do but that which is for the greater
good of the soul You understand now to be Yours and which
places itself in Your power so as to follow You wherever You
go, even to death on the cross, and is determined to help You
bear it and not leave You alone with it? . . . [I] desire to . . .
trust in [Your] goodness [for You] never fail . . . [Your]
friends. . . . [I] believe that all is for [my] own greater
good. . . . Lead [me] along the path [You] desire. . . . [I] belong no longer to [myself]. . . . Do, Lord, what You desire.
May I not offend You. Don't let the virtues be lost, if You
only out of Your goodness have already given me some. I
desire to suffer, Lord, since You suffered. Let Your will be
done in me in every way, and may it not please Your Majesty
that something as precious as Your love be given to anyone
who serves You only for the sake of consolations.   (L 11:12)

May You be blessed, Lord, who have made me so unable
and unprofitable! But I praise You very much because You
awaken so many to awaken us. Our prayer for those who give
us light should be unceasing. In the midst of tempests as
fierce as those the Church now endures, what would we be

without them? If some have gone bad, the good ones shine more brilliantly. May it please the Lord to keep them in His hands and help them so that they might help us. Amen.

(L 13:21)

O my Lord and my God! I cannot say this without tears and great joy of soul! How You desire, Lord, thus to be with us and to be present in the Sacrament (for in all truth this can be believed since it is so, and in the fullness of truth we can make this comparison); and if it were not for our fault we could rejoice in being with You, and You would be glad to be with us since You say that Your delight is to be with the children of men. O my Lord! What is this? As often as I hear these words, they bring me great consolation; they did so even when I was very far gone. Is it possible, Lord, that there be a soul that reaches the point where You bestow similar favors and gifts, and understands that You are to be with it, that goes back to offending You after so many favors and after such striking demonstrations of the love You have for it which cannot be doubted since the effects of it are obvious? Yes, there certainly is one, and not one who has done this once but done it many times—for it is I. And may it please Your goodness, Lord, that I might be the only ungrateful one and the only one who has done such terrible evil and shown such excessive ingratitude.

(L 14:10)

How many are the reasons I can sing Your mercies forever! I beseech You, my God, that it may be so and that I may sing them without end since You have deigned to bestow upon me mercies so outstanding. . . . They frequently carry me out of myself to praise You the better. By remaining in myself without You, I could do nothing, my Lord, but return to cutting the garden flowers in such a way that this miserable ground would once more serve for a trash heap as it did previously. Do not permit it, Lord, or desire the loss of the soul You bought with so many labors and which You have so often gone back again to rescue.   (*L* 14:10–11)

May You be blessed forever, Lord! May all things praise You forever! Since while I write this I am not freed from such holy, heavenly madness coming from Your goodness and mercy—for You grant this favor without any merits on my part at all—either desire, my King, I beseech You, that all to whom I speak become mad from Your love, or do not permit that I speak to anyone! Either ordain, Lord, that I no longer pay attention to anything in the world, or take me out of it! . . .

O true Lord and my Glory! How delicate and extremely heavy a cross You have prepared for those who reach this state! "Delicate" because it is pleasing; "heavy" because there come times when there is no capacity to bear it; and yet the soul would never want to be freed from it unless it were for the sake of being with You. When it recalls that it hasn't served You in anything and that by living it can serve You, it would want to carry a much heavier cross and never die until the end of the world. It finds no rest in anything except in doing You some small service. It doesn't know what it wants, but it well understands that it wants nothing other than You.

(*L* 16:4–5)

When, my God, will my soul be completely joined together in Your praise and not broken in pieces, unable to make use of itself?   (*L* 17:5)

O my Lord, how good You are! May You be blessed for-ever! May all things praise You, my God, for You have so loved us that we can truthfully speak of this communication which You engage in with souls even in our exile! And even in the case of those who are good, this still shows great generosity and magnanimity. In fact, it is Your communica-tion, my Lord; and You give it in the manner of who You are. O infinite Largess, how magnificent are Your works! It frightens one whose intellect is not occupied with things of the earth that he has no intellect by which he can understand divine truths. That You bestow such sovereign favors on souls that have offended You so much certainly brings my intellect to a halt; and when I begin to think about this, I'm unable to continue. Where can the intellect go that would not be a turning back since it doesn't know how to give You thanks for such great favors? Sometimes I find it a remedy to speak absurdities.   (L 18:3)

Lord, look what You are doing. Don't forget so quickly my great wickedness. Now that in order to pardon me You have forgotten it, I beseech You to remember it that You might put a limit on Your favors. Don't, my Creator, pour such precious liqueur in so broken a bottle; You have already seen at other times how I only spill and waste it. Don't place a treasure like this in a place where cupidity for life's consola-tions is still not cast off as it should be; otherwise it will be badly squandered. How is it that You surrender the strength of this city and the keys to its fortress to so cowardly a mayor who at the enemy's first attack allows him entrance? Don't let Your love be so great, eternal King, as to place in risk such precious jewels. It seems, my Lord, that the occasion is given for esteeming them but little since You put them in the

power of a thing so wretched, so lowly so weak and miserable, and of so little importance. For although she strives
with Your help not to lose them (and there is need for more
than a little effort because of what I am), she cannot make
good use of them to win over anyone. In sum, she is a
woman; and not a good but a wretched one. It seems that the
talents are not only hidden but even buried by being placed
in such vile earth. You are not accustomed, Lord, to bestow
on a soul grandeurs and favors like these unless for the profit
of many. You already know, my God, that with all my heart
and will I beseech You and have besought You at times in the
past that You grant these favors to someone who would make
better use of them for the increase of Your glory—and that I
would consider it a blessing to lose the greatest earthly good
possessable in order that You do so.   (L 18:4)

May You be blessed, my Lord, that from such filthy mud as
I, You make water so clear that it can be served at Your table!
May You be praised, O Joy of the angels, for having desired
to raise up a worm so vile!   (L 19:2)

O my Jesus! What a sight it is when You through Your
mercy return to offer Your hand and raise up a soul that has
fallen in sin after having reached this stage! How such a soul
knows the multitude of Your grandeurs and mercies and its
own misery! In this state it is in truth consumed and knows
Your splendors. Here it doesn't dare raise its eyes, and here it
raises them up so as to know what it owes You. Here it
becomes a devotee of the Queen of heaven so that she might
appease You; here it invokes the help of the saints that fell
after having been called by You. Here it seems that everything You give it is undeserved because it sees that it doesn't

merit the ground on which it treads. Here, in approaching the sacraments, it has the living faith to see the power that God has placed in them; it praises You because You have left such a medicine and ointment for our wounds and because this medicine not only covers these wounds but also takes them away completely. It is amazed by all this. And who, Lord of my soul, wouldn't be amazed by so much mercy and a favor so large for a betrayal so ugly and abominable? I don't know why my heart doesn't break as I write this! For I am a wretched person! (*L* 19:5)

O Lord! Were You to give me the office by which I could shout this aloud, they would not believe me, as they do not believe many who know how to say this better than I; but at least it would be satisfying to me. It seems to me I would have held my life in little account in order to make known only one of these truths; I don't know what I might have done afterward, for I am not trustworthy. In spite of what I am, I experience great consuming impulses to tell these truths to those who are rulers. When I can do no more, I turn to You, my Lord, to beg of You a remedy for all. And You know well that I would very willingly dispossess myself of the favors You have granted me and give them to the kings, providing I could remain in a state in which I do not offend You; because I know that it would then be impossible for them to consent to the things that are now consented to, nor would these favors fail to bring the greatest blessings.

O my God! Give kings an understanding of their obligations. (*L* 21:2–3)

May You be pleased, my God, that there come a time in which I may be able to repay You even one mite of all I owe You. Ordain, Lord, as You wish, how this servant of Yours may in some manner serve You. . . . Fortify my soul and dispose it first, Good of all goods and my Jesus, and then ordain ways in which I might do something for You, for there is no longer anyone who can suffer to receive so much and not repay anything. Cost what it may, Lord, do not desire that I come into Your presence with hands so empty, since the reward must be given in conformity with one's deeds. Here is my life, here is my honor and my will. I have given all to You, I am Yours, make use of me according to Your will. I see clearly, Lord, the little I'm capable of. But having reached You, having climbed to this watchtower, I see truths. I can do all things, providing You do not leave me.   (*L* 21:5)

O Lord of my soul, who has the words to explain what You give to those who trust in You and to explain what those lose who reach this state and yet remain with themselves! Do not desire a loss like this, Lord, since You do so much in coming to a dwelling place as shabby as mine. May You be blessed forever and ever!

O Lord of my soul and my Good, Jesus Christ crucified! At no time do I recall this opinion I had without feeling pain; it seems to me I became a dreadful traitor—although in ignorance.

And what a pity it was for me to have left You, my Lord, under the pretext of serving You more! When I was offending You I didn't know You; but how, once knowing You, did I think I could gain more by this path! Oh, what a bad road I was following, Lord! Now it seems to me I was walking on no path until You brought me back, for in seeing You at my side I saw all blessings. There is no trial that it wasn't good for

me to suffer once I looked at You as You were, standing
before the judges.   (L 22:17)

O my Lord, how You are the true friend; and how powerful! When You desire You can love, and You never stop
loving those who love You! All things praise You, Lord of the
world! Oh, who will cry out for You, to tell everyone how
faithful You are to Your friends! All things fail; You, Lord of
all, never fail! Little it is, that which You allow the one who
loves You to suffer! O my Lord! How delicately and smoothly
and delightfully You treat them! Would that no one ever
pause to love anyone but You! It seems, Lord, You try with
rigor the person who loves You so that in extreme trial he
might understand the greatest extreme of Your love. O my
God, who has the understanding, the learning, and the new
words with which to extol Your works as my soul understands them? All fails me, my Lord; but if You do not abandon me, I will not fail You. Let all learned men rise up
against me, let all created things persecute me, let the devils
torment me; do not You fail me, Lord, for I already have
experience of the gain that comes from the way You rescue
the one who trusts in You alone.   (L 25:17)

Oh, how good a Lord and how powerful! He provides
not only the counsel but also the remedy! His words are
works! Oh, God help me; and how He strengthens faith and
increases love!   (L 25:18)

O admirable kindness of God, You allow me to gaze upon
You with eyes that have so badly gazed as have those of my
soul. May they, Lord, become accustomed through this

vision not to look at base things, so that nothing outside of You might satisfy them! O ingratitude of mortals! To what extremes will you go? For I know through experience that what I say is true and that what can be said is the least of what You do, Lord, for a soul You bring to such frontiers.

(L 27:11)

O my Jesus! Who could make known the majesty with which You reveal Yourself! And, Lord of all the world and of the heavens, of a thousand other worlds and of numberless worlds, and of the heavens that You might create, how the soul understands by the majesty with which You reveal Yourself that it is nothing for You to be Lord of the world!

In this vision the powerlessness of all the devils in comparison with Your power is clearly seen, my Jesus, and it is seen how whoever is pleasing to You can trample all hell under foot. . . . I see that You want the soul to know how tremendous this majesty is and the power that this most sacred humanity joined with the Divinity has. In this vision there is a clear representation of what it will be like on Judgment Day to see the majesty of this King and to see its severity toward those who are evil. This vision is the source of the true humility left in the soul when it sees its misery, which it cannot ignore. This vision is the source of confusion and true repentance for sins; although the soul sees that He shows love, it doesn't know where to hide, and so it is completely consumed.

(L 28:8–9)

O superb contrivance of my Lord! What delicate skill You use with Your miserable slave! You hide Yourself from me and afflict me with Your love through a death so delightful that the soul would never want to escape from it.

(L 29:8)

O my Lord! What a shame it is to see so much wickedness and to tell about some grains of sand, which even then I didn't lift from the ground for Your service, since everything I did was enveloped in a thousand miseries! The waters of Your grace didn't flow yet under these grains of sand in order to raise them up. O my Creator! Who could find among so many evils something of substance to relate, since I am telling about the great favors I've received from You! So it is, my Lord, that I don't know how my heart can bear it or how anyone who reads this can fail to abhor me in observing that such marvelous favors were so poorly repaid and that I have no shame, in the end, to recount these services as my own. Yes, I am ashamed, my Lord; but having nothing else to tell about the part I played makes me speak of such lowly beginnings so that anyone who did great things in the beginning may have hope; since it seems the Lord has taken my early actions into account, He will do so more with theirs. May it please His Majesty to give me grace so that I might not always remain at the beginning, amen. (L 31:25)

My Lord, how is it You command things that seem impossible? For if I were at least free, even though I am a woman! But bound on so many sides, without money or the means to raise it or to obtain the brief or anything, what can I do, Lord? (L 33:11)

Lord, You must not deny me this favor; see how this individual is fit to be our friend.

O goodness and great humanity of God! You don't look at the words but at the desires and the will with which they are spoken! How do You bear that one like myself should speak so boldly to Your Majesty! May You be blessed forever and ever.   (*L* 34:8–9)

O my Jesus, what a soul inflamed in Your love accomplishes! How highly we must esteem such a soul and how we must beg the Lord to let it remain in this life! Whoever has this same love must follow after these souls if he can.

(*L* 34:15)

O my Lord, how obvious it is that You are almighty! There's no need to look for reasons for what You want. For, beyond all natural reason, You make things so possible that You manifest clearly there's no need for anything more than truly to love You and truly to leave all for You, so that You, my Lord, may make everything easy. It fits well here to say that You feign labor in Your law. For I don't see, Lord, nor do I know how the road that leads to You is narrow. I see that it is a royal road, not a path; a road that is safer for anyone who indeed takes it. Very far off are the occasions of sin, those narrow mountain passes and the rocks that make one fall. What I would call a path, a wretched path and a narrow way, is the kind which has on one side, where a soul can fall, a valley far below, and on the other side a precipice: as soon as one becomes careless one is hurled down and broken into pieces.   (*L* 35:13)

He who really loves You, my Good, walks safely on a broad and royal road. He is far from the precipice. Hardly has he begun to stumble when You, Lord, give him Your hand. One fall is not sufficient for a person to be lost nor are many, if he loves You and not the things of the world. He journeys in the valley of humility. I cannot understand what it is that makes people afraid of setting out on the road of perfection. May the Lord, because of who He is, give us understanding of how wretched is the security that lies in such manifest dangers as following the crowd and how true security lies in striving to make progress on the road of God. Let them turn their eyes to Him and not fear the setting of this Sun of Justice, nor, if we don't first abandon Him, will He allow us to walk at night and go astray. (L 35:14)

O King of Glory and Lord of all kings! How true that Your kingdom . . . has no end! . . . There is no need for intermediaries with You! Upon beholding Your person one sees immediately that You alone . . . merit to be called Lord.

O my Lord! O my King! Who now would know how to represent Your majesty! It's impossible not to see that You in Yourself are a great Emperor, for to behold Your majesty is startling; and the more one beholds along with this majesty, Lord, Your humility and the love You show to someone like myself the more startling it becomes. Nevertheless, we can converse and speak with You as we like, once the first fright and fear in beholding Your majesty passes; although the fear of offending You becomes greater. But the fear is not one of punishment, for this punishment is considered nothing in comparison with losing You. (L 37:6)

Indeed, I took delight in the Lord today and dared to complain of His Majesty, and I said to Him: "How is it, my God, that it's not enough that You keep me in this miserable life and that for love of You I undergo it and desire to live where everything hinders the enjoyment of You, in that I have to eat and sleep and carry on business and talk with everyone (and I suffer all for love of You, as You well know, my Lord, because it's the greatest torment for me); how is it that when there is so little time left over to enjoy Your presence You hide from me? How is this compatible with Your mercy? How can the love You bear me allow this? I believe, Lord, that if it were possible for me to hide from You as it is for You to hide from me that the love You have for me would not suffer it; but You are with me and see me always. Don't tolerate this, my Lord! I implore You to see that it is injurious to one who loves You so much."

. . . May so good a king be praised! (L 37:8–9)

O my Lord! If You did not hide Your grandeur, who would approach so often a union of something so dirty and miserable with such great majesty! May the angels and all creatures praise You, for You so measure things in accordance with our weakness that when we rejoice in Your sovereign favors Your great power does not so frighten us that, as weak and wretched people, we would not dare enjoy them. (L 38:19)

O Wealth of the poor, how admirably You know how to sustain souls! And without their seeing such great wealth, You show it to them little by little. When I behold majesty as extraordinary as this concealed in something as small as the host, it happens afterward that I marvel at wisdom so wonderful, and I fail to know how the Lord gives me courage or strength to approach Him. If He who has granted, and still does grant me so many favors, did not give this strength, it would be impossible to conceal the fact or resist shouting aloud about marvels so great. (L 38:21)

Certainly, my Lord and my glory, I am about to say that in some way in these great afflictions my soul feels I have done something in Your service. Alas! I don't know what I'm saying to myself, because almost without my uttering this I'm already putting it down in writing. I find I'm disturbed and somewhat outside myself since I have brought these things back to mind. If this sentiment had come from me, I might truly have said that I had done something for You, my Lord; but since there can be no good thought if You do not give it, there's no reason to be thankful to myself. I am the debtor, Lord, and You the offended one. (L 38:22)

May He be blessed forever who gives so much, and to whom I give so little. For what does he do, my Lord, who doesn't get rid of everything for You? How I fail, how I fail, how I fail—and I could say it a thousand times—to get rid of everything for You! There's no reason on this account to want to live (although there are other reasons), because I don't live in conformity with what I owe You. How many imperfections I see in myself! What laxity in serving You! Indeed I think sometimes I would like to be without consciousness in order not to know so much evil about myself. May He who is able provide the remedy. (L 39:6)

Yet pardon me, my Lord, and don't blame me for having to console myself with something, for I don't serve You in anything. If I served You in great matters, I wouldn't be paying attention to trifles. Blessed are those persons who serve You with great deeds! If it were taken into account that I envy them and desire these deeds, I wouldn't be very far behind in pleasing You; but I'm not worth anything, my Lord. Give me worth Yourself since You love me so much.

(*L* 39:13)

O my Grandeur and Majesty! What are You doing, my all-powerful Lord? Look upon whom You bestow such sovereign favors! Don't You recall that this soul has been an abyss of lies and a sea of vanities, and all through my own fault? For even though You gave me the natural temperament to abhor the lie, I myself in dealing with many things have lied. How do You bear it, my God? How is such great consolation and favor compatible with one who so poorly deserves this from You?

(*L* 40:4)

May it please the Lord, since He is powerful and can hear me if He wants, that I might succeed in doing His will in everything. May His Majesty not allow this soul to be lost, which, with so many artifices, in so many ways, and so often, He has rescued from hell and brought to Himself. Amen.

(*L* 40:24)

THE WAY OF PERFECTION

O my Redeemer, my heart cannot bear these thoughts without becoming terribly grieved. What is the matter with Christians nowadays? Must it always be those who owe You the most who afflict You? Those for whom You performed the greatest works, those You have chosen for Your friends, with whom You walk and commune by means of Your sacraments? Aren't they satisfied with the torments You have suffered for them?

(*WP* 1:3)

It seems bold that I think I could play some role in obtaining an answer to these petitions. I trust, my Lord, in these Your servants who live here, and I know they desire and strive for nothing else than to please You. For You they renounced the little they had—and would have wanted to have more so as to serve You with it. Since You, my Creator, are not ungrateful, I think You will not fail to do what they beg of You. Nor did You, Lord, when You walked in the world, despise women; rather, You always, with great compassion, helped them. . . . When we ask You for honors, income, money, or worldly things, do not hear us. But when we ask You for the honor of Your Son, why wouldn't You hear us, eternal Father, for the sake of Him who lost a thousand honors and a thousand lives for You? Not for us, Lord, for we don't deserve it, but for the blood of Your Son and His merits.   (*WP* 3:7)

How then, my Creator, can a heart as loving as Yours allow that the deeds done by Your Son with such ardent love and so as to make us more pleasing to You (for You commanded that He love us) be esteemed so little? For nowadays these heretics have so little regard for the Blessed Sacrament that they take away its dwelling places. . . . Was something still to be done to please You? But He did everything. . . . Hasn't He already paid far more than enough for the sin of Adam? Whenever we sin again must this loving Lamb pay? Don't allow this, my Emperor! Let Your Majesty be at once appeased! . . .

O my God, would that I might have begged You much. . . . Lord . . . , perhaps I am the one who has angered You so that my sins have caused these many evils to come about. Well, what is there for me to do, my Creator, but offer this most blessed bread to You, and even though You have given it to us, return it to You and beg You through the merits of Your Son to grant me this favor since in so many ways He has merited that You do so? Now, Lord, now; make the sea calm! May this ship, which is the Church, not always have to journey in a tempest like this. Save us, Lord, for we are perishing. (*WP* 3:8; 35:5)

May You be blessed, my God, and all creatures praise You! One cannot repay You for this favor—as is likewise so for many others You have granted me—for my vocation to be a nun was a very great favor! Since I have been so miserable, You did not trust me, Lord. Instead of keeping me where there were so many living together and where my wretchedness would not have been so clearly seen during my lifetime, You have brought me to a place where, since there are so few nuns, it seems impossible for this wretchedness not to be known. That I might walk more carefully, You have removed from me all opportunities to conceal it. Now I confess there is no longer an excuse for me, Lord, and so I have greater need of Your mercy that You might pardon any fault I may have. (*WP* 8:2)

O my Lord, when I think of the many ways You suffered and how You deserved none of these sufferings, I . . . do not know where my common sense was when I didn't want to suffer, nor where I am when I excuse myself. You already know, my Good, that if I have some good it is a gift from no one else's hands but Yours. Now, Lord, what costs You more, to give much or little? If it is true that I have not merited this good, neither have I merited the favors You have granted me. Is it possible that I have wanted anyone to feel good about a thing as bad as I after so many evil things have been said about You who are the Good above all goods? Don't allow, don't allow, my God—nor would I ever want You to allow—that there be anything in Your servant that is displeasing in Your eyes. Observe, Lord, that mine are blind and satisfied with very little. Give me light and grant that I may truly desire to be abhorred by all since I have so often failed You who have loved me so faithfully.

The fact is that since we are inclined to ascend—even though we will not ascend to heaven by such an inclination—there must be no descending. O Lord, Lord! Are You our Model and Master? Yes, indeed! Well then, what did Your honor consist of, You who honored us? Didn't You indeed lose it in being humiliated unto death? No, Lord, but You won it for all. (*WP* 15:5; 36:5)

What is this, my God? What do we expect to obtain from pleasing creatures? What does it matter if we are blamed a lot by all of them if in Your presence we are without fault?

(*WP* 15:6)

O my Lord, how often do we make You fight the devil in arm to arm combat! Isn't it enough that You allowed him to take You in his arms when he carried You to the pinnacle of the temple so that You might teach us how to conquer him? But what would it be like, daughters, to see him, with his darknesses, next to the Sun. And what fear that unfortunate one must have borne without knowing why, for God didn't allow him to understand it. Blessed be such compassion and mercy. What shame we Christians ought to have for making Him wrestle arm to arm, as I have said, with so foul a beast. It was truly necessary, Lord, that You have such strong arms. But how is it that they didn't weaken by the many torments

You suffered on the cross? Oh, how everything that is suffered with love is healed again! And so I believe that had You survived, the very love You have for us would have healed Your wounds, for no other medicine was necessary. . . . O my God, grant that I might put medicine like this in everything that causes me pain and trial! How eagerly I would desire these if I could be sure that I'd be healed with so soothing a balm!   (*WP* 16:7)

O Lord, how true that all harm comes to us from not keeping our eyes fixed on You; if we were to look at nothing else but the way, we would soon arrive. But we meet with a thousand falls and obstacles and lose the way because we don't keep our eyes—as I say—on the true way. It seems so new to us that you would think we had never walked on it. It's certainly something to excite pity, that which sometimes happens.   (*WP* 16:11)

O my Lord, and who will find himself so immersed in this living water that he will die! But, is this possible?   (*WP* 19:8)

O my Lord, defend Yourself! See how they understand Your words in reverse. Don't permit such weaknesses in Your servants.   (*WP* 21:8)

Oh, our Emperor, supreme Power, supreme Goodness, Wisdom itself, without beginning, without end, without any limit to Your works; they are infinite and incomprehensible, a fathomless sea of marvels, with a beauty containing all beauty, strength itself! Oh, God help me, who might possess here all human eloquence and wisdom together in order to know how to explain clearly—insofar as is possible here below...—a number of the many things we can consider in order to have some knowledge of who this Lord and God of ours is!   (*WP* 22:1, 4, 6)

O Lord of the world, my true Spouse!... Are You so in need, my Lord and my Love, that You would want to receive such poor company as mine, for I see by Your expression that You have been consoled by me? Well then, how is it Lord that the angels leave You and that even Your Father doesn't console You? If it's true, Lord, that You want to endure everything for me, what is this that I suffer for You? Of what am I complaining? I am already ashamed, since I have seen You in such a condition. I desire to suffer, Lord, all the trials that come to me and esteem them as a great good enabling me to imitate You in something. Let us walk together, Lord. Wherever You go, I will go; whatever You suffer, I will suffer.
                                        (*WP* 26:6)

O Son of God and my Lord! How is it that You give so much all together in the first words? Since You humble Yourself to such an extreme in joining with us in prayer and making Yourself the Brother of creatures so lowly and wretched, how is it that You give us in the name of Your Father everything that can be given? For You desire that He consider us His children, because Your word cannot fail. You oblige Him to be true to Your word, which is no small burden since in being Father He must bear with us no matter how serious the offenses. If we return to Him like the prodigal son, He has to pardon us. He has to console us in our trials. He has to sustain us in the way a father like this must. For, in effect, He must be better than all the fathers in the world because in Him everything must be faultless. And after all this He must make us sharers and heirs with You.

$\qquad$ (*WP* 27:2)

Couldn't You, my Lord, have concluded the Our Father with the words: "Give us, Father, what is fitting for us"? It doesn't seem there would have been need to say anything else to One who understands everything so well.

O Eternal Wisdom! Between You and Your Father these words would have sufficed. Your petition in the garden was like this. You manifested Your own desire and fear, but You abandoned them to His will. Yet, You know us, my Lord, that we are not as surrendered to the will of Your father as You were. You know that it was necessary for You to make those specific requests so that we might pause to consider if what we are seeking is good for us, so that if it isn't we won't ask for it. If we aren't given what we want, being what we are, with this free will we have, we might not accept what the Lord gives. For although what He gives is better, we don't think we'll ever become rich, since we don't at once see the money in our hand.

$\qquad$ (*WP* 30:1–2)

Your will be done on earth as it is in heaven." You did well, good Master of ours, to make this petition so that we might accomplish what You give on our behalf. For certainly, Lord, if You hadn't made the petition, the task would seem to me impossible. But when Your Father does what You ask Him by giving us His kingdom here on earth, I know that we shall make Your words come true by giving what You give for us. For once the earth has become heaven, the possibility is there for Your will to be done in me. But if the earth hasn't—and earth as wretched and barren as mine—I don't know, Lord,

how it will be possible. It is indeed a great thing, that which
You offer!   (*WP* 32:2)

Now I freely give [my will] to You, O Lord, even though I
do so at a time in which I'm not free of self-interest. For I
have felt and have had great experience of the gain that
comes from freely abandoning my will to Yours. . . . Your
will, Lord, be done in me in every way and manner that You,
my Lord, want. If You want it to be done with trials,
strengthen me and let them come; if with persecutions, illnesses, dishonors, and a lack of life's necessities, here I am; I
will not turn away, my Father.   (*WP* 32:4, 10)

Oh, God help me, what great love from the Son and what
great love from the Father! Yet I am not so surprised about
Jesus, for since He had already said, *fiat voluntas tua*, He had
to do that will, being who He is. Yes, for He is not like us!
Since, then, He knows that He does it by loving us as Himself, He went about looking for ways of doing it with greater
perfection, even though His fulfillment of this commandment was at a cost to Himself. But You, Eternal Father, how
is it that You consented? Why do You desire to see Your Son
every day in such wretched hands? Since You have already
desired to see Him in these hands and given Your consent,
You have seen how they treated Him. How can You in Your
compassion now see Him insulted day after day? And how
many insults will be committed today against this Most
Blessed Sacrament! In how many enemies' hands must the
Father see Him! How much irreverence from these heretics!
    O eternal Lord! Why do You accept such a petition? Why
do You consent to it? Don't look at His love for us, because
in exchange for doing Your will perfectly, and doing it for us,

He allows Himself to be crushed to pieces each day. It is for You, my Lord, to look after Him, since He will let nothing deter Him. Why must all our good come at His expense? Why does He remain silent before all and not know how to speak for Himself, but only for us? Well, shouldn't there be someone to speak for this most loving Lamb?   (*WP* 33:3–4)

Well, what is this, my Lord and my God! Either bring the world to an end or provide a remedy for these very serious evils. There is no heart that can suffer them, not even among those of us who are wretched. I beseech You, Eternal Father, that You suffer them no longer. Stop this fire, Lord, for if You will You can. Behold that Your Son is still in the world. Through His reverence may all these ugly and abominable and filthy things cease. In His beauty and purity He doesn't deserve to be in a house where there are things of this sort. Do not answer for our sakes, Lord; we do not deserve it. Do it for Your Son's sake. We don't dare beseech You that He be not present with us; what would become of us? For if something appeases You, it is having a loved one like this here below. Since some means must be had, my Lord, may Your Majesty provide it.   (*WP* 35:4)

O my God, would that I might have begged You much and served You diligently so as to be able to ask for this great favor in payment for my services, since You don't leave anyone without pay! But I have not done so, Lord; rather, perhaps I am the one who has angered You so that my sins have caused these many evils to come about. Well, what is there for me to do, my Creator, but offer this most blessed bread to You, and even though You have given it to us, return it to You and beg You through the merits of Your Son to grant me this favor since in so many ways He has merited that You do so? Now, Lord, now; make the sea calm! May this ship, which is the Church, not always have to journey in a tempest like this. Save us, Lord, for we are perishing.

(*WP* 35:5)

And forgive us, Lord, our debts, as we forgive our debtors."

But, my Lord, are there some persons in my company who have not understood this? If there are, I beg them in Your name to remember this and pay no attention to the little things they call wrongs. It seems that, like children, we are making houses out of straw with these ceremonious little rules of etiquette. Oh, God help me, Sisters, if we knew what honor is and what losing honor consists in! . . .

O Lord, Lord! Are You our Model and Master? Yes, indeed! Well then, what did Your honor consist of, You who honored us? Didn't You indeed lose it in being humiliated unto death? No, Lord, but You won it for all. (*WP* 36:1, 3, 5)

. . . Grant, that our love may never be small, but always most ardent, like a great fire that cannot but shine brightly.

(*WP* 40:4)

May the Lord give [this love] to me because of Who His Majesty is. Let me not leave this life, O my Lord, until I no longer desire anything in it; neither let me know any love outside of You, Lord, nor let me succeed in using this term "love" for anyone else. Everything is false since the foundation is false, and so the edifice doesn't last.   (*WP* 41:1)

I beseech the Lord to deliver me from all evil forever since I do not make up for what I owe; it could be that each day I become more indebted. And what is unendurable, Lord, is not to know for certain that I love You or that my desires are acceptable before You. O my Lord and my God, deliver me now from all evil and be pleased to bring me to the place where all blessings are. . . . How our will deviates in its inclination from that which is the will of God. He wants us to love truth; we love the lie. He wants us to desire the eternal; we, here below, lean toward what comes to an end. He wants us to desire sublime and great things; we, here below, desire base and earthly things. He would want us to desire only what is secure; we, here below, love the dubious. Everything is a mockery . . . except beseeching God to free us from these dangers forever and draw us at last away from every evil. . . . What does it cost us to ask for a great deal? We are asking it of One who is powerful. . . . His name be forever hallowed in heaven and on earth, and may His will be always done in me. Amen.   (*WP* 42:2, 4)

Deliver me, Lord, from this shadow of death, deliver me from so many trials, deliver me from so many sufferings, deliver me from these many changes, from so many compliments that we are forced to receive while still living, from so many, many, many things that tire and weary me, that would tire anyone reading this if I mentioned them all. There's no longer anyone who can bear to live here. This weariness must come to me because I have lived very badly, and from seeing that the way I live now is still not the way I should live since I owe so much. . . .

O my Lord and my God, deliver me now from all evil and be pleased to bring me to the place where all blessings are.

(*WP* 42:2)

MEDITATIONS ON THE SONG OF SONGS

O my Lord, how poorly we profit from the blessing You grant us! You seek ways and means and You devise plans to show Your love for us; we, inexperienced in loving You, esteem this love so poorly that our minds, little exercised in love, go where they always go and cease to think of the great mysteries this language, spoken by the Holy Spirit, contains within itself. . . . Being what we are, the love that He had and has for us surprises and bewilders me more; for knowing that He has such love I already understand that there is no exaggeration in the words by which He reveals it to us, for He has shown this love even more through His deeds.

(*M* 1:4, 7)

May You be blessed, Lord, my God, for You show us so much pity that it seems You forget Your greatness so as not to punish—as would be right—a betrayal as treacherous as this.

(*M* 2:19)

O Lord of heaven and earth, how is it possible that even while in this mortal life one can enjoy You with so special a friendship? . . . May You be blessed, Lord, because we don't lose anything through Your fault. Along how many paths, in how many ways, by how many methods You show us love! With trials, with a death so harsh, with torments, suffering offenses every day and then pardoning; and not only with these deeds do You show this love, but with words so capable of wounding the soul in love with You that You say them in this Song of Songs and teach the soul what to say to You. . . .

My Lord, I do not ask You for anything else in life but that *You kiss me with the kiss of Your mouth*, and that You do so in such a way that although I may want to withdraw from this friendship and union, my will may always, Lord of my life, be subject to Your will and not depart from it. . . .   (*M* 3:14–15)

Great is this favor, my Spouse; a pleasing feast. Precious wine do You give me, for with one drop alone You make me forget all of creation and go out from creatures and myself, so that I will no longer want the joys and comforts that my sensuality desired up until now. Great is this favor; I did not deserve it.   (*M* 4:6)

What am I, Lord? If I am not close to You, what am I worth? If I stray a little from Your Majesty, where will I end up?

Oh, my Lord, my Mercy, and my Good! And what greater good could I want in this life than to be so close to You, that there be no division between You and me? With this companionship, what can be difficult? What can one not undertake for You, being so closely joined? . . . Never, with Your favor and help, will I turn my back on You.

Now I see, my Bridegroom, that *You are mine.* I cannot deny it. You came into the world for me; for me You underwent severe trials; for me You suffered many lashes; for me You remain in the most Blessed Sacrament. . . . With what ardor I have said . . . "What can I do for my Spouse?" . . .

What can one who has used so unskillfully the favors You have granted do for You? What can be expected of her services? Since with Your help she does something, consider what a poor worm will be able to do. Why does a Lord so powerful need her? Oh, love! How I would want to say this word everywhere because love alone is that which can dare say with the bride, *I am my Beloved's.* He gives us permission to think that He, this true Lover, My Spouse and my Good, needs us. . . .

If You come to me, why do I doubt that I will be able to serve You? From here on, Lord, I want to forget myself and look only at how I can serve You and have no other desire than to do Your will. But my desire is not powerful, my God; You are the powerful One. What I can do is be determined; thus from this very moment I am determined to serve You through deeds.   (*M* 4:8–12)

It seems to me the Holy Spirit must be a mediator between the soul and God, the One who moves it with such ardent desires, for He enkindles it in a supreme fire, which is so near. O Lord, how great are these mercies You show to the soul here! May You be blessed and praised forever, for You are so good a Lover. O my God and my Creator! Is it possible that there is no one who loves You? Oh, alas, and how often it is I who do not love You! . . .

And the Lord is not content with all this—something marvelous, worthy of careful attention—for He understands that the soul is totally His, without any other interests. This means that things must not move it because of what they are, but that it be moved because of Who its God is and out of love for Him, since He never ceases to commune with it in so many ways and manners, as One Who is Wisdom itself. . . .

Well now, what more could we desire than this favor just mentioned? Oh, God help me, how little we desire to reach

Your grandeurs, Lord! How miserable we would remain if Your giving were in conformity with our asking!   (*M* 5:5–6)

W*ho is this that is as bright as the sun?* O true King, and how right the bride was in giving You this name! For in a moment You can give riches and place them in a soul that they may be enjoyed forever. How well ordered love is in this soul!

(*M* 6:11)

I don't believe that souls brought to this state by the Lord . . . think of themselves, and of whether they will lose or gain. . . . They look only at serving and pleasing the Lord. And because they know the love He has for His servants, they like to leave aside their own satisfaction and good so as to please Him and serve and tell souls beneficial truths by the best means they can. Nor do they . . . think about whether or not they will themselves lose. They keep before their minds the benefit of their neighbor, nothing else. So as to please God more, they forget themselves for their neighbor's sake, and they lose their lives in the challenge, as did many martyrs.   (*M* 7:5)

SOLILOQUIES

I

[1]   . . . O Lord, how gentle are Your ways! But who will walk them without fear? I fear to live without serving You; and when I set out to serve You, I find nothing that proves a satisfactory payment for anything of what I owe. It seems I want to be completely occupied in Your service, and when

I consider well my own misery I see I can do nothing good, unless You give me this good.

[2]   O my God and my Mercy! What shall I do so as not to undo the great things You've done for me? Your works are holy, they are just, they are priceless and done with great wisdom, since You, Lord, are wisdom itself. If my intellect busies itself with this wisdom, my will complains. It wouldn't want anything to hinder it from loving You, because the intellect cannot reach the sublime grandeurs of its God. And my will desires to enjoy Him, but it doesn't see how it can since it is placed in a prison as painful as is this mortality. Everything hinders my will, although it was helped by the consideration of Your grandeurs, by which my countless miseries are better revealed.

[3]   Why have I said this, my God? To whom am I complaining? Who hears me but You, my Father and Creator? That You might hear of my sorrow, what need have I to speak, for I so clearly see that You are within me? This is foolish of me. But, alas, my God, how can I know for certain I'm not separated from You? O my life, how can you live with such little assurance of something so important? Who will desire you, since the gain one can acquire or hope for from you, that is, to please God in all, is so uncertain and full of dangers?

2

[1]   I often reflect, my Lord, that if there is something by which life can endure being separated from You, it is solitude. For the soul rests in the quiet of solitude; yet, since it is not completely free for the enjoyment of solitude, the torment is

often doubled. But the torment arising from the obligation
to deal with creatures and from not being allowed to be
alone with one's Creator makes the soul consider that first
torment a delight. But why is this, my God, that quiet tires
the soul that aims only at pleasing You? Oh, powerful love
of God, how different are your effects from those of the
world's love! This latter love doesn't want company since
company would seem to oblige it to give up what it possesses. In the case of the love of my God, the more lovers
that love knows there are, the more it increases; and so its
joys are tempered by seeing that not all enjoy that good. O
my God, what is this that happens: in the greatest favors and
consolations coming from You, the memory grieves over the
many there are who don't want these consolations and over
those who will lose them forever! So the soul looks for ways
to find company, and willingly sets aside its joy when it
thinks it can be of some help that others might strive to
enjoy it.

[2]   But, my heavenly Father, wouldn't it be more worthwhile to
leave aside these desires until a time when the soul has less
experience of Your favors, and now be completely occupied
in enjoying You? Oh, my Jesus, how great is the love You
bear the children of men, for the greatest service one can
render You is to leave You for their sake and their benefit—
and then You are possessed more completely. For although
the will isn't so satisfied through enjoyment, the soul rejoices
because it is pleasing You. And it sees that while we live this
mortal life, earthly joys are uncertain, even when they seem
to be given by You, if they are not accompanied by love of
neighbor. Whoever fails to love his neighbor, fails to love
You, my Lord, since we see You showed the very great love

You have for the children of Adam by shedding so much blood.

3

[1]   My soul grew greatly distressed, my God, while considering the glory You've prepared for those who persevere in doing Your will, the number of trials and sufferings by which Your Son gained it, and how much love in its greatness, which at such a cost taught us to love, deserves our gratitude. How is it possible, Lord, that all this love is forgotten and that mortals are so forgetful of You when they offend You? O my Redeemer, and how completely forgetful of themselves they are! What great goodness is Yours, that You then remember us, and that though we have fallen through the mortal wound we inflicted on You, You return to us, forgetful of this, to lend a hand and awaken us from so incurable a madness, that we might seek and beg salvation of You! Blessed be such a Lord; blessed be such great mercy; and praised forever such tender compassion!

[2]   Oh, my soul, bless forever so great a God. How is it possible to turn against Him? Oh, how the greatness of Your favor, Lord, harms those who are ungrateful? May You, my God, provide the remedy. Children of the earth, how long will you be hard of heart and keep your hearts opposed to this most meek Jesus? What is this? Shall our wickedness against Him perhaps endure? No, for the life of humans comes to an end like the flower of the field, and the Virgin's Son must come to give that terrible sentence. O my powerful God! Since even though we may not so desire, You must judge us, why don't we consider how important it is to please You before

that hour comes? But who, who will not want so just a Judge? Blessed will they be who in that fearful moment rejoice with You, my God and Lord! The soul You have raised up has known how miserably lost it was for the sake of gaining a very brief satisfaction, and it is determined to please You always. Since You, my soul's Good, do not fail those who desire You or cease to respond to those who call upon You, what remedy, through Your favor, Lord, will You provide that the soul may be able to live afterward and not be dying over the remembrance of having lost the great good it once possessed through the innocence that came from baptism? The best life it can have is to die always with this feeling of compunction. But the soul that loves You tenderly, how can it bear this?

[3]   Yet what foolishness I'm asking You, my Lord! It seems I've forgotten Your grandeurs and mercies and how You've come into the world for sinners and have purchased us at so great a price and have paid for our false joys by suffering such cruel torments and blows.

You have cured my blindness with the blindfold that covered Your divine eyes and my vanity with that cruel crown of thorns!

O Lord, Lord! All this saddens more the one who loves You. The only consolation is that Your mercy will be praised forever when my wickedness is known. Nevertheless, I don't know if this weariness will be taken away until all the miseries of this mortal life are removed by seeing You.

4

[1]   It seems, my Lord, my soul finds rest in considering the joy it

will have if through Your mercy the fruition of Yourself is granted it. But first it would want to serve You since it will be enjoying what You, in serving it, have gained for it. What shall I do, my Lord? What shall I do, my God? Oh, how late have my desires been enkindled and how early, Lord, were You seeking and calling that I might be totally taken up with You! Do You perhaps, Lord, abandon the wretched or withdraw from the poor beggar when he wants to come to You? Do Your grandeurs or Your magnificent works, Lord, perhaps have a limit? O my God and my Mercy, how You can show them now in Your servant! You are mighty, great God! Now it can be known whether my soul understands itself in being aware of the time it has lost and of how in a moment You, Lord, can win this time back again. It seems foolish to me, since they usually say lost time cannot be recovered. May You be blessed, my God!

[2]   O Lord, I confess Your great power. If You are powerful, as You are, what is impossible for You who can do everything? Please my Lord, give the order, give the order, for although I am miserable, I firmly believe You can do what You desire. And the more I hear of Your greater marvels and consider that You can add to them, the more my faith is strengthened; and I believe with greater determination that You will do this. What is there to marvel at in what the Almighty does? You know well, my God, that in the midst of all my miseries I never failed to acknowledge Your great power and mercy. May that in which I have not offended You, Lord, help me.

Recover, my God, the lost time by giving me grace in the present and future so that I may appear before You with wedding garments; for if You want to, You can do so.

5

[1]   O my Lord, how does anyone who has so poorly served You and so poorly known how to keep what You have given her dare ask for favors? What can be entrusted to one who has often been a traitor? What, then, shall I do, Consoler of the disconsolate and Cure for anyone who wants to be cured by You? Would it be better, perhaps, to keep still about my needs, hoping You will provide the remedy for them? Certainly not: for You, my Lord and my delight, knowing the many needs there must be and the comfort it is for us to rely on You, tell us to ask You and that You will not fail to give.

[2]   I sometimes remember the complaint of that holy woman, Martha. She did not complain only about her sister, rather, I hold it is certain that her greatest sorrow was the thought that You, Lord, did not feel sad about the trial she was undergoing and didn't care whether she was with You or not. Perhaps she thought You didn't have as much love for her as for her sister. This must have caused her greater sorrow than did serving the one for whom she had such great love; for love turns work into rest. It seems that in saying nothing to her sister but in directing her whole complaint to You, Lord, that love made her dare to ask why You weren't concerned. And even Your reply seems to refer to her complaint as I have interpreted it, for love alone is what gives value to all things; and a kind of love so great that nothing hinders it is the one thing necessary. But how can we possess, my God, a love in conformity with what the Beloved deserves, if Your love does not join love with itself? Shall I complain with this holy woman? Oh, I have no reason at all, for I have always seen in my God much greater and more extraordinary signs of love

than I have known how to ask for or desire! If I don't complain about the many things Your kindness has suffered for me, I have nothing to complain about. What, then, can so miserable a thing as I ask for? That You, my God, give to me what I might give to You, as St. Augustine says, so that I may repay You something of the great debt I owe You; that You remember that I am the work of Your hands; and that I may know Who my Creator is in order to love Him.

6

[1] O my delight, Lord of all created things and my God! How long must I wait to see You? What remedy do You provide for one who finds so little on earth that might give some rest apart from You? O long life! O painful life! O life that is not lived! Oh, what lonely solitude; how incurable! Well, when, Lord, when? How long? What shall I do, my God, what shall I do? Should I, perhaps, desire not to desire You? Oh, my God and my Creator, You wound and You do not supply the medicine; You wound and the sore is not seen; You kill, leaving one with more life! In sum, my Lord, being powerful You do what You will. Well, my God, do You want so despicable a worm to suffer these contradictions? Let it be so, my God, since You desire it, for I desire nothing but to love You.

[2] But, alas, alas, my Creator, what great pain it causes to complain and speak of what has no remedy until You give one! And the soul so imprisoned wants its freedom, while desiring not to depart one iota from what You want. Desire, my Glory, that its pain increase; or cure it completely. O death, death, I don't know who fears you, since life lies in you! But

who will not fear after having wasted a part of life in not loving God? And since I am one of these, what do I ask for and what do I desire? Perhaps the punishment so well deserved for my faults? Don't permit it, my Good, for my ransom cost You a great deal.

[3]   Oh, my soul! Let the will of God be done; this suits you. Serve and hope in His mercy, for He will cure your grief when penance for your faults will have gained some pardon for them. Don't desire joy but suffering. O true Lord and my King! I'm still not ready for suffering if Your sovereign hand and greatness do not favor me, but with these I shall be able to do all things.

7

[1]   O my Hope, my Father, my Creator, and my true Lord and Brother! When I consider how You say that Your delights are with the children of the earth, my soul rejoices greatly. O Lord of heaven and earth, what words these are that no sinner might be wanting in trust! Are You, Lord, perhaps lacking someone with whom to delight that You seek such a foul-smelling little worm like myself? That voice that was heard at the Baptism says You delight in Your Son. Well, will we all be equal, Lord? Oh, what extraordinary mercy and what favor so beyond our ability to deserve! And that mortals forget all of this! Be mindful, my God, of so much misery, and behold our weakness, since You are the Knower of everything.

[2]   O my soul: Consider the great delight and great love the Father has in knowing His Son and the Son in knowing His

Father; and the enkindling love with which the Holy Spirit is joined with them; and how no one of them is able to be separate from this love and knowledge, because they are one. These sovereign Persons know each other, love each other, and delight in each other. Well, what need is there for my love? Why do You want it, my God, or what do You gain? Oh, may You be blessed! May You be blessed, my God, forever! May all things praise You, Lord, without end, since in You there can be no end.

[3] Be joyful, my soul, for there is someone who loves your God as He deserves. Be joyful, for there is someone who knows His goodness and value. Give thanks to Him, for He has given us on earth someone who thus knows Him, as His only Son. Under this protection you can approach and petition Him, for then His Majesty takes delight in you. Don't let any earthly thing be enough to separate you from your delight, and rejoice in the grandeur of God; in how He deserves to be loved and praised; that He helps you to play some small role in the blessing of His name; and that you can truthfully say: *My soul magnifies and praises the Lord.*

8

[1] O Lord, my God, how You possess the words of eternal life, where all mortals will find what they desire if they want to seek it! But what a strange thing, my God, that we forget Your words in the madness and sickness our evil deeds cause! O my God, God, God, author of all creation! And what is creation if You, Lord, should desire to create more? You are almighty; Your works are incomprehensible. Bring it about, then, Lord, that my thoughts not withdraw from Your words.

[2]   You say: *Come to me all who labor and are burdened, for I will comfort you.* What more do we want, Lord? What are we asking for? What do we seek? Why are those in the world so unhappy if not because of seeking rest? God help me! Oh, God help me! What is this, Lord? Oh, what a pity! Oh, what great blindness, that we seek rest where it is impossible to find it! Have mercy, Creator, on these Your creatures. Behold, we don't understand or know what we desire, nor do we obtain what we ask for. Lord, give us light; behold, the need is greater than with the man born blind, for he wanted to see the light and couldn't. Now, Lord, there is no desire to see. Oh, how incurable an illness! Here, my God, is where Your power must be demonstrated; here, Your mercy.

[3]   Oh, what a difficult thing I ask You, my true God; that You love someone who doesn't love You, that You open to one who doesn't knock, that You give health to one who likes to be sick and goes about looking for sickness. You say, my Lord, that You come to seek sinners; these, Lord, are real sinners. Don't look at our blindness, my God, but at all the blood Your Son shed for us. Let Your mercy shine upon evil that has so increased; behold, Lord, we are Your handiwork. May Your goodness and mercy help us.

9

[1]   O compassionate and loving Lord of my soul! You likewise say: *Come to me all who thirst, for I will give you drink.* How can anyone who is burning in the living flames of cupidity for these miserable earthly things fail to experience great thirst? There is an extraordinary need for water so that one might not be completely consumed by this fire. I already know, my Lord, that out of Your goodness You will give it. You Your-

self say so; Your words cannot fail. Well, if those accustomed to living in this fire and to being reared in it, no longer feel it or, like fools, do not succeed in recognizing their great need, what remedy is there, my God? You've come into the world as a remedy for needs such as these. Begin, Lord! Your compassion must be shown in the most difficult situations. Behold, my God, Your enemies are gaining a great deal. Have pity on those who have no pity on themselves; now that their misfortune has placed them in a state in which they don't want to come to You, come to them Yourself, my God. I beg this of You in their name; and I know that as they understand and turn within themselves and begin to taste You, these dead ones will rise.

[2] O Life, who gives life to all! Do not deny me this sweetest water that You promise to those who want it. I want it, Lord, and I beg for it, and I come to You. Don't hide Yourself, Lord, from me, since You know my need and that this water is the true medicine for a soul wounded with love of You. O Lord, how many kinds of fire there are in this life! Oh, how true it is that one should live in fear! Some kinds of fire consume the soul, other kinds purify it that it might live ever rejoicing in You. O living founts from the wounds of my God, how you have flowed with great abundance for our sustenance, and how surely those who strive to sustain themselves with this divine liqueur will advance in the midst of the dangers of this life.

10

[1] O God of my soul, how we hasten to offend You and how You hasten even more to pardon us! What reason is there, Lord, for such deranged boldness? Could it be that we have

already understood Your great mercy and have forgotten that Your justice is just?

The sorrows of death surround me. Oh, oh, oh, what a serious thing sin is, for it was enough to kill God with so many sorrows! And how surrounded You are by them, my God! Where can You go that they do not torment You? Everywhere mortals wound You.

[2]   O Christians, it's time to defend your King and to accompany Him in such great solitude. Few are the vassals remaining with Him, and the great multitude accompanying Lucifer. And what's worse is that these latter appear as His friends in public and sell Him in secret. He finds almost no one in whom to trust. O true Friend, how badly they pay You back who betray You! O true Christians, help your God weep, for those compassionate tears are not only for Lazarus but for those who were not going to want to rise, even though His Majesty call them. O my God, how You bear in mind the faults I have committed against You! May they now come to an end, Lord, may they come to an end, and those of everyone. Raise up these dead; may Your cries be so powerful that even though they do not beg life of You, You give it to them so that afterward, my God, they might come forth from the depth of their own delights.

[3]   Lazarus did not ask You to raise him up. You did it for a woman sinner; behold one here, my God, and a much greater one; let Your mercy shine. I, although miserable, ask life for those who do not want to ask it of You. You already know, my King, what torment it is for me to see them so forgetful of the great endless torments they will suffer if they don't return to You.

O you who are accustomed to delights, satisfactions, and consolations, and to always doing your own will, take pity on yourselves! Recall that you will have to be subject forever and ever, without end, to the infernal furies. Behold, behold that the Judge who will condemn you now asks you; and that your lives are not safe for one moment. Why don't you want to live forever? Oh, hardness of human hearts! May Your boundless compassion, my God, soften these hearts.

11

[1]   Oh, God, help me! Oh, God, help me! How great a torment it is for me when I consider what a soul that has always here below been valued, loved, served, esteemed, and pampered will feel when after having died finds itself lost forever, and understands clearly that this loss is endless. (Forgetting about the truths of faith will be no help there, as it is here below.) Also what a torment it is for me to consider what a soul will feel when it finds itself separated from what seemingly it will not yet have begun to enjoy (and rightly so, for all that which ends with life is but a breath of wind), and surrounded by that deformed and pitiless company with whom it will always have to suffer. It will be placed in that fetid lake filled with snakes, and the bigger the snake, the bigger the bite; in that miserable darkness where it will only see what gives it torment and pain, without seeing any light other than a dark flame! Oh, how ineffective exaggeration is in expressing what this suffering is!

[2]   O Lord, who placed so much mud in the eyes of this soul that it has not seen these things before it sees them there? O Lord, who stopped its ears that it didn't hear the many times

these things were explained to it or of the eternity of these torments? O life that shall not end! O torment without end! O torment without end! How is it they don't fear you, those who are afraid to sleep on a hard bed lest they cause their body discomfort?

[3]   O Lord, my God! I weep for the time I didn't understand; and since You know, my God, the great number who don't want to understand, I now beg You, Lord, let there be at least one, at least one who will see Your light so that many might possess it. Not through my merits, Lord, for I don't deserve it, but through the merits of Your Son. Behold His wounds, Lord, and since He pardoned those who inflicted them, may You pardon us.

12

[1]   O my God and my true Fortitude! What is this, Lord, that we are cowards about everything except being against You? In opposing You, all the strength of the children of Adam is used up. And if their reason weren't so blind, the reasonings of all together wouldn't suffice for them to dare to take up arms against their Creator, and sustain a continual war against one who in a moment can plunge them into the abyss. But since they are blind, they are like madmen seeking their death because in their imagination it seems to them that by death they gain life. In sum, they are like people without reason. What can we do, my God, with those who have this infirmity of madness? It is said that evil itself brings them great strength. Thus, those who withdraw from my God are sick people because all their fury is turned against You Who give them every good.

[2] O incomprehensible Wisdom! How necessary is all the love You have for creatures in order to endure so much madness and to wait for our cure and strive to bring it about through a thousand ways and means and remedies! It is something frightening to me when I consider that we lack the strength to be restrained in some very light matter (for they are truly convinced that they are unable to give up an occasion and withdraw from a danger where they may lose their souls), and yet we have strength and courage to attack a Majesty as great as Yours. What is this, my God? What is this? Who gives this strength? Isn't the captain, whom they follow in this battle against You, Your slave banned to eternal fire? Why does one rise up against You? How does the conquered one give courage? How is it they follow one so poor that he is driven away from the heavenly riches? What can anyone give who has nothing himself, other than a lot of unhappiness? What is this, my God? What is this, my Creator? Where does all this strength against You come from, and all this cowardice against the devil? Such an attitude would be the wrong way to attain what You have kept for us eternally and to realize that all the devil's joys and promises are false and traitorous, even if You, my Prince, did not favor Your own, even if we owed something to this prince of darkness. What can we expect from him who was against You?

[3] Oh, great blindness, my God! What extraordinary ingratitude, my King! What incurable madness, that we serve the devil with what You, my God, give us! Shall we repay the great love You bear us by loving the one who so abhors You and must abhor You forever? After the blood You shed for us, and the blows and great sorrows You suffered, and the severe torments You endured, do we, as a substitute for avenging

Your heavenly Father (since He doesn't want vengeance, and pardons the great disrespect with which His Son was treated), accept as companions and friends those who disrespectfully treated Him? Since we follow their infernal captain, it is clear we shall all be one and live forever in his company, if Your compassion does not provide a remedy and bring us back to our senses and pardon us for the past.

[4]   O mortals, return, return, to yourselves! Behold your King, for now you will find Him meek; put an end to so much wickedness; turn your fury and your strength against the one who makes war on you and wants to take away your birthright. Turn, turn within yourselves, open your eyes, with loud cries and tears seek light from the one who gave it to the world. Understand for love of God that you with all your strength are about to kill the one who to give you life lost His own. Behold that it is He who defends you from your enemies. And if all this is not enough, let it be enough for you to know that you cannot do anything against His power and that sooner or later you shall have to pay through eternal fire for such great disrespect and boldness. Why is it you see this Majesty bound and tied by the love He bears us? What more did those who delivered Him to death do, but inflict blows and wounds on Him after He was bound?

[5]   Oh, my God, how much You suffer for one who grieves so little over Your pains! The time will come, Lord, when You will have to make known Your justice and whether it is the equal of Your mercy. Behold, Christians, let us consider it carefully and we shall never finish understanding the splendor of the Lord's mercies and what we owe Him. For if His justice is so great, alas, what will become of those who

have deserved that it be carried out and that it shine forth in them?

13

[1] O souls that without fear already have fruition of your joy and are always absorbed in praises of my God, happy has been your lot! What great reason you have for being ever engaged in these praises. How my soul envies you, for you are already free from the sorrow such terrible offenses committed against my God cause in these unfortunate times, and from the sorrow of seeing so much ingratitude, and seeing that there is no awareness of the multitude of souls that are being carried away by Satan. O blessed heavenly souls! Help our misery and be our intercessors before the divine mercy that we may be given some of your joy and a share in this clear knowledge you possess.

[2] Give us understanding, my God, of what it is that is given to those who fight valiantly in the dream of this miserable life. Obtain for us, O loving souls, understanding of the joy it gives you to see the eternal character of your fruition, and how it is so delightful to see certainly that it will have no end. Oh, how fortunate we are, my Lord! For we believe in everlasting joy and know the truth well; but with so pronounced a habit of failing to reflect on these truths, they have already become so foreign to our souls that these souls neither know about them nor desire to know about them. O selfish people, greedy for your pleasures and delights; not waiting a short time in order to enjoy them in such abundance, not waiting a year, not waiting a day, not waiting an hour—and perhaps it will take no more than a moment—you lose everything, because of the joy of that misery you see present!

[3] Oh, oh, oh, how little we trust You, Lord! How much greater the riches and treasures You entrusted to us, since after His thirty-three years of great trials and so unbearable and pitiable a death, You have given us Your Son; and so many years before we were born! Even knowing that we wouldn't repay You, You didn't want to cease trusting us with such an inestimable treasure, so that it wouldn't be Your fault, merciful Father, if we fail to acquire what through Him we can obtain from You.

[4] O blessed souls who with this precious price knew so well how to profit and buy an inheritance so delightful and permanent, tell us how you gained such an unending good! Help us, since you are so near the fount; draw water for those here below who are perishing of thirst.

14

[1] O my Lord and true God! Whoever does not know You does not love You. What a great truth this is! But, alas, Lord, there are those who don't want to know You! A dreadful thing is the hour of death. But, alas, my Creator, how frightful will be the day when Your justice will have to be exercised! I often consider, my Christ, how pleasing and delightful Your eyes are to one who loves You; and You, my God, want to look with love. It seems to me that only one such gentle glance toward souls that You possess as Yours is enough reward for many years of service. Oh, God help me, how hard it is to explain this unless to those who have already understood how gentle the Lord is.

[2] Christians, Christians! Behold the communion you have with this great God; recognize it and don't despise it, for just

as this glance is agreeable to His lovers, it is frightful with a terrifying wrath for His persecutors. Oh, how we fail to understand that sin is a battle pitched against God with all our soul's senses and faculties. He who can commit more sins, invents more treachery against his King. You already know, my Lord, that recalling that I might see Your divine face angered with me on this frightful day of the final judgment caused me greater fear than all the pains and furies of hell shown to me. I beg You that Your mercy may protect me from a thing that would be so sad for me, and thus I beg it of You now, Lord. What can happen to me on earth that would resemble this? I want to possess all, my God. May I not fail to enjoy peacefully so much beauty. Your Father gave You to us, may I not lose, my Lord, so precious a jewel. I confess, eternal Father, I have kept it poorly. But there is still a remedy, Lord, there is still a remedy while we live in this exile. . . .

[4] O Lord, God, help me! Oh what hardness! Oh, what foolishness and blindness! If when something is lost (a needle or a sparrow hawk that isn't worth anything other than to give a little pleasure upon seeing it fly through the air) we feel sad, why don't we feel sad upon losing this royal eagle of God's majesty and a kingdom of endless enjoyment? What is this? I don't understand it. My God, cure such a great foolishness and blindness.

15

[1] Woe is me, woe is me, Lord, how very long is this exile! And it passes with great sufferings of longing for my God! Lord, what can a soul placed in this prison do? O Jesus, how long is the life of humans, even though it is said to be short!

It is short, my God, for gaining through it a life that cannot end; but it is very long for the soul that desires to come into the presence of its God. What remedy do You provide for this suffering? There isn't any, except when one suffers for You.

[2]   I desire, Lord, to please You; but my happiness I know well doesn't lie with any mortal beings. Since this is true, You will not blame my desire. See me here, Lord, if it's necessary to live in order to render You some service, I don't refuse all the trials that can come to me on earth, as Your lover St. Martin said.

[3]   But alas, woe is me, Lord, for he had works and I have only words, because I'm not good for anything else! May my desire be worthwhile, my God, before Your divine Presence, and don't look at my lack of merit. May we all merit to love You, Lord. Now that we must live may we live for You, may our desires and self-interests come to an end. What greater thing can be gained than to please You? O my Happiness and my God, what shall I do to please You? Miserable are my services, even though I may have rendered many to my God. Why, then, must I remain in this miserable wretchedness? That the will of the Lord may be done. What greater sin, my soul? Wait, wait, for you know neither the day nor the hour. Watch with care, for everything passes quickly, even though your desire makes the certain doubtful and the short time long. Behold the more you struggle the more you show the love you have for your God and the more you will rejoice in your Beloved with a joy and delight that cannot end.

16

[1] O true God and my Lord! It is a great consolation for the soul wearied by the loneliness of being separated from You to see that You are everywhere. But when the vehemence of love and the great impulses of this pain increase, there's no remedy, my God. For the intellect is disturbed and the reason is so kept from knowing the truth of Your omnipresence that it can neither understand nor know. It only knows it is separated from You and it accepts no remedy. For the heart that greatly loves receives no counsel or consolation except from the very one who wounded it, because from that one it hopes its pain will be cured. When You desire, Lord, You quickly heal the wound You have caused; prior to this there is no hope for healing or joy, except for the joy of such worthwhile suffering.

[2] O true Lover, with how much compassion, with how much gentleness, with how much delight, with how much favor and with what extraordinary signs of love You cure these wounds, which with the darts of this same love You have caused! O my God and my rest from all pains, how entranced I am! How could there be human means to cure what the divine fire has made sick? Who is there who knows how deep this wound goes, or how it came about, or how so painful and delightful a torment can be mitigated? It would be unreasonable were so precious a sickness able to be mitigated by something so lowly as are the means mortals can use. How right the bride of the Canticles is in saying: *My Beloved is for me and I for my Beloved,* . . . for it is impossible that a love like this begin with something so lowly as is my love.

[3]   Well, if it is lowly, my Spouse, how is it that it is not so lowly in rising from the creature to its Creator? Oh, my God, why "I for my Beloved"? You, my true Lover, have begun this war of love, because this love doesn't seem to be anything else than a restlessness and dereliction on the part of all the faculties and senses; for they go out into the streets and squares entreating the daughters of Jerusalem to tell of their God. Once, Lord, this battle was begun, who are these faculties to fight against, if not against the one who has been made lord of this fortress where they dwell, which is the highest part of the soul? They are driven out so that they might return to conquer their Conqueror. And now, tired of seeing themselves without Him, they quickly surrender and lose all their forces, and fight better; and by surrendering they win the victory over their Victor.

[4]   O my soul, what a wonderful battle you have waged in this pain, and how literally true is what happens here! Since *my Beloved is for me and I for my Beloved*, who will be able to separate and extinguish two fires so enkindled? It would amount to laboring in vain, for the two fires have become one.

17

[1]   O my God and my infinite Wisdom, measureless and boundless and beyond all the human and angelic intellects! O love that loves me more than I can love myself or understand! Why, Lord, do I want to desire more than what You want to give me? Why do I want to tire myself in asking You for something decreed by my desire? For with regard to everything my intellect can devise and my desire can want You've already understood my soul's limits, and I don't understand how my desire will help me. In this that my soul thinks it will

gain, it will perhaps lose. For I ask You to free me from a trial, and the purpose of that trial is my mortification, what is it that I'm asking for, my God? If I beg You to give the trial, it perhaps is not a suitable one for my patience, which is still weak and cannot suffer such a forceful blow. And if I suffer it with patience and am not strong in humility, it may be that I will think I've done something, whereas You do it all, my God. If I want to suffer, but not in matters in which it might seem unfitting for Your service that I lose my reputation—since as for myself I don't know of any concern in me about honor—it may be that for the very reason I think my reputation might be lost, more will be gained on account of what I'm seeking, which is to serve You.

[2] I could say many more things about this, Lord, in order to explain that I don't understand myself. But since I know You understand these things, why am I speaking? So that when I awaken to my misery, my God, and see my blind reason, I might be able to see whether I find this misery in what I write. How often I see myself, my God, so wretched, weak, and fainthearted. For I go about looking for what Your servant has done, since it already seemed to her she had received favors from You to fight against the tempests of this world. But no, my God, no; no more trust in anything I can desire for myself. Desire from me what You want to desire, because this is what I want; for all my good is in pleasing You. And if You, my God, should desire to please me by fulfilling all my desire seeks, I see that I would be lost.

[3] How miserable is the wisdom of mortals and how uncertain their providence! May You through Your providence, Lord, provide the necessary means by which my soul may serve

You at Your pleasure rather than at its own. Don't punish me by giving me what I want or desire if Your love, which lives in me always, doesn't desire it. May this "I" die, and may another live in me greater than I and better for me than I, so that I may serve Him. May He live and give me life. May He reign, and may I be captive, for my soul doesn't want any other liberty. . . . Happy are those who with the strong fetters and chains of the kindnesses of the mercy of God find themselves prisoners and deprived of the power to break loose. *Love is strong as death, and unyielding as hell.* Oh, that I might be slain by Him and thrown into this divine hell where there is no longer any hope of coming out; or better, any fear of finding oneself outside! But, woe is me, Lord; while this mortal life lasts, eternal life is ever in danger!

[4]   O life at enmity with my good; who has leave to bring you to an end? I bear with you because God bears with you; I maintain you because you are His; do not be a traitor or ungrateful to me.

Nonetheless, woe is me, Lord, for my exile is long! Short is all life in exchange for Your eternity; very long is one day alone and one hour for those who don't know and who fear whether they will offend You! O free will, so much the slave of your freedom if you don't live fastened with fear and love of your Creator! Oh, when will that happy day arrive when you will see yourself drowned in the infinite sea of supreme truth, where you will no longer be free to sin! Nor will you want to sin, for you will be safe from every misery, naturalized by the life of your God!

[6]   . . . Don't abandon me, Lord, because I hope that in You my hope will not be confounded; may I always serve You; and do with me whatever You will.   (*CWT* 1)

THE FOUNDATIONS

My desires to be of some help to some soul as time went on had grown much greater. And I often felt like one who has a great treasure stored up and desires that all enjoy it, but whose hands are bound and unable to distribute it. . . . I was so grief-stricken over the loss of so many souls that I couldn't contain myself. . . . I cried out to the Lord, begging Him that He give me the means to be able to do something to win some souls to His service, . . . and that my prayer would do some good since I wasn't able to do anything else. I was very envious of those who for love of our Lord were able to be engaged in winning souls, though they might suffer a thousand deaths. This is the inclination the Lord has given me, for it seems to me that He prizes a soul that through our diligence and prayer we gain for Him, through His mercy, more than all the services we can render Him.   (F 1:6–7)

O greatness of God! How You manifest Your power in giving courage to an ant! How true, my Lord, that it is not because of You that those who love You fail to do great works but because of our own cowardice and pusillanimity. . . . Who is more fond than You of giving, or of serving even at a cost to Yourself, when there is someone open to receive?   (F 2:7)

Since, my Lord, we see that You often free us from the dangers in which we place ourselves, even in opposition to You, how can one believe that You will fail to free us when we aim after nothing more than to please You and delight in You? Never can I believe this!   (F 4:4)

In matters touching on obedience He doesn't want the soul who truly loves Him to take any other path than the one He did: *obediens usque ad mortem.*   (F 5:3)

O Lord, how different are Your paths from our clumsy imaginings! And how from a soul that is already determined to love You and is abandoned into Your hands, You do not want anything but that it obey, that it inquire well into what is for Your greater service, and that it desire this! There's no need for it to be seeking out paths or choosing them, for its will is Yours. You, my Lord, take up this care of guiding it to where it receives the most benefit. The prelate who is the superior may not be concerned for what benefits the soul. . . . Yet, You, my God, do have concern and go about disposing the soul and the things with which it is dealing in such a way that, without understanding how, we find in ourselves spiritual improvement, so great that we are afterward left amazed.   (F 5:6)

O Lord! What a great favor You grant to those children whose parents love them so much as to want them to possess their estates, inheritance, and riches in that blessed life that has no end! . . . Open the eyes of parents, my God. Make them understand the kind of love they are obliged to have for their children so that they do not do these children so much wrong and are not complained about before God in that final judgment where, even though they may not want to know it, the value of each thing will be understood.   (F 10:9)

O Son of the Eternal Father, Jesus Christ, our Lord, true King of all! What did You leave in the world? What could we, Your descendants, inherit from You? What did You possess, my Lord, but trials, sufferings, and dishonors? You had nothing but a wooden beam on which to swallow the painfully difficult drink of death. In sum, my God, it does not fit those of us who want to be Your true children, and hold on to their inheritance, to flee suffering. Your heraldry consists of five wounds. . . . This must be our badge if we are to inherit His kingdom. Not with rest, not with favors, not with honors, not with riches will that which He bought with so much blood be gained.   (F 10:11)

May You be blessed forever and ever, my God, for within a moment You undo a soul and remake it. What is this, Lord? I would want to ask here what the apostles asked You when You cured the blind man, whether it was his parents who had sinned. . . . Oh, great are Your judgments, Lord! You know what You are doing, but I do not know what I am saying since Your works and judgments are incomprehensible. May You be ever glorified, for You have the power to do even more. What would become of me if this were not so? . . . Sometimes I think You grant similar favors to those who love You, and You do them so much good that You give them that by which they may serve You.   (F 22:7)

O Jesus! How many fears I have suffered before taking possession of these foundations! I reflect on the fact that if one can feel so much fear in doing something good, for the service of God, what must be the fear of those who do evil, deeds that are against God and against neighbor? I don't know what they can gain or what satisfaction they can find as a counterbalance to all that fear.   (F 25:8)

O my Lord, how certain it is that anyone who renders You some service soon pays with a great trial! And what a precious reward a trial is for those who truly love You if we could at once understand its value!

(F 31:22)

THE INTERIOR CASTLE

The will is inclined to love after seeing such countless signs of love; it would want to repay something; it especially keeps in mind how this true Lover never leaves it, accompanying it and giving it life and being. Then the intellect helps it realize that it couldn't find a better friend, even were it to live for many years, that the whole world is filled with falsehood, and that so too these joys the devil gives it are filled with trials, cares, and contradictions. . . .

But, oh, my Lord and my God, how the whole world's habit of getting involved in vanities vitiates everything! Our faith is so dead that we desire what we see more than what faith tells us. And, indeed, we see only a lot of misfortune in those who go after these visible vanities. . . . Ah, my Lord! Your help is necessary here; without it one can do nothing. In Your mercy do not consent to allow this soul to suffer deception and give up what was begun. Enlighten it that it may see how all its good is within this castle.   (<i>IC</i> 2, 1:4–6)

PRAYERS IN POETRY

Self-Surrender

How blessed is the heart with love fast bound
On God, the center of its every thought!
Renouncing all created things as naught,
In Him its glory and its joy are found.
Even from self its cares are now set free;
To God alone its aims, its actions tend—
Joyful and swift it journeys to its end
O'er the wild waves of life's tempestuous sea!   (CP)

In the Hands of God

I am Yours and born for You,
What do You want of me?

Majestic Sovereign,
Unending wisdom,
Kindness pleasing to my soul;
God sublime, one Being Good,
Behold this one so vile.
Singing of her love to You:
What do You want of me?

Yours, You made me,
Yours, You saved me,
Yours, You endured me,
Yours, You called me,
Yours, You awaited me,
Yours, I did not stray.
What do You want of me?

Good Lord, what do You want of me,
What is this wretch to do?
What work is this,
This sinful slave, to do?
Look at me, Sweet Love,
Sweet Love, look at me,
What do You want of me?

In Your hand
I place my heart,
Body, life and soul,
Deep feelings and affections mine,
Spouse—Redeemer sweet,
Myself offered now to You,
What do You want of me?

Give me death, give me life,
Health or sickness,
Honor or shame,
War or swelling peace,
Weakness or full strength,
Yes, to these I say,
What do You want of me?

Give me wealth or want,
Delight or distress,
Happiness or gloominess,
Heaven or hell,
Sweet life, sun unveiled,
To You I give all.
What do You want of me?

Give me, if You will, prayer;
Or let me know dryness,
An abundance of devotion,

Or if not, then barrenness.
In You alone, Sovereign Majesty,
I find my peace,
What do You want of me?

Give me then wisdom.
Or for love, ignorance,
Years of abundance,
Or hunger and famine.
Darkness or sunlight,
Move me here or there:
What do You want of me?

If You want me to rest,
I desire it for love;
If to labor,
I will die working:
Sweet Love say
Where, how and when.
What do You want of me?

Calvary or Tabor give me,
Desert or fruitful land;
As Job in suffering
Or John at Your breast;
Barren or fruited vine,
Whatever be Your will:
What do You want of me?

Be I Joseph chained
Or as Egypt's governor,
David pained
Or exalted high,
Jonas drowned,
Or Jonas freed:

What do You want of me?

Silent or speaking,
Fruitbearing or barren,
My wounds shown by the Law,
Rejoicing in the tender Gospel;
Sorrowing or exulting,
You alone live in me:
What do You want of me?

Yours I am, for You I was born:
What do You want of me?

(*CWT* 3:377–79)

Aspirations toward Eternal Life

I live without living in myself,
And in such a way I hope,
I die because I do not die.

Since I die of love,
Living apart from love,
I live now in the Lord,
Who has desired me for Himself.
He inscribed on my heart
When I gave it to Him:
I die because I do not die.

Within this divine prison,
Of love in which I live,
My God my captive is.
My heart is free
To behold my prisoner-God,
Passion welling in my heart,
I die because I do not die.

Ah, how weary this life!
These exiles so hard!
This jail and these shackles
By which the soul is fettered!
Longing only to go forth
Brings such terrible sorrow,
I die because I do not die.

Ah, how bitter a life
When the Lord is not enjoyed!
While love is sweet,
Long awaiting is not.
O God, take away this burden
Heavier than steel,
I die because I do not die.

Only with that surety
I will die do I live,
Because in dying
My hope in living is assured.
Death, bringing life,
Do not tarry; I await you,
I die because I do not die.

See how love is strong.
Life, do not trouble me.
See how all that remains
Is in losing you to gain.
Come now, sweet death,
Come, dying, swiftly.
I die because I do not die.

That life from above,
That is true life,
Until this life dies,

Life is not enjoyed.
Death, be not aloof;
In dying first, may life be,
I die because I do not die.

Life, what can I give
To my God living in me,
If not to lose you,
Thus to merit Him?
In dying I want to reach
Him alone whom I seek:
I die because I do not die.

(*CWT* 3:375–76)

Loving Colloquy

If the love You have for me,
Is like the love I have for
    You,
My God, what detains me?
Oh, what is delaying You?
—Soul, what is it you desire
    of me?
—My God, nothing other than to
    see You.
—What is it that you fear more
    than self?
—What I fear most is the loss
    of You.
A soul hidden in God,
What has it to desire
Save to love more and more,
And, in love all hidden
Again and again to love You?

One all possessing love I ask
My God, my soul centered in You,
Making a delightful nest,
A resting place most pleasing.

(*CWT* 3:380)

Oh Exceeding Beauty

Oh Beauty exceeding
All other beauties!
Paining, but You wound not,
Free of pain You destroy
The love of creatures.

Oh, knot that binds
Two so different,
Why do You become unbound
For when held fast You strengthen
Making injuries seem good.

Bind the one without being
With being unending;
Finish, without finishing,
Love, without having to love,
Magnify our nothingness.

(*CWT* 3:381–82)

Sighs in Exile

My God, how sad is
Life without You!
Longing to see You,
Death I desire.

This earth's journey
How long it is;
A painful dwelling,
An exile drear.
Oh, Master adored,
Take me away!
Longing to see You,
Death I desire.

Dismal is life,
Bitter as can be:
The soul lifeless,
Apart from You.
O my sweet Goodness,
How sad am I!
Longing to see You,
Death I desire.

O kind death
Free me from trials!
Gentle are your blows,
Freeing the soul.
Oh, my Beloved, what joy
To be oned to You!
Longing to see You,
Death I desire.

To this life
Worldly love adheres;
Love divine
For the other sighs.
Eternal God, without You,
Who can live?

Longing to see You,
Death I desire.

Unending sorrow
Of this earthly life;
Life that is true
In heaven alone is found.
My God, allow
That there I may dwell.
Longing to see You,
Death I desire.

Who fears
The body's death
If one then gains
Pleasure so great?
Oh, yes, in loving You,
Forever, my God!
Longing to see You,
Death I desire.

Afflicted, my soul
Sighs and faints.
Ah, who can stay apart
From her Beloved?
Oh! end now,
This my suffering.
Longing to see You,
Death I desire.

The fish caught
On the painful hook,
In death's embrace
Its torment ending.

Ah, how I suffer,
Without You, my Love.
Longing to see You,
Death I desire.

Master, my soul
In vain seeks You!
Always unseen
You leave me anxiously longing.
Ah! the very longing inflames
Until I cry out:
Longing to see You,
Death I desire.

When at last
You enter my heart,
My God, then at once
I fear Your leaving.
The pain that touches me
Makes me say,
Longing to see You,
Death I desire.

Lord, end now
This long agony.
Comfort Your servant
Sighing for You.
Shatter the fetters
Let her rejoice.
Longing to see You,
Death I desire.

Ah, no, Beloved Master,
It is only that I suffer
My sins to atone

My guilt unbounded
Ah! may my tears gain
Your listening to me:
Longing to see You,
Death I desire.   (*CWT* 3:382–84)

Seeking God

Soul, you must seek yourself in Me
And in yourself seek Me.

With such skill, soul,
Love could portray you in Me
That a painter well gifted
Could never show
So finely that image.

For love you were fashioned
Deep within me
Painted so beautiful, so fair;
If, my beloved, I should lose you,
Soul, in yourself seek Me.

Well I know that you will discover
Yourself portrayed in my heart
So lifelike drawn
It will be a delight to behold
Yourself so well painted.

And should by chance you do not know
Where to find Me,
Do not go here and there;
But if you wish to find Me,
In yourself seek Me.

Soul, since you are My room,
My house and dwelling,
If at any time,
Through your distracted ways
I find the door tightly closed,

Outside yourself seek Me not,
To find Me it will be
Enough only to call Me,
Then quickly will I come,
And in yourself seek Me.   (*CWT* 3:385)

Efficacy of Patience

Let nothing trouble you,
Let nothing scare you,
All is fleeting,
God alone is unchanging.
Patience
Everything obtains.
Who possesses God
Nothing wants.
God alone suffices.   (*CWT* 3:386)

To the Birth of Jesus

Ah, shepherds watching,
Guarding your flocks!
Behold, a Lamb born for you,
Son of our Sovereign God.

Poor and despised He comes,
Begin now guarding Him,
Lest the wolf carry Him off.

Before rejoicing in Him,
Bring me your crook, Giles.
Firmly will I grasp it,
Preventing theft of the Lamb:
See you not He is Sovereign God?

Come now, bewildered am I
By joy and sorrow joined.
If today God be born,
How can He then die?
Oh, since He is man as well,

Life in His hands will be!
In this Lamb behold,
The Son of our Sovereign God.

Why do they ask for Him
And then against Him war.
Giles, in faith it would be better
For Him to return to His land.
If by sin we are banished,
In His hand all good lies
Since to suffer He came,
This God truly sovereign.

His suffering so little troubles you:
Oh, how true of men.
When profit comes,
Evil we ignore!
Do you see He gains renown
As the Shepherd of the great flock?
Terrible it is nonetheless
That the Sovereign God should die.

(*CWT* 3:387–88)

At the Birth of Jesus

Giles, today there comes to redeem us
A shepherd boy, our kinsman,
God Omnipotent!

He frees us from
Satan's prison;
But He is kin of Bras,
Menga, and Llorente.
Oh, He is God Omnipotent!

If He be God, why sold

And crucified dies?
Giles, in His suffering innocently,
Do you see, He vanquished sin?
He is God Omnipotent.

Oh, I saw Him being born
Of a shepherdess most fair.
If He is God, why did He desire
Among such poor folk to be?
See you not that He is Omnipotent?

No more questioning,
Let us serve Him.
Llorente, since He comes to die,
Let us die with Him.
He is God Omnipotent.   (*CWT* 3:388–89)

For the Profession of Isabel de los Angeles

In weeping be my joy,
My rest in fright,
In sorrowing my serenity,
My wealth in losing all.

Amid storms be my love,
In the wound my delight.
My life in death,
In rejection my favor.

In poverty be my riches,
My triumph in struggling,
Rest in laboring,
In sadness my contentment.

In darkness be my light,
My greatness in the lowly place,
My way on the short road,
In the cross my glory.

In humiliation be my honor,
My palm in suffering
Increase in my wanting
In losing my gain.

My fullness be in hunger,
In fearing my hope,
My rejoicing in fear,
In grieving my delight.

In forgetting be my memory,
Humiliation my exalting,
In lowliness my repute,
Affronts my victory.

My laurels be in contempt,
In afflictions my fondness,
My dignity a lowly nook,
In solitude my esteem.

In Christ be my trust,
My affection in Him alone.
In His weariness my vigor,
My repose in His imitation.

My strength is found here,
In Him alone my surety,
My integrity's proof,
In His likeness my Purity.

(*CWT* 3:402–4)

VIII

Saint John of the Cross

(1542–1591)

Juan de Yepes y Alvarez was born in 1542 in Fontiveros, Spain, twenty-four miles north of Avila. He was born into a poor family and had two brothers. After the early death of his father, the family moved to Medina del Campo. Juan was able to assist with finances by working at carpentry, tailoring, and then at a hospital.

When he was seventeen he enrolled at the Jesuit College, taking humanities courses. Upon graduation he realized he had a vocation to the Carmelite Order. He entered in 1563, taking the name Juan de Santo Matía. During his formation period he took classes at the University of Salamanca. He was such an outstanding student that he was named prefect of studies.

Fray Juan was ordained to the priesthood in 1567. It was at this time that he met Teresa of Avila, who was making her second foundation of the Reform. She wanted to find a suitable friar to begin the Reform among the friars. After they met and discussed this, Fray Juan agreed, but on the condition it would happen quickly. He had been thinking of entering the Carthusian Order to have a life of deeper prayer and more solitude. The following summer he began this endeavor, but only after having been trained by Teresa of Avila. The Reform seemed to be taking hold, and several discalced ("without shoes", i.e., wearing sandals) monasteries were established under Fray Juan. The Calced Carmelites

(i.e., "wearing shoes") were not pleased with what was happening. There were misunderstandings and disobedience on the part of the Calced, to the extent that in December 1577 Fray Juan ended up in prison. He was held captive in a little cell, six feet by ten feet, and was scourged regularly by each one of the friars. After six months he was given a pen and paper by one of his captors, and there he composed some of his amazingly beautiful poems. The darkness of the prison could not exclude the flames of light and love that emanated from this holy man.

He managed to escape to one of the Reform monasteries in Toledo, where he stayed until he regained his health. Then he became prior at El Calvario and spiritual director to the nuns at Beas. It was for one of them that he wrote the *Spiritual Canticle*. In 1579 he founded and became rector of a college for the students of the Reform in southern Spain.

Fray Juan served very high positions in the Order after this and continued to spread the Reform, despite opposition from within and without the Discalced Order. He wrote many of his works during this period.

When he developed leg ulcers and a fever he asked to be sent to a place where he was unknown. There, the prior, who was jealous of his reputation for holiness, greeted him with less than a welcome. He was given the poorest cell in the monastery in which to suffer alone. His wish was to die "not as a superior, not in a place where he was known, and after having suffered much". This poet, mystic, spiritual director par excellence, and gentle teacher died December 13, 1591, uttering the words: "Into Your hands I commend my spirit." He is now known as Saint John of the Cross, Doctor of the Church.

PRAYERS

THE ASCENT OF MOUNT CARMEL

[1] One dark night,
Fired with love's urgent longings
—Ah, the sheer grace!—
I went out unseen,
My house being now all stilled;

[2] In darkness, and secure,
By the secret ladder, disguised,
—Ah, the sheer grace!—
In darkness and concealment,
My house being now all stilled;

[3] On that glad night,
In secret, for no one saw me,
Nor did I look at anything,
With no other light or guide
Than the one that burned in my heart;

[4] This guided me
More surely than the light of noon
To where He waited for me
—Him I knew so well—
In a place where no one else appeared.

[5] O guiding night!
O night more lovely than the dawn!
O night that has united
The Lover with His beloved,
Transforming the beloved in her Lover.

[6] Upon my flowering breast
Which I kept wholly for Him alone,
There He lay sleeping,
And I caressing Him
There in a breeze from the fanning cedars.

[7] When the breeze blew from the turret
Parting His hair,
He wounded my neck
With His gentle hand,
Suspending all my senses.

[8] I abandoned and forgot myself,
Laying my face on my Beloved;
All things ceased; I went out from myself,
Leaving my cares
Forgotten among the lilies.   (*CWJC* 68–69)

May God extend and show forth His infinite mercy in this
matter!   (*A* 3, 31:5)

How many festivals, my God, do the children of men celebrate in Your honor in which the devil has a greater role than
You! And the devil, like a merchant, is pleased with these
gatherings because he does more business on those days. How
many times will You say of them: *This people honors Me with
their lips alone, but their heart is far from Me, because they serve Me
without cause* [Mt 15: 8–9].   (*A* 3, 38:3)

THE DARK NIGHT

Ah, my Lord and my God! How many go to You looking
for their own consolation and gratification and desiring that
You grant them favors and gifts, but those wanting to give
You pleasure and something at a cost to themselves, setting
aside their own interests, are few. What is lacking is not that
You, O my God, desire to grant us favors again, but that we
make use of them for Your service alone and thus oblige You
to grant them to us continually.   (*DN* 2, 19:4)

THE SPIRITUAL CANTICLE

Bride   [1]   Where have You hidden,
            Beloved, and left me moaning?
            You fled like the stag
            After wounding me;
            I went out calling You, and You were gone.

        [2]   Shepherds, you that go
            Up through the sheepfolds to the hill,
            If by chance you see
            Him I love most,
            Tell Him that I sicken, suffer, and die.

        [3]   Seeking my Love
            I will head for the mountains and for watersides,
            I will not gather flowers,
            Nor fear wild beasts;
            I will go beyond strong men and frontiers.

        [4]   O woods and thickets
            Planted by the hand of my Beloved!

O green meadow,
Coated, bright, with flowers,
Tell me, has He passed by you?

[5] Pouring out a thousand graces,
He passed these groves in haste;
And having looked at them,
With His image alone,
Clothed them in beauty.

[6] Ah, who has the power to heal me?
Now wholly surrender Yourself!
Do not send me
Any more messengers,
They cannot tell me what I must hear.

[7] All who are free
Tell me a thousand graceful things of You;
All wound me more
And leave me dying
Of, ah, I-don't-know-what behind their
    stammering.

[8] How do you endure
O life, not living where you live?
And being brought near death
By the arrows you receive
From that which you conceive of your Beloved.

[9] Why, since You wounded
This heart, don't You heal it?
And why, since You stole it from me,
Do You leave it so,
And fail to carry off what You have stolen?

[10]   Extinguish these miseries,
       Since no one else can stamp them out;
       And may my eyes behold You,
       Because You are their light,
       And I would open them to You alone.

[11]   Reveal Your presence,
       And may the vision of Your beauty be my death;
       For the sickness of love
       Is not cured
       Except by Your very presence and image.

[12]   O spring like crystal!
       If only, on your silvered-over face,
       You would suddenly form
       The eyes I have desired,
       Which I bear sketched deep within my heart.

[13]   Withdraw them, Beloved,
       I am taking flight!

Bridegroom   Return, dove,
       The wounded stag
       Is in sight on the hill,
       Cooled by the breeze of your flight.

Bride   [14]   My Beloved is the mountains,
       And lonely wooded valleys,
       Strange islands,
       And resounding rivers,
       The whistling of love-stirring breezes.

[15]   The tranquil night
       At the time of the rising dawn,
       Silent music,
       Sounding solitude,
       The supper that refreshes, and deepens love.

[16] Catch us the foxes,
For our vineyard is now in flower,
While we fashion a cone of roses
Intricate as the pine's;
And let no one appear on the hill.

[17] Be still, deadening north wind;
South wind come, you that waken love,
Breathe through my garden,
Let its fragrance flow,
And the Beloved will feed amid the flowers.

[18] You girls of Judea,
While among the flowers and roses
The amber spreads its perfume,
Stay away, there on the outskirts;
Do not so much as seek to touch our thresholds.

[19] Hide Yourself, my Love;
Turn Your face toward the mountains,
And do not speak;
But look at those companions
Going with her through strange islands.

Bridegroom [20] Swift-winged birds,
Lions, stags, and leaping roes,
Mountains, lowlands, and river banks,
Waters, winds, and ardors,
Watching fears of night:

[21] By the pleasant lyres
And the siren's song, I conjure you
To cease your anger
And not touch the wall,
That the bride may sleep in deeper peace.

[22]   The bride has entered
       The sweet garden of her desire,
       And she rests in delight,
       Laying her neck
       On the gentle arms of her Beloved.

[23]   Beneath the apple tree:
       There I took you for My own,
       There I offered you My hand,
       And restored you,
       Where your mother was corrupted.

Bride   [24]   Our bed is in flower,
       Bound round with licking dens of lions,
       Hung with purple,
       Built up in peace,
       And crowned with a thousand shields of gold.

[25]   Following Your footprints
       Maidens run along the way;
       The touch of a spark,
       The spiced wine,
       Cause flowings in them from the balsam of God.

[26]   In the inner wine cellar
       I drank of my Beloved, and, when I went abroad
       Through all this valley
       I no longer knew anything,
       And lost the herd which I was following.

[27]   There He gave me His breast:
       There He taught me a sweet and living knowledge;
       And I gave myself to Him,
       Keeping nothing back;
       There I promised to be His bride.

Christ Crucified:
A drawing by Saint John of the Cross

[28]   Now I occupy my soul
       And all my energy in His service;
       I no longer tend the herd,
       Nor have I any other work
       Now that my every act is love.

[29]   If, then, I am no longer
       Seen or found on the common,
       You will say that I am lost;
       That, stricken by love,
       I lost myself, and was found.

[30]   With flowers and emeralds
       Chosen on cool mornings
       We shall weave garlands
       Flowering in Your love,
       And bound with one hair of mine.

[31]   You considered
       That one hair fluttering at my neck;
       You gazed at it upon my neck
       And it captivated You;
       And one of my eyes wounded You.

[32]   When You looked at me
       Your eyes imprinted Your grace in me;
       For this You loved me ardently;
       And thus my eyes deserved
       To adore what they beheld in You.

[33]   Do not despise me;
       For if, before, You found me dark,
       Now truly You can look at me
       Since You have looked
       And left in me grace and beauty.

Bridegroom [34] The small white dove
Has returned to the ark with an olive branch;
And now the turtledove
Has found its longed-for mate
By the green river banks.

[35] She lived in solitude,
And now in solitude has built her nest;
And in solitude He guides her,
He alone, Who also bears
In solitude the wound of love.

Bride [36] Let us rejoice, Beloved,
And let us go forth to behold ourselves in
    Your beauty,
To the mountain and to the hill,
To where the pure water flows,
And further, deep into the thicket.

[37] And then we will go on
To the high caverns in the rock
Which are so well concealed;
There we shall enter
And taste the fresh juice of the pomegranates.

[38] There You will show me
What my soul has been seeking,
And then You will give me,
You, my Life, will give me there
What You gave me on that other day:

[39] The breathing of the air,
The song of the sweet nightingale,
The grove and its living beauty
In the serene night,
With a flame that is consuming and painless.

[40]   No one looked at her,
        Nor did Aminadab appear;
        The siege was still;
        And the cavalry,
        At the sight of the waters, descended.

(CWJC 410–15)

My Spouse, in that touch and wound of Your love, You have not only drawn my soul away from all things, but have also made it go out from self—indeed, it even seems that You draw it out of the body—and You have raised it up to Yourself, while it was calling after You, now totally detached so as to be attached to You.   *(SC* 1:20)

At the time I desired to hold fast to Your presence, I did not find You, and the detachment from one without attachment to the other left me suspended in air and suffering, without any support from You or from myself.   *(SC* 1:21)

Do not let my knowledge of You, communicated through these messengers of news and sentiments about You, any longer be so measured, so remote and alien to what my soul desires. How well You know, my Spouse, that messengers redouble the sorrow of one who grieves over Your absence: first, through knowledge they enlarge the wound; second, they seem to postpone Your coming. From now on do not send me this remote knowledge. If up to this time I could be content with it, because I did not have much knowledge or love of You, now the intensity of my love cannot be satisfied with these messages; therefore: "Now wholly sur-render Yourself!"   *(SC* 6:6)

My Lord, my Spouse, You have given Yourself to me partially; now may You give me Yourself more completely. You have revealed Yourself to me as through fissures in a rock; now may You give me that revelation more clearly. You have communicated by means of others, as if joking with me; now may You truly grant me a communication of Yourself by Yourself. In Your visits, at times, it seems You are about to give me the jewel of possessing You; but when I become aware of this possession, I discover that I do not have it, for You hide this jewel as if You had given it jokingly. Now wholly surrender Yourself by giving Yourself entirely to all of me, that my entire soul may have complete possession of You.   (*SC* 6:6)

Do not send me
Any more messengers,
They cannot tell me what I must hear.

I desire complete knowledge of You, and they have neither knowledge nor ability to tell of You entirely. Nothing in heaven or on earth can give the soul the knowledge she desires of You. Thus, "they cannot tell me what I must hear." Instead of these other messengers, may You, then, be both the messenger and the message.   (*SC* 6:7)

There You will teach me (wisdom and knowledge and love), *and I shall give you a drink of spiced wine* (my love spiced with Yours, transformed in Yours).   (*SC* 26:6)

Why, since You wounded this heart until it has become sorely wounded, do You not heal it by wholly slaying it with love? Since You cause the sore wound in the sickness of love, may You cause health in the death of love. As a result, the heart, wounded with the sorrow of Your absence, will be healed with the delight and glory of Your sweet presence.

(*SC* 9:3)

Why do You fail to carry off the heart You have stolen through love; and why do You fail to fill, satisfy, accompany, and heal it, giving it complete stability and repose in You?

(*SC* 9:7)

Since the delight arising from the sight of Your being and beauty is unendurable, and since I must die in seeing You, may the vision of Your beauty be my death.   (*SC* 11:6)

O faith of Christ, my Spouse, would that you might show me clearly now the truths of my Beloved, which you have infused in my soul and which are covered with obscurity and darkness (for faith, as the theologians say, is an obscure habit), in such a way that, what you communicate to me in inexplicit and obscure knowledge, you would show suddenly, clearly, and perfectly, changing it into a manifestation of glory!   (*SC* 12:2)

Oh, if only on your silvered-over face (the articles we mentioned) by which you cover the gold of the divine rays (the eyes I have desired), and she adds: You would suddenly form the eyes I have desired.   (*SC* 12:4–5)

Oh, if only the truths hidden in Your articles, which You teach me in an inexplicit and dark manner, You would give me now completely, clearly, and explicitly, freed of their covering, as my desire begs!   (SC 12:5)

Withdraw them, Beloved," that is, these Your divine eyes, "for they cause me to take flight and go out of myself to supreme contemplation, which is beyond what the sensory part can endure."   (SC 13:2)

My dear Spouse, withdraw to the innermost part of my soul and communicate Yourself in secret, manifest Your hidden wonders, alien to every mortal eye.   (SC 19:3)

Let Your divinity shine on my intellect by giving it divine knowledge, and on my will by imparting to it the divine love, and on my memory with the divine possession of glory.
                    (SC 19:4)

Do not speak as before when the communications You granted me were such that You spoke them to the exterior senses; that is, You spoke things apprehensible to the senses, since these things were not so high and deep that the sensory part could not attain to them. But now let these communications be so lofty and substantial and interior that You do not speak of them to the senses, that is, such that the senses may be unable to attain to the knowledge of them.   (SC 19:5)

Since I go to You through a spiritual knowledge strange and foreign to the senses, let Your communication be so interior and sublime as to be foreign to all of them.   (SC 19:7)

But Beloved, first turn to the interior of my soul, and be enamored of the company—the riches—You have placed there, so that loving the soul through them You may dwell and hide in her. For, indeed, even though they are Yours, since You gave them to her, they also belong to her.

(*SC* 19:6)

You dried up and subdued in me the appetites and passions which in our flesh are the breasts and milk of mother Eve, and an impediment to this state. And when this is accomplished "that I may find You alone outside," that is, outside of all things and of myself, in solitude and nakedness of spirit, which is attained when the appetites are dried up. And alone there, "kiss You" alone, that is, that my nature now alone and denuded of all temporal, natural, and spiritual impurity may be united with You alone, with Your nature alone, through no intermediary.   (*SC* 22:7)

My Beloved, all that is rough and toilsome I desire for Your sake, and all that is sweet and pleasant I desire for Your sake.

(*SC* 28:10)

My faculties, the eyes through which I can see You, my Spouse, have merited this elevation which enables them to look at You.   (*SC* 32:8)

Let us so act that by means of this loving activity we may attain to the vision of ourselves in Your beauty in eternal life. That is: That I be so transformed in Your beauty that we may be alike in beauty, and both behold ourselves in Your beauty, possessing now Your very beauty; this, in such a way that each looking at the other may see in the other his own beauty, since both are Your beauty alone, I being absorbed in Your beauty; hence, I shall see You in Your beauty, and You shall see me in Your beauty, and I shall see myself in You in Your beauty, and You will see Yourself in me in Your beauty; that I may resemble You in Your beauty, and You resemble me in Your beauty, and my beauty be Your beauty and Your beauty my beauty; wherefore I shall be You in Your beauty, and You will be me in Your beauty, because Your very beauty will be my beauty; and therefore we shall behold each other in Your beauty. *(SC 36:5)*

What You gave me (that weight of glory to which You predestined me, O my Spouse, on the day of Your eternity when You considered it good to decree my creation), You will give me then on the day of my espousals and nuptials and on my day of gladness of heart . . . , when loosed from the flesh and within the high caverns of Your chamber, gloriously transformed in You, I shall drink with You the juice of the sweet pomegranates. *(SC 38:9)*

My soul is now divested, detached, alone, and withdrawn from all created things, both from those above and from those below; and it has entered so deeply into interior recollection with You that none of them can discern the intimate delight I now possess in You; that is, these creatures cannot move my soul to relish their sweetness or become displeased and disturbed by their misery and lowness. Since my soul stays so far from them and abides in such profound delight with You, none of them can get a view of me. *(SC 40:2)*

THE LIVING FLAME OF LOVE

[1]   O living flame of love
That tenderly wounds my soul
In its deepest center! Since
Now You are not oppressive,
Now Consummate! if it be Your will:
Tear through the veil of this sweet encounter!

[2]   O sweet cautery,
O delightful wound!
O gentle hand! O delicate touch
That tastes of eternal life
And pays every debt!
In killing You changed death to life.

[3]   O lamps of fire!
In whose splendors
The deep caverns of feeling,
Once obscure and blind,
Now give forth, so rarely, so exquisitely,
Both warmth and light to their Beloved.

[4]   How gently and lovingly
You wake in my heart,
Where in secret You dwell alone;
And in Your sweet breathing,
Filled with good and glory,
How tenderly You swell my heart with love.   (*CWJC* 578–79)

O enkindled love, with your loving movements you are pleasantly glorifying me according to the greater capacity and strength of my soul, bestowing divine knowledge according to all the ability and capacity of my intellect, and communicating love according to the greater power of my will, and rejoicing the substance of my soul with the torrent of your delight by your divine contact and substantial union, in harmony with the greater purity of my substance and the capacity and breadth of my memory! . . .   (*LF* 1:17)

O flame of the Holy Spirit that so intimately and tenderly pierces the substance of my soul and cauterizes it with Your glorious ardor! Previously, my requests did not reach Your ears, when, in the anxieties and weariness of love in which my sense and my spirit suffered because of considerable weakness, impurity, and lack of strong love, I was praying that You loose me and bring me to Yourself, because my soul longed for You, and impatient love did not allow me to be so conformed to the conditions of this life in which You desired me still to live. The previous impulses of love were not enough, because they did not have sufficient quality for the attainment of my desire; now I am so fortified in love that not only do my sense and spirit no longer faint in You, but my heart and my flesh, reinforced in You, rejoice in the living God [Ps 83:3], with great conformity between the sensory and spiritual parts. What You desire me to ask for, I ask for; and what You do not desire, I do not desire, nor can I, nor does it even enter my mind to desire it. My petitions are now more valuable and estimable in Your sight, since they come from You, and You move me to make them, and I make them in the delight and joy of the Holy Spirit, my judgment now issuing from Your countenance [Ps 16:2], that is, when You esteem and hear my prayer. Tear then the thin veil of this life and do not let old age cut it naturally, that from now on I may love You with plenitude and fullness my soul desires forever and ever.   (*LF* 1:36)

O happy wound, wrought by one who knows only how to heal! O fortunate and choicest wound; you were made only for delight, and the quality of your affliction is delight and gratification for the wounded soul! You are great, O delightful wound, because He who caused you is great! And your delight is great, because the fire of love is infinite and makes you delightful according to your capacity and greatness. O, then, delightful wound, so much more sublimely delightful the more the cautery touched the intimate center of the substance of the soul, burning all that was burnable in order to give delight to all that could be delighted!   (*LF* 2:8)

O hand, You are as gentle to my soul, which You touch by resting gently, as You would be powerful enough to submerge the entire world if You rested somewhat heavily, for by Your look alone the earth trembles [Ps 103:32], the nations melt and faint, and the mountains crumble! [Heb 3:6] Oh, then, again, great hand, by touching Job somewhat roughly, You were as hard and rigorous with him [Job 19:21] as You are friendly and gentle with me; how much more lovingly, graciously, and gently do You permanently touch my soul! You cause death, and You give life, and no one flees from Your hand. For You, O divine life, never kill unless to give life, never wound unless to heal. When You chastise, Your touch is gentle, but it is enough to destroy the world. When You give delight, You rest very firmly, and thus the delight of Your sweetness is immeasurable. You have wounded me in order to cure me, O divine hand, and You have put to death in me what made me lifeless, deprived me of God's life in which I now see myself live. You granted this with the liberality of Your generous grace, which You used in contacting me with the touch of the splendor of Your glory and the figure of

Your substance [Heb 1:3] which is Your only begotten Son, through Whom, being Your substance, You touch mightily from one end to the other [Wis 8:1].   (*LF* 2:16)

O You, then, delicate touch, the Word, the Son of God, through the delicacy of Your divine being, You subtly penetrate the substance of my soul and, lightly touching it all, absorb it entirely in Yourself in divine modes of delights and sweetnesses unheard of in the land of Canaan and never before seen in Theman! [Bar 3:22]. O, then, very delicate, exceedingly delicate, touch of the Word, so much the more delicate for me insofar as, after overthrowing the mountains and smashing the rocks to pieces on Mount Horeb with the shadow of might and power that went before You, You gave the prophet the sweetest and strongest experience of Yourself in the gentle breeze! [3 Kings 19:11–12]. O gentle breeze, since You are a delicate and mild breeze, tell us: How do You, the Word, the Son of God, touch mildly and gently, since You are so awesome and mighty?   (*LF* 2:17)

Oh, happy is the soul that You, being terrible and strong, gently and lightly touch! Proclaim this to the world! but You are unwilling to proclaim this to the world because it does not know of a mild breeze and will not experience You, for it can neither receive nor see you [Jn 14:17]. But they, O my God and my life, will see and experience Your mild touch, who withdraw from the world and become mild, bringing the mild into harmony with the mild, thus enabling themselves to experience and enjoy You. You touch them the more gently the more You dwell permanently hidden within them, for the substance of their soul is now refined, cleansed, and purified, withdrawn from every creature and every touch and trace of creature. As a result, *You hide them in the secret of Your face*, which is the Word, *from the disturbance of men* [Ps 30:21].   (*LF* 2:17)

O, then again, repeatedly delicate touch, so much the stronger and mightier the more You are delicate, since You detach and withdraw the soul from all the other touches of created things by the might of Your delicacy, and reserve it for and unite it to Yourself alone, so mild an effect do You leave in the soul that every other touch of all things both high and low seems coarse and spurious. It displeases the soul to look at these things, and to deal with them is a heavy pain and torment to it.   (*LF* 2:18)

O then, delicate touch, the more abundantly You pervade my soul, the more substantial You are and the purer is my soul! It should also be known that the more subtle and delicate the touch, and the more delight and gratification it communicates there where it touches, the less volume and bulk it has. This divine touch has no bulk or volume, because the Word who grants it is alien to every mode and manner, and free from all the volume of form, figure, and accident which usually encircles and imposes boundaries or limits to the substance. This touch we are discussing is indescribable insofar as it is substantial, that is, from the divine substance. Finally, then, O Word, indescribably delicate touch, produced in the soul only by Your most simple being, which, since it is infinite, is infinitely delicate and hence touches so subtly, lovingly, eminently, and delicately!   (*LF* 2:18–20)

O abyss of delights! You are so much the more abundant the more Your riches are concentrated in the infinite unity and simplicity of Your unique being, where one attribute is so known and enjoyed as not to hinder the perfect knowledge and enjoyment of the other; rather, each grace and virtue within You is a light for each of Your other grandeurs. By Your purity, O divine Wisdom, many things are beheld in You through one. For You are the deposit of the Father's treasures, the splendor of the eternal light, the unspotted mirror and image of His goodness.   (*LF* 3:2, 17)

How gentle and loving (that is, extremely loving and gentle) is Your awakening, O Word, Spouse, in the center and depth of my soul, which is its pure and intimate substance, in which secretly and silently, as its only lord, You dwell alone, not only as in Your house, nor only as in Your bed, but also as in my own heart, intimately and closely united to it. And how delicately You captivate me and arouse my affections toward You in the sweet breathing You produce in this awakening, a breathing delightful to me and full of good and glory.   (*LF* 4:3)

Awaken and enlighten us, my Lord, that we might know and love the blessings which You ever propose to us, and that we might understand that You have moved to bestow favors · on us and have remembered us.   (*LF* 4:9)

SAYINGS OF LIGHT AND LOVE

O Lord, my God, who will seek You with simple and pure love and not find You are all he desires, for You show Yourself first and go out to meet those who desire You?   (*SL* 2)

O Sweetest love of God, so little known, he who has found its veins is at rest!   (*SL* 16)

A soul that is hard because of its self-love grows harder. O good Jesus, if You do not soften it, it will ever continue in its natural hardness.   (*SL* 28)

I didn't know You, my Lord, because I still desired to know and relish things.   (*SL* 30)

Well and good if all things change, Lord God, provided we are rooted in You.   (*SL* 31)

My spirit has become dry because it forgets to feed on You.
                                                  (*SL* 36)

Lord, You return gladly and lovingly to lift up the one who offends You and I do not turn to raise and honor him who annoys me.   (*SL* 44)

O mighty Lord, if a spark from the empire of Your justice effects so much in the mortal ruler who governs the nations, what will Your all-powerful justice do with the righteous and the sinner?   (*SL* 45)

Lord, my God, You are not a stranger to him who does not estrange himself from You. How do they say that it is You who absent Yourself?   (*SL* 47)

Going everywhere, my God, with You, everywhere things will happen as I desire for You.   (*SL* 50)

Prayer of a Soul Taken with Love

Lord God, my Beloved, if You remember still my sins in suchwise that You do not do what I beg of You, do Your will concerning them, my God, which is what I most desire, and exercise Your goodness and mercy, and You will be known through them. And if it is that You are waiting for my good works so as to hear my prayer through their means, grant them to me, and work them for me, and the sufferings You desire to accept, and let it be done. But if You are not waiting for my works, what is it that makes You wait, my most clement Lord? Why do You delay? For if, after all, I am to receive the grace and mercy which I entreat of You in Your Son, take my mite, since You desire it, and grant me this blessing, since You also desire that.

Who can free himself from the lowly manners and limitations if You do not lift him to Yourself, my God, in purity of love? How will a man begotten and nurtured in lowliness rise up to You, Lord, if You do not raise him with Your hand which made him?

You will not take from me, my God, what You once gave me in Your only Son, Jesus Christ, in Whom You gave me all I desire. Hence I rejoice that if I wait for You, You will not delay.

With what procrastinations do You wait, since from this very moment you can love God in your heart?

Mine are the heavens and mine is the earth. Mine are the nations, the just are mine, and mine the sinners. The angels are mine, and the Mother of God, and all things are mine; and God Himself is mine and for me, because Christ is mine and all for me.

What do you ask, then, and seek, my soul? Yours is all of this, and all is for you. Do not engage yourself in something less, nor pay heed to the crumbs which fall from your Father's table. Go forth and exult in your Glory! Hide yourself in It and rejoice, and you will obtain the supplications of your heart.   (*SL* 25)

MAXIMS AND COUNSELS

All for You and nothing for me.   (*MC* 32)

Oh, how sweet Your presence will be to me, You Who are the supreme good! I must draw near You in silence and uncover my feet before You that You may be pleased to unite me to You in marriage [Ruth 3:7], and I will not rest until I rejoice in Your arms. Now I ask You, Lord, not to abandon me at any time in my recollection, for I am a squanderer of my soul.   (*MC* 45)

IX

Saint Mary Magdalen de' Pazzi

(1566–1607)

Saint Mary Magdalen was born in Florence, Italy. She entered the Carmel there, where she was wholly given to a hidden life of prayer. For Saint Mary Magdalen, liturgical prayer was a most important prayer form, and she insisted that the nuns be most attentive. During the recitation of the Divine Office she found it difficult to keep from being carried away.

According to Saint Mary Magdalen, prayer is important because through it "the soul detaches itself from created things and is united with God."

Her graces were of the highest mystical order. She went from meditation to deep insights, raptures, ecstatic states, prayer of recollection, absorption in God, and finally transforming union. Her experiences were recorded by her superiors and fill seven volumes. The following excerpts represent, therefore, only a small part of her work. She died in 1607.

PRAYERS

O Goodness, O Goodness, O Goodness, You do not want to be surpassed by the creature! . . . Such is the heart of God! It hides our heart within itself as a sponge hides water in itself; and if a person does not press the sponge, he does not see what is there. (*CWMM*)

O my beloved Spouse and loving Word, you engender the Body of the holy Church in a way which you alone know and understand. . . . By means of your Blood, you make a well-organized, well-formed body of which you are the head. The angels delight in its beauty, the archangels admire it, the seraphim are enraptured by it, all the angelic spirits marvel at it, and all the souls of the blessed in heaven rejoice in it. The Blessed Trinity takes delight in it in a manner beyond our comprehension.   (*DI 1. Colloquies. CWMM* 3)

O Mary, anyone who looks at you is comforted in any anxiety or tribulation or pain, and is victorious over any temptation. Anyone who does not know something about God, let him have recourse to you, O Mary. Anyone who does not find mercy in God, let him have recourse to you, O Mary. Anyone whose will is not in conformity, let him have recourse to you, O Mary. Anyone who falters on account of weakness, let him have recourse to you who are all strong and powerful. Anyone in constant struggle, let him have recourse to you who are a tranquil sea. . . . Whoever is tempted, . . . let him have recourse to you, who are the mother of humility, and nothing drives away the devil more than humility. Let them, one and all, have recourse to you, O Mary!

(*DI 2. Colloquies. CWMM* 3)

O Lord, if I see my neighbor committing sin, I shall make an excuse for him on the grounds of his intention, which being hidden cannot be seen, and even if I see plainly that his intention was distorted and evil, help me to know how to make allowance for the temptation, which is something from which no mortal is excluded.

And if someone should come to speak to me of my

neighbor's faults, I do not want to listen, and I shall answer that I will pray for him and ask the Lord to let me first amend myself. Besides, it will be easier for me to speak to my erring neighbor himself about his fault than to talk about it with others, because instead of remedying that fault, many others, much more serious, may be committed than those that are being discussed.   (*DI 3. Probation*)

O Lord, the soul's mouth . . . lovingly tastes you; it savors the purity of the divine essence and of your humanity and attains to such a knowledge of your purity that that which used to seem virtue to it, now seems like a shortcoming both in itself and in others. Receiving the Holy Sacraments which draw strength from your Blood and from your passion, we come by their means to taste the sweetness of the passion, and of the Blood that was shed therein. We savor this most fully when we receive the holy Sacrament of your Body and Blood, for there more than anywhere else this sweetness and grace are found hidden, when the Sacrament is really received with purity and honesty. Let whoever wishes to taste of your gentleness and sweetness approach this Blood and there he will find all rest and consolation. The soul will be washed with this Blood, cleansed in this Blood, nourished by this Blood.   (*DI 3. Colloquies 1. CWMM 3*)

O Holy Spirit, you show us what we must do to please the Trinity, interiorly through your inspirations, and exteriorly through preaching and warnings, and that all proceeds from you, since no one can say the sweet and holy name of Jesus unless he is moved by you.

    You are the dispenser of the treasures hidden in the bosom of the Father and treasurer of the counsels which pass between the Father and the Word. You are that rod that strikes the rock and makes it bring forth the water that satisfies every creature. The cataracts of heaven are always open to send down grace, but we do not have the mouth of our desire open to receive it.

Come, come, O most gentle Spirit! Spirit of goodness! I contemplate you as you leave the bosom of the Father, and enter the side of the Word, then leaving by the heart of the Word, come to us here on earth. From the bosom of the Father, bring us power, from the Heart of the Son burning love. *(DI 4. Revelations and Enlightenments. CWMM 4)*

Your wisdom, O Word, is like the bush you showed to Moses, which burned, but was not consumed. . . . Those who seek and go after the wisdom that is human abhor your wisdom, but to God human wisdom is foolishness. . . . In addition, by abhorring your wisdom, they deny themselves union with you, for by offending you they deprive themselves both of you and of it. . . .

What do you do, O wisdom of my Word? You raise up the soul and you submerge it in the depths: you erect and tear down every building; always weeping and singing, watching and sleeping, walking and never moving—you are wisdom, containing in yourself every treasure and remaining far from foolishness. . . .

And how is this wisdom acquired? It is acquired by an enlightened understanding of God's being, by continual affection and desire for God in God. Those who have reached this point have acquired the pleasure of wisdom. Those who savor it, taste it; and those who know nothing, understand it. Oh, why do we not pursue this wisdom continually without ever stopping?

O wisdom, you give stability to the ever-moving heavens, you make angelic and human spirits glorious, you nourish the brides of the Word and make his christs strong; you confound all wisdom and exalt all ignorance, verify every truth and confound every lie. O wisdom, you are the crown of your bride the Church, and the wealth of your bride the soul!   (*DI 4. Colloquies 2. CWMM* 3)

O my God, if I might be made worthy to give my life for the good of souls and to put an end to all this malice, what a comfort this would be! How strange it is to live and to be continually dying! What anguish to see that I might be of some help to your creatures by giving my life, and yet not be able to do so! O charity, you are a file that little by little is wearing away soul and body, and you are also continuously nourishing both soul and body. . . .

O Trinity, O Father, O Word, O Spirit, give your light to your creatures, one by one, so that they may understand their malice; and give me the grace to be able to satisfy for them, even by giving my life when this might be necessary. Oh, why can I not give this light to all? Would that we all together could make reparation for the offenses you receive, even though we could not satisfy for them except by your own goodness. . . . O immeasurable goodness, diffuse your-self in the hearts of your elect!   (*DI 4. Colloquies. CWMM* 3)

O eternal Word, when you were nailed to the most hard wood of the cross, you did not aim at anything else but bringing creatures to you. . . . You said: "I thirst," and you showed that you thirsted not only for those souls then present, but also for those that were yet to come. You suffered thirst, O sweet God, you suffered thirst, O good and all-loving God. . . . O how can it be that one who relieves his thirst with the very blood of the eternal Word does not relieve him also of the thirst that he has for his creatures?

(*DI* 4. *CWMM* 1)

O eternal Father lend me your power, so that . . . I can enter everywhere. For if I would have so much grace as to be able to enter into hearts, I would do so much that that charity would penetrate into them! O eternal Father . . . at least let there be some soul that acquires this charity, with which all good things are possessed, and without which no good can be had that is a true good.

Oh, if I could give my life and be consumed so that someone would acquire this charity, oh, how willingly I would do it! O Father, infuse your Spirit (into hearts). . . . And yet it is necessary that they be disposed in order to be able to receive him. Do you, O Word, dispose them, with that love with which you shed your blood. O eternal Father, I offer you your Word with all that is within him, plus that blood, for all creatures. O eternal Father, infuse this charity, infuse it, for I beg you, . . . O Father, fulfill your Truth. You know that he said: "I came to bring fire to the earth, and what else do I want except that it be lighted!" . . .

O eternal Father, you make me desire this charity so much among creatures that all those who do not want to receive the infusion of the blood of your Word—through which they become able to receive that charity within themselves— are for me as many hells as there are creatures.

(*DI* 4. *Colloquies* 2. *CWMM* 3)

On being told hidden things or things to come: "Keep it to Yourself, O God; keep it to Yourself!"   (*SAA*)

Looking at myself, O God of Love, I would never raise my mind and my will to ask for this Comforter. But looking again at Your Being, which is goodness and love, and mercy, I cannot but long for the coming of Your Holy Spirit.

I know, though not as well as I should, that I am not in any way a vessel suitable to receive You. But considering that you are He Who makes suitable every heart that desires this grace, I yearn for you in my inmost heart; and with the offering of the Blood of the Word, . . . which offering I pray the saints to make for me to the Most Holy Trinity. . . . I take courage to ask and beg for this Holy Spirit.

Wherefore I pray you, all you angelic spirits and saintly souls in heaven, in your act of love and through that same continued act of love that is yours, pray to the Holy Ghost that He may come to dwell in my and in all the other daughters of Mary. Moreover, in asking for this Holy Spirit, I intend to receive the entire Holy Trinity.   (*SAA*)

May He come Who by coming upon Mary caused the Word to be Incarnate, and may He do in us by grace what He did in her by nature. . . . Oh, come, You Who are the refreshment, the consolation and the nourishment of our souls! Oh, come and take away from within me all that is mine and pour in only what is Yours! . . . Yet I beseech You to come not only to me, but also to all those who have chosen You . . . or better, whom you have chosen as You have written, for "You have not chosen Me, but I have chosen you" (Jn 15:16) . . . and to whom You are the crown of their virginity. Oh, come You Who are the nourishment of every chaste thought, the circle of all clemency and the cumulus of all purity! Oh, come and destroy in me all that is a reason why I cannot be consumed by You! Come, O

Spirit of Goodness, You Who are always in the Father and
with the Son!   (*SAA*)

O Love, come to dwell within my heart. Make me all
on fire with You, so that I can love You. Come, O Love!
O Love, if You find rest in those who seek Your love and
honor, why should I ever ask anything else? . . . Yet, do hurry
Your steps and come within me, my Love. If You, O Love,
repose in the bosom of the Father, so too have I been present
in Your mind from all eternity. You will say that You are God
Himself, and that I am made to Your image and likeness. If
You find repose in pure vessels, behold, here is one that has
never desired aught but purity.   (*SAA*)

In Ecstasy:

Which was the way by which this purest love came down
to earth? You, O child Mary! And in you was placed the
hook to catch it. And which is the food by which creatures
are drawn to desire this love? . . . The glory that is prepared
for those who love. . . . But please do tell me, O child Mary,
which way could one follow to acquire a love so high? . . .
An anxious and constant desire for that love, and removing
from ourselves self-love! For, love hinders love. The loves
that hinder this high love are of three kinds: a great and
grand self-love; a great and anxious love of created things;
and a great and a restless love of creatures.   (*CWMM*)

But, O Mary, I cannot but love the creatures of my God! He
has commanded me to do so. He has created us all out of
love, and to me in particular He has given a certain power to
love. Looking into Himself, God saw love and was moved to

create man to share in that love; hence we exist for love, through love and with love, and so that in the end we may enjoy love itself, which is God. How, then, can I do without love? But please, Mary, tell me a little, in what way am I to love this neighbor of mine?   (*CWMM*)

Oh, Mary, you have gone too high in telling me to love him as my Bridegroom loved him! And how did He love him? For them He left, so to speak in a certain way, the bosom of the Eternal Father, with His power, His wisdom and, in a way of speaking, His purity, in order to be able to dwell with the impurity of creatures. He left His substance and His faculties, and finally gave Himself and His own blood. And I too ought to leave myself and the love of all created things, and be prepared, should it be necessary for their salvation, to give my own blood.   (*CWMM*)

O most pure Mary, I offer and give myself to you, not only with that purity and innocence that I received when I consecrated myself to you, but adorned beyond that, and then repurified, and then adorned again. Receive me, therefore, O Mary, and keep me within yourself.   (*CWMM*)

O my Bridegroom—for I shall indeed call You thus—there is no comparison between the horrible sight of the devil and the so beautiful and admirable sight of You, my God! For You are, as the prophet said, "*beautiful in form above the sons of men*" (Ps 44:3).

And so, just as in the past there was neither time nor place that I did not have that sight (of the devil), so now, while walking, remaining still, working, talking, I shall always see

You, my Beloved. And just as they sometimes also showed themselves in various forms to my bodily eyes, besides my mental sight of them, so also will You not wish to do less than they; for sometimes You will be present not only in my mind, but You will show Yourself also to my bodily eyes, in order to make me rejoice and exult to their (devils') belittlement.

Inasmuch as You are one God in three persons, I also shall be content to see You in three ways, to wit: as You were during the time You stayed in Egypt, I mean Your infancy; then in Your boyhood, as You were precisely when Your mother lost You in the temple; finally in Your young manhood, during which time You left us Your self and Your teaching. You suffered, and finally You gave us Your blood. When I shall go to give food to my body, I shall see You as a little Child, because at that age You also took milk from Your most pure Mother.

(He appears as an Infant) Oh, behold Him, my Little One, precisely at the age of three or four years! He is, in truth, so pretty! He has those beautiful little eyes, so happy and laughing, but also compelling and grave. . . . Oh, what an admirable thing: You are so little and still You are God! But Your littleness makes me know Your greatness. Oh, the greatness and the littleness of my God! And as I take food for my body, I shall see with the eyes of my mind this beautiful little Child, where before I saw those ugly monkeys, my adversaries; and in exchange for what they had on their heads, You have that beautiful and sweet-smelling little garland. I shall never have enough of looking at You, O my little and great God, You are so beautiful and attractive. I am afraid that sometimes Your beautiful presence will cause me so much joy that I shall show it also externally. . . .

In Your boyhood You will show me Yourself during the

time of darkness; for, just as You were hidden from creatures at that age, and Your words were known only to Your Eternal Father and to Your mother, so shall I be hidden during that time, and my words shall be known only to You and to Your mother.   (*CWMM*)

And suddenly Jesus presented Himself to her in that age of young manhood, at which sight she greatly rejoiced and remained for a long while looking upon His beauty with great admiration. Then she began to speak, saying:

My Jesus, in this flowery age of Your young manhood, I shall see You everywhere, excepting those places in which I am to see You as a child and as a youth. When I shall see You in this so beautiful and gracious age when You left us Yourself and suffered Your Passion. . . . I am much pleased to look upon You as You show me Yourself now, that is, sitting on the well, where You were asking questions and giving enlightening answers. . . . If I were desirous of change, I could go on discoursing with my intellect in many places, for You worked so much during this time; but I shall be content to stay with You and sit on the well. And sometimes I shall also anoint You with the Magdalen. . . . The ointment will be love of my neighbor. . . . The tears with which I have to wash Your holy feet will be that charity of which St. Paul spoke: "Weep with them that weep; rejoice with them that rejoice," etc. (Rom 12:15). The hair, which is something almost superfluous, will be the condescension that the soul which understands You in an exalted way must practice; for it must accommodate itself to the weakness and littleness of its neighbor. . . .

I will now return to looking at You on the well, where I see that on the right You have a cross, dark and resplendent;

for, although my intense suffering of soul, known to You, has ended, nevertheless I shall still have this cross of seeing that You are neither loved nor known, and that that which is Your will is not put into effect. I am speaking of the work of renewal of Your bride, the Church, the work so well understood by me and which, in every case, will be a cross for me. For whether it is understood or not understood, whether it is carried out or not carried out, it will be a cross for me, but a cross resplendent and glorious. . . . You have written in Your hands all my words.

O my God, to say that You take words for works, how can this be? . . . Oh yes, I understand. It is because You crown the intense desire to do a work, where there is no possibility of doing it, more than a work done without the desire. And if Your work will not be accomplished, it will not be for this reason, that it is not Your will, but because there is not the proper disposition in creatures, or generous hearts to do it, as would be necessary. . . . My Lord, whether it is accomplished or not accomplished, in any case it will be to my glory; but not to the others', because it will be for them the loss of salvation and reward.   (*CWMM*)

O Eternal Father, that You are blessed and glorious in Yourself is no cause for wonder. That all creatures are blessed and glorious through You is no cause for wonder. But that You communicate Yourself to, and take pleasure in, a creature so vile, this is a cause for wonder. . . . Then He leads the soul into so much grandeur and into so much light! And still it gives You more pleasure that we give belief, obedience, to creatures, even though we know such grandeur. But this is not understood by creatures; and therefore so few give You this pleasure. . . . Yes, I have understood.   (*CWMM*)

X

Venerable Cyril of the Mother of God

(1590–1675)

Father Cyril was born Nicholas Schockwilerg in 1590 at Luxemburg. He entered the Carmelite Order at an early age and was ordained a priest in 1624 and was later elected a prior. In 1628 he left his monastery to join the more austere Discalced Carmelites at Prague.

Father Cyril is known chiefly for his work in promoting devotion to the statue of the Infant of Prague. It was he who rescued the statue from the rubble of a church, after it had been ransacked by the Saxons. The statue had been damaged and the hands broken off. One day when Father Cyril was praying in the oratory he heard the words: "Have pity on Me and I will have pity on you. Give Me back my hands and I will give you peace. The more you honor Me, the more I will bless you." Father Cyril was able with much difficulty to have the statue repaired, and immediately the friars were blessed with relief from their financial difficulties. Many miracles have been received throughout the centuries through the intervention of the Divine Child. Father Cyril died in 1675 and is entombed in the catacombs beneath the church where the statue is enshrined.

PRAYERS

Jesus, you decided to become a child,
And I'm coming to you full of trust.
I believe that your attentive love
Forestalls all my needs.
Even for the intercession of your holy Mother,
You can meet my necessities,
spiritual as well as material.
If I pray according to your holy will.
I love you with all my heart, all my strength.
I beg your pardon if my weakness makes me sin.
I repeat with the Gospel
"Lord, if you want you can heal me."
I leave you decide how and when.
I'm ready to accept suffering, if this is your will,
but help me not to become hardened to it,
rather to bear fruit.
Help me to be a faithful servant
And for your sake, holy Child,
To love my neighbor as myself.
Almighty Child, unceasingly I pray you
To support me in my necessities
Of the present moment.
Grant me the grace to remain in you,
To be possessed and to possess you entirely,
With your parents, Mary and Joseph,
In the eternal praise
Of your heavenly servants.   (*IJOP*)

O Infant Jesus

[Revealed to Father Cyril of the Mother of God by our Lady]

O Infant Jesus! I have recourse to You.
I beg of You by Your holy Mother, deliver me
from (*mention your petition here*) for
I firmly believe Your Divinity will protect me.
I hope with all confidence to obtain Your holy grace.

I love You with all my heart and soul
I repent of my sins and I beseech You,
O Jesus, to pardon them.
I firmly resolve to correct myself and never more to
    offend You.

Therefore I offer myself to You,
In order to suffer much and patiently.
Moreover, I wish to serve You patiently
And to love myself for Your sake.

O holy Infant Jesus!
I adore You, O powerful Child.
I beg of You to deliver me from
(*here mention your particular need*)
In order that I may enjoy You
With the angels eternally. Amen.   (*IJOP*)

Perpetual Adoration Chapel,
St. Patrick's Church, Carlisle, Pennsylvania

XI

Venerable Seraphina of God

(1621–1699)

Venerable Seraphina was born in 1621 in Capri, Italy. She was intensely prayerful even from her youth. She praised God in all things, and she found Him everywhere. She continually found Him when she entered the Carmelite monastery in Naples. Mother Seraphina even praised God when told that her niece had apparently committed suicide. She prayed: "The Lord gave, the Lord takes away, blessed be the name of the Lord." This demonstrated her unflagging trust in Divine Providence. In her lifetime she founded seven monasteries. She is often called the Saint Teresa of Naples. She had a very deep devotion to the Blessed Sacrament and explained to her sisters that where He was present in a given place, there was a fragrance He exuded throughout the monastery—not just in the chapel. Venerable Seraphina died in 1699.   (CD)

PRAYER

Speaking of the Trinity... O brightest of truths! O bright obscurity, so apparent to the person who loves you!

(PLC)

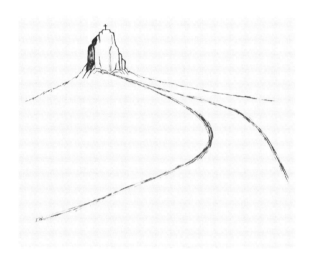

Ascending Mount Carmel

XII

Brother Lawrence of the Resurrection

(1611–1691)

Brother Lawrence was born Nicolas Herman in French Lorraine. He was not a learned man and served as a footman and a soldier before entering the Discalced Carmelites as a lay brother in 1666. The prayer of Brother Lawrence was constant and simple. He found his converse with God as easily in his work among the pots and pans as in the chapel. He would console himself with some thought such as: "Let what may come of it, however many be the days remaining to me, I will do all things for the love of God". Thus in *forgetting self* he had in truth *found God*. He died in 1691 in Paris.

PRAYERS

My God, I believe You are really present in my heart and see all that passes and will pass within me and in all creatures. What can I fear when I am with You? Do with me as You please, for I wish nothing but Yourself and to be all Yours.

(GA)

Your treasure, my God, is like an infinite ocean, yet a little wave of feeling, passing with the moment, contents us. Blind as we are, we hinder you and stop the current of your graces. But when you find a soul permeated with a living faith, you

169

pour your graces plenteously into it; they flow into the soul
like a torrent, which after being forcibly stopped against its
ordinary course, has found a passage, and spreads its pent-up
flood with great impetuosity.

O Lord, grant that I may make it my only business to
persevere always in your holy presence, keeping myself there
in a simple attention and a most loving regard . . . in a silent
and secret conversation of my soul with you. O Lord, I
contemplate you as my Father, present in my heart; and
there I adore you, . . . keeping my mind in your holy presence and calling it back every time I surprise it wandering in
distraction.   (*DI* 2)

O my God, since Thou art with me, and I must now, in
obedience to Thy commands, apply my mind to these out-
ward things, I beseech Thee to grant me the grace to continue in Thy presence; and to this end do Thou prosper me
with Thy assistance, receive all my works, and possess all my
affections.   (*PPG*)

My God I worship Thee in my infirmities. Now, now, I
shall have something to bear for Thee,—good, be it so, may I
suffer and die with Thee. (Then he would repeat those verses
of Psalm 51: "Create in me a clean heart, O God. Cast me
not away from Thy Presence. Restore unto me the joy of
Thy salvation.")   (*PPG*)

O Lord, O God of gods, how wonderful Thou art in all
Thy thoughts, beyond our understanding, how profound in
all Thy purposes, Almighty in the works of Thy Hands!

                                                        (*PPG*)

O Lord, the sense of Thy love well-nigh overwhelms me. If it be Thy will, bestow these many tokens of Thy loving-kindness on those who know Thee not, to draw them to Thy service; for me it is enough to have the riches that faith brings in the knowledge of thee. Yet forasmuch as I must not reject the favors of Thy bounteous Hand, accept my praises, Lord. And, I entreat, receive again these gifts, which Thou hast granted; for, O Lord, enlarge the chambers of my heart that I may find room for Thy love. Sustain me by Thy power, lest the fire of Thy love consume me.   (*PPG*)

Lord, Thou knowest that it is not Thy gifts I seek, but Thee Thyself, and my heart will know no rest, till it has found Thee.

O Loving-Kindness so old and still so new, I have been too late of loving Thee.   (*PPG*)

XIII

Saint Teresa Margaret Redi of the Sacred Heart

(1747–1770)

Anna Maria Redi was born in 1747 in Italy. From the earliest years she would seek solitude and be found with her eyes lifted as if her heart were already soaring to heaven. She lived at home until she was nine years old and then attended a boarding school run by Benedictine nuns. There she received spiritual direction and began to realize she had a vocation. In 1763 she received a very definite call to Carmel: "I am Teresa of Jesus—I want you among my daughters." It was not until 1764 that she entered Carmel. There she was noted for her humility, obedience, heroic charity, and utter joy, which radiated from her person. She practiced penance at every opportunity. Sister Teresa Margaret became ill quite suddenly and flew to heaven on March 5, 1770, at the Carmel of Florence.

PRAYERS

Lord, give me greater patience, that I may be able to suffer still more for Thee. (GA)

O my God, reflecting that You have made me to love and serve You, I am determined to renounce my own inclinations in order to follow the way it pleases You to lead me. I shall strive always to obey. May I learn from You, my God,

Who made Yourself obedient for me in far more difficult circumstances. *(GA)*

Prayer to the Trinity

To you be love, praise, honor, glory,
To you be expressions of deep gratitude,
O most holy, blessed and glorious Trinity,
Our one God.

(GIL)

My God, I desire nothing save to become your perfect image; and since yours was a hidden life of humiliation, love and sacrifice, so also I wish mine to be. I desire to enclose myself henceforth within your most loving Heart as in a desert, so that I may live in you, and with you, and for you, this hidden life of love and sacrifice.

O my Lord, you know my great desire to become a victim of your Sacred Heart wholly consumed by the fire of your holy love. May your Heart be the altar upon which my holocaust shall be made, and you be the priest who will consume this victim by the flames of your burning Love.

But how confused I am, my God, when I see what a worthless victim I am, and how unfitting is this sacrifice I ask you to accept. Yet, I am confident that all will be accomplished by the fire of divine love. *(GIL)*

My God, how well you know my great need of your help. I trust in your infinite mercy, and I shall always do so, regardless of the spiritual state in which I might find myself. Always and everywhere I shall endeavor to recognize your will in all things, even though my eyes see only contradiction and uncertainty. I know that I cannot depend upon myself, and so I shall trust completely in you. "Nothing shall separate me from the love of Christ", for in you, O Lord, I have hoped; I shall never be confounded.   (GIL)

Reflecting on the end for which Thou, O my God, hast conjured me out of nothing and called me to the religious life, I propose and resolve to give myself up to a complete reform of myself, to divest myself entirely of my own inclinations, to adhere solely to Thee, considering the means Thou hast given me for sanctification. I resolve in the future to esteem those means more highly and even should it be in little things, to avail myself of them for no other end than Thy glory, and to love and serve Thee, O my Jesus, in that way and manner which in Thy mercy Thou dost please to lead me and in this I will not cease, because without perseverance there can be no salvation. Having pondered with care over the thought that no one can call herself a true spouse of Christ who cannot restrain her predominant passions, I resolve to fight them with all my heart and at all costs in the continual abnegation of my will with a complete obedience to my superiors, but also to my equals and inferiors, so as to learn from Thee, O my God, Who made Thyself obedient in far harder circumstances than I find myself.

Knowing that a bride cannot be pleasing to her spouse if she does not endeavor to become what He wishes her to be, I intend to study with all my faculties how to imitate Thee in every way, to crucify myself with Thee, with a most meticulous mortification of all my powers, passions and senses.

I will always think of my neighbors as beings made to Thy likeness, produced by Thy Divine Love, at the price of Thy Blood. I will try to always look upon them with true

Christian charity, which is Thy command. I intend henceforth always to pity them and excuse their faults, always to
speak well of them and finally to never fail, of my will, in
charity towards them either in thought, word or deed.

Seeing that with regard to Thee, O my Jesus, I am nothing
but a heap of misery and ingratitude towards Thee, and that
I am full of defects, I mean to flee from and abhor praise of
myself and never to say directly or indirectly anything to call
it forth.

Thou dost clearly show me, O my God, that a soul cannot
be all Thine unless she rids her mind and heart of every
mundane affection to think only of Thee. I resolve never to
talk of worldly matters nor to be curious about them, even
the trivial ones, but only to occupy my thoughts with things
that can lead me to Thee.

With this aim in view, I propose to attend in the convent
only to the things that are my own duties and not seek to
know what my Sisters are doing, to be blind to their con-
cerns and deaf to their conversations, wishing to employ all
my capacities to serve, praise and bless Thee, my God, my
supreme Good.

Knowing, O my Jesus, that he who is ever with Thee
cannot perish and that Thy divine and sweet conversation
makes one despise the things of this world and produce in the
soul a real peace and contentment, I wish with my whole
heart never to be separated from Thee and to enjoy at all
times Thy divine blessings, never to lose sight of the Divine
Presence, to cultivate more than of yore the practice, never
neglecting it except under obedience or for grave necessity,
and to suffer with humility and resignation that aridity, anguish, fear and desolation that it may please Thee to afflict
me with in the exercise of the above.

Knowing well that he who hears Thy ministers hears

Thee, O my Jesus, who refers to them refers to Thee, being convinced of this, I resolve to lay aside and conquer all the aversion I have to opening my heart and showing my inner thoughts to those who are in Thy place for my safe spiritual guidance. I make a firm resolution, moreover, to follow the teaching of our holy Mother who says: "To your confessor and your superiors you will discover all your temptations, imperfections and repugnances, so that they may counsel you, give you the remedies to overcome them" and to render to my spiritual directors a simple, ready, blind and constant obedience. (STM)

Saint Theresa Margaret had a secret longing to unite herself to "Him", but was afraid others would find out. She prayed: "My God, let me keep my secret inviolate." (STM)

During her spiritual exercises in 1768, she wrote: "My God, I only wish to become a perfect copy of Thee, nothing else. Because Thy life was a hidden one of humility, love and sacrifice, so must mine be, since Thou knowest that I desire nothing else but to become a victim of the Sacred Heart entirely consumed in the fire of Thy Divine Love." (STM)

In all things I shall be content, knowing that the route I travel leads to Calvary. The thornier the path, the heavier the cross, the more consoled I shall be, because I desire to love you with a suffering love, a selfless love, an active love, with a firm, undivided, persevering love. . . . I have promised you many things, but in no wise do I depend upon my own indolent spirit. You have enlightened me as to what I must do; now help me to execute it. All this I hope of your infinite mercy. (GIL)

O Jesus, sweet Captain, as you raise the emblem of your cross you lovingly tell me: "Take the cross I am giving you, and however heavy it may seem to you, follow me and do not hesitate." In order to correspond with your invitation, I promise you, my heavenly Bridegroom, never more to resist your love. But I already see that you are on the road to Calvary, and here is your bride following promptly. . . . Always do with me whatever pleases you most, because I am content with everything, provided I may follow you on the road to Calvary; the more thorny I find it, and the heavier the cross, the more I shall be consoled, for I want to love you with an enduring love . . . a firm and undivided love.

Willingly I offer my heart as prey for afflictions and sadness and labor. I rejoice at not rejoicing, for fasting in this life must precede the eternal banquet that awaits me.

My Lord, you are on the cross for me, and I for you. Oh, if it could be understood even once how sweet and of how great value it is to suffer and be silent for your sake, O Jesus! O dear, suffering, good Jesus!   (DI 3)

> Elpina the shepherdess
> Burning with a great desire
> To know how God
> Could be loved upon earth,
> Wept alone one day
> And in the woods
> Uttered these words:
> "Eh! Who can teach me
> to love God Who loves me
> and Who, before the existence
> of the world He created
> with this same love

of His Heart Divine,
loved me . . ."
While thus grieved
she wept to herself
not being able to console
the pain of her heart;
the virgin, now a hermit,
swooned and fell—
a prey to languor . . .
Behold, there before her,
ornate with gilded wings,
brimming with celestial delight,
stood suddenly a gracious spirit,
and his loving lips
like lilies and roses
opened into these beautiful accents:
"Elpina, how can you say
You do not love God,
When your very desire
Of loving is love itself?
It is the sweet flame
Which escapes from
The secret furnace of your Heart."   (*FSH*)

I desire to love You with a patient love, a love dead to self—that is, a love which completely abandons me to You; an active love; to sum it all up, a solid love with no division within itself and which will stand regardless of what may happen.   (*FSH*)

When shall I come and appear before Thy Face?   (*FSH*)

Glory be to the Trinity!   (*FSH*)

Holy, Holy, Holy...   (*FSH*)

I venerate you a thousand times, O true Mother of my Lord Jesus Christ:—Hail Mary.

I venerate you, O sovereign Queen of the Angels, Empress of the Universe:—Hail Mary.

I venerate you, most kindly Virgin Mary, most worthy mother of my one Savior Jesus:—Hail Mary.   (*MMC* 2)

XIV

The Martyrs of Compiègne

(D. 1794)

There were in Compiègne, France, sixteen Carmelites who lived during the Reign of Terror. They were part of a community that was known for its fervor and fidelity to the Teresian spirit. When war broke out they would not don civilian clothes, choosing to remain in their habit. They saw the horror of the bloodshed by so many and could see no end in sight. With the encouragement of the prioress, Mother Teresa of Saint Augustine, they all made an act of oblation daily, offering themselves as victims in order that peace would come. Their names are important, for their sacrifice was complete. They are:

Sister Jesus Crucified, age 78
Sister Charlotte of the Resurrection, age 78
Sister Euphrasia of the Immaculate Conception, age 58
Sister Julie Louise of Jesus, age 52
Sister Teresa of the Heart of Mary, age 52
Sister Saint Martha, age 52
Sister Catherine, age 52
Sister Marie of the Holy Spirit, age 51
Sister Teresa of Saint Ignatius, age 51
Mother Henriette of Jesus, age 49
Sister Teresa, age 46
Sister Saint Louis, age 42
Mother Teresa of Saint Augustine (Lidoine), age 41

Sister Marie Henriette of the Divine Providence, age 34
Sister Saint Francis Xavier, age 30
Sister Constance, age 29

While in prison, they were models of serene confidence
and also tranquility. They spread joy and even composed a
song of jubilee in anticipation of their martyrdom. All died
at the guillotine at the Place de la Nation, Paris, on July 17,
1794, singing of their love for Jesus.

The sixteen Blessed Carmelites of Compiègne

PRAYERS

Composed by Mother Teresa of Saint Augustine

O Infant God, naught else can fill my longing,
Yea, nothing else can satisfy my heart!
It's settled then, henceforth I'm Thy belonging,
And of Thy love, I've now become a part.
My criminal soul, heal of its sin so shameful,
Wound Thou my heart, with pain or love's delight.
Let wounds divine, wounds for my soul most gainful,
Martyr my heart to suffer day and night!

O Love divine, I now with all my being
Here at Thy creche abandon all my soul.
I thus yield up my reasoning and my seeing
From this time forth: my faith in Thee is bold!
Thy heart alone! Thy heart shall be my master!
Thoughts and desires I sacrifice as weak.
Within thy heart, I would now be clasped faster,
The martyrdom of love alone I seek.

Oh! Fix my hope, oh fix it all on dying!
Truly I die from not dying for Thee.
And hasten, Lord, the end of all my sighing
Freed from these chains to Thee alone I'll flee!
Let Thy blade cut, completing all my offerings,
For nothing but Thy will for me is sweet.
My one desire is that Thy hand be hovering
O'er me Thy bride, the sacrifice complete!

Thy shepherd's crook, let it rule as the master
O'er this Thy flock entrusted to my care.
Here at thy creche, I yield to Thee, O Pastor,

Mother and flock, abandoning all I dare!
O loving Queen, Mother of might most holy,
O deign to place us all within Thy breast!
For in Thy power, the children all, though lowly,
Do set their hope, trusting in thy behest.   (*TQT*)

Composed by Sister Julie Louise

Let our hearts be giv'n to joyfulness
The day of glory now is here!
Let us banish all of our weakness,
We can see that the cross now is near!
Let's prepare ourselves for the victory!
Let us each as a conqueror go forth!
Under the cross, God's great banner,
Let's all run, let's all fly toward glory!
Let our ardor be enflamed!
Let's give our bodies in His name!
Let's climb, let's climb, the scaffold high!
We'll give God the victory!

Happiness that's ever beckoning
To all the Catholics of France
To take up the path of the martyrs
Where many another's advanced!
The martyrs go off to their passion
As did Jesus, followed by our King.
Our faith as Christians let us bring,
God's righteousness let us adore!
So let the priest with zeal,
And all believers seal,
Their faith, their faith, with all their blood,
In a God who like them died.

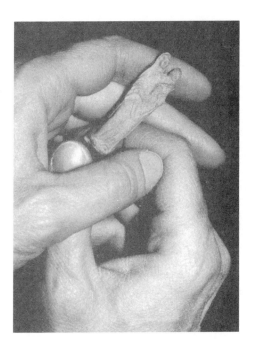

*Statue kissed by the Martyrs of Compiègne
before dying on the scaffold*

Great God who seest all my weaknesses
Although I'm eager, still I fear.
Confidently ardor now guides me,
O do Thou lend Thine aid and be near!
I can't hide from Thine eyes my poor heart,
Thinking that it's with death I must pay.
Be Thou my comfort, be my stay,
And I'll say, come, let's make our start!

Hasten now the sacrifice!
Thou canst change me in a trice!
O Lord, O Lord, with no delay,
To my heart give joy today.

Holy Virgin, our example,
Of martyrs all the august Queen,
Do thou deign to sustain our great ardor
Cleanse our desires, make us all pure and clean!
Still protect sweet France, our dear country
From heaven's heights lend us all now thine aid
Let us all feel here in these places
The effects of all thy graces.
We, thine own, await thy power;
Submit, obey thee in this hour.
We'll die as did Jesus our God,
And our believing King!

Behold O divine Mary
The holy zeal of us, thine own.
Since it's God who us life has given
We accept this death as our own.
Reveal thyself as our tender mother,
And present us all to Jesus Christ
That, given life by His Spirit
We may, in taking leave of life:
With the fire of His great love
Join with all the saints above,
And sing, and sing, on heaven's shore,
All His goodness evermore!   (*TQT*)

XV

Blessed Francis Palau y Quer

(1811–1872)

Blessed Francis was born in 1811 in Aytona, Lerida, to a poor peasant family. In 1828 he entered the diocesan seminary at Lerida, where he was to study for three years. At the end of this time he decided to enter the Teresian Carmelite seminary at Barcelona. He was there clothed with the habit, but it was a time of great persecution of the Church and soon after community life ceased. He was ordained a priest in Barbastro in 1836. He was never again able to step into a Carmelite cloister. For more than ten years Blessed Francis was exiled in France, where he lived the eremitical life rigorously. He returned to Spain in 1851, to Barcelona, where he exercised his apostolic ministry. He was very involved in religious education and also in resisting the civil and military authorities who interfered in religious affairs. This caused him to be exiled to Ibiza until 1860. During this time he went through a very dark night. The solitude replenished his spirit with the strength to face what would lie ahead. He was freed by a decree of Queen Isabel II in July 1860. His activities resumed, but not without serene moments of solitude in the caves of Santa Cruz of Horta, Barcelona, and El Vedra, in Ibiza. He served as a catechist, prolific writer whose works are still published today, exorcist, and founder. Blessed Francis knew that the faith in Spain needed to be restored, and to assure this he was able to found congregations of Carmelite brothers and sisters to pray for this end. These

congregations were reformed as Saint Teresa of Avila had done previously. As exorcist he prayed with many of the sick the prayers that the priest has the authority to use. As Carmelite he followed in the footsteps of Elias. Many of the sick were cured. He came under suspicion of the authorities and was imprisoned, charged with illegal medical practice. He died without knowing that he had been previously absolved of any wrongdoing in 1872.

PRAYERS

Model of the Church

Mary, Mother of God all pure,
Mary, Mother of Jesus.

I am a perfect complete model
Of your loved
Holy Church
The communion of all the saints
The Virgin of Carmel.   (*FPP*)

For the Church

I give myself to you, the Church, such as I am,
With everything I have now,
During my lifetime and in eternity.   (*FPP*)

Mary

Mary, you are the standard, the model,
The mirror, support, and firm strength
Of the virtues.   (*FPP*)

XVI

Saint Raphael Kalinowski

(1835–1907)

Joseph Kalinowski was born in Poland in 1835. He lived an active life, becoming an engineer, a military officer, and a leader in the 1863 insurrection against Russian domination. He was exiled in Siberia and then entered Carmel after his release. His entrance was at Graz, where he was clothed in the habit and received the name Raphael of Saint Joseph. He was a true contemplative and considered prayer essential. However, he also spent his life serving in very demanding positions that required much of his attention. He was an educator and even tutored a prince who was an invalid. He took care of the desperate and the needy, considering the welfare of others before his own. Saint Raphael was an outstanding confessor and spiritual director, saying that "when he was receiving penitents, he felt himself to be a treasury of Divine Mercy." He was like a "Father" to his children and was available day and night. He insisted that Church unity could be achieved through the devotion to our Lady that both the Orthodox and Catholics have in common. His maxim was "Mary always and in everything". He died on November 15, 1907, the feast for all Carmelite souls who are deceased.

PRAYERS

Jesus, hope of suffering humanity, our refuge and our strength, whose light pierces the black clouds that hang over our stormy sea, enlighten our eyes so that we can direct ourselves toward You Who are our harbor. Guide our bark with the rudder of the nails of Your cross, lest we drown in the storm. With the arms of this cross rescue us from the turbulent waters and draw us to Yourself, our only repose, Morning Star, Sun of Justice, for with our eyes obscured by tears, we can catch a glimpse of You there, on the shores of our heavenly homeland. Redeemed by You, we pray: *Salvos nos fac propter nomen tuum*—"Save us for the sake of Your holy name." And all this through Mary.   (*SRK*)

We entrust our task to our Most Holy Mother, the Virgin Mary, under her maternal care.

If there is anything to correct, let it be corrected once and for all; may the good that is done continue to increase.

Toward this purpose, may God's love flood your souls along this earthly life, and finally lead you to the fountain of love, that is, to God Himself in eternity.   (*SRK*)

In a letter written from Siberia he prayed: "O God, what a great treasure You grant to those who hope in You."   (*FRK*)

In the midst of great suffering: "Oh, my God, mercy!" "Oh, God, God, give me patience!"   (*FRK*)

XVII

Saint Henry de Osso

(1840–1896)

Henry de Osso y Cervello was born into a good Catholic family in Vinebre, Spain. His dream was to become a teacher. At the age of thirteen he lost his mother, and like Saint Teresa of Avila he took our Lady as his Mother. At this point he decided to run away and become a hermit. He went on foot to Montserrat and there promised himself to Jesus forever.

Henry realized he needed to study if he was to carry out his promise, so he went to the seminary at Tortosa. His zeal and virtue did not go unnoticed, and upon his ordination he was named professor at the seminary. He served in that position from 1866 to 1867. He was much loved, but he wanted to go and convert as much of Spain as possible.

To accomplish this he used his pen. He was a journalist and initiated *St. Teresa's Magazine*. He also began an Association of Catholic Action. He had three hundred young girls for his beginning. This movement was quite successful and spread rapidly. Because of this it was raised to the rank of archconfraternity.

He had great devotion to Saint Teresa of Avila and founded an order of nuns, the Society of Saint Teresa of Jesus. They were educators who reformed the schools in Spain, Portugal, Africa, and America.

Saint Henry wrote numerous prayers, poems, novenas, and litanies. Many were directed to the Mother of God. They are not translated yet, so his prayers in this work are limited.

Before Henry died in January 1896, he asked that he be buried at his beloved Montserrat. He was told that he would be buried at his monastery. He said if they would not bury him at Montserrat, they could bury him in a Franciscan monastery!

This teacher, reformer, and holy man was quickly recognized as exceptional and given the title of Blessed in 1979 and Saint in 1993.

PRAYERS

Saint Teresa

My beloved Saint Teresa, beautiful, powerful, gracious, and a charmer of hearts, may you be blessed. May the results of your Centennial not be passing glories. May your reign not end here. Wherever there be a heart that beats and a mind that knows, may there also be always an admirer of your greatness, a lover of your glories, and someone to celebrate your valor and imitate your virtues. (PP)

At Montserrat

I found my vocation. You guided me without remembering how, Star of the Sea, Morning Star, Star of Barcelona, you shone in my eyes; I followed your light; and when you showed me Jesus, the blessed fruit of your womb, I said, "I will always belong to Jesus, I will be His minister, His apostle, His missionary of peace and love." (HDO)

Novena to the Holy Spirit

Oh, my Jesus and my all! You know all things; you know that I love You! Oh, my Jesus and my all! Engrave Your divine name in my understanding, my memory, on my lips and especially in my heart, so that I may remember You more, speak more of You, and love You more.

Oh, my Jesus and my all! To love or to die! Do not let me leave this world, my Jesus, without having loved You, and made You known and loved. (*HDO*)

My Jesus, I want to have my name written perpetually in Your heart; I want to possess a heart like Yours. (*EE*)

Speak, Lord, your servant is listening. Lord, I do not speak to men, nor the prophets, but You alone, Who are my God. Lord, You have the words of eternal life. Speak them to my heart, my soul, my strength and senses. (*EE*)

O Lord Jesus! My Spouse and my Love! You promised me that You would grant Your pity on them. I come to You, therefore, on this day, to carry out Your word of peace to my Spain. Keep my eyes from continuing to weep. . . . Many tears have been shed for the disasters of all my Spanish people, their whole spiritual life has been consumed. . . . To see the stream of tribulations of the people of my village, when the temples were destroyed or profaned, the persecution and assassination of the priests, the uprooting of the homes of the virgins consecrated to You, the conversion of the convents, the houses of prayer into houses of perdition, or barns, the calling and spoiling in order that the Protestant heresies would be deeply rooted in my country. O Eternal

God, mercy and patience! To have opened my country to bitterness; the drunkenness of belonging to others. Enough, Lord, of punishment; let Your mercy shine [on us]. I invoke Your holy name with tears to the door of Your compassionate heart—that You reign in Spain—that You do not close Your ears to my cries. (*EE*)

XVIII

Blessed Mary of Jesus Crucified

(1846–1878)

Mariam Baouardy was born in 1846 at Abellin, Galilee. Her family was Lebanese and lived in the hill country. They belonged to the Greek Melkite Catholic rite. Her parents had lost twelve sons before her birth, so they traveled to Bethlehem and petitioned the Blessed Virgin for a child, promising to name her Mariam if it was a girl. Two years after Mariam's birth, her parents were also blessed with a boy, Boulos. However, the joy was not to last long. Both parents died soon after, and Mariam was taken in by her paternal uncle; Boulos, by a maternal aunt. Mariam was attracted to penance and humility from an early age. She loved to enjoy the orchards and vineyards and especially spent her time thinking of God. She had no formal education, but had a deep devotion to the Blessed Virgin. Her new family decided to move from Abellin to Egypt. Her life was marked by a deep hunger for the Eucharist, drawing her to receive her First Communion before she was given permission. At that moment she saw Jesus give Himself to her as a most beautiful child. At the age of thirteen she had been promised in marriage to an uncle. In her heart the night before the wedding she heard: "Everything passes! If you wish to give Me your heart, I will always remain with you." Her response was to cut off her braids to signify her intention to remain a virgin. She was treated as a slave. One day she decided to send a letter to her brother through a Muslim friend of the family. He wanted her to become a Muslim, and when she refused he slashed her throat with a scimitar, leaving her for dead in a pool of blood. The Blessed Virgin came and nursed her back to health.

In 1870 she entered the Carmel of Pau. Her whole religious life was marked with supernatural gifts. She had eight ecstatic levitations from 1873 to 1874. She possessed the stigmata and gave off a strong, sweet fragrance. Her heart was transpierced; she had apparitions and received prophecies that were fulfilled. Mariam had mysterious knowledge and even bilocated. She also had the gift of poetry, which was remarkable considering her lack of schooling. Blessed Mary traveled to Mangalore, India, and then returned to Pau. This "Little Arab" founded the monastery in Bethlehem and died in 1878.

PRAYERS

I am a daughter of Holy Church, my Mother.

How I wish to give my blood for the Church! I offer everything for Her, for the unity, for the triumph of the Church. (*MLA*, from *Revue du Rosaire*)

To what shall I liken me?
To little birds in their nest.
If the father and mother do not bring them food,
   they die of hunger.
Thus is my soul without You, Lord; it does not have
   its nourishment, it cannot live!
To what shall I liken me?
To the little grain of wheat cast into the earth. If the
   dew falls not, if the sun does not warm it, the grain
   molds.

But if You give Your dew and Your sun, the little
    grain will be refreshed and warmed; it will take
    root and will produce a beautiful plant with many
    grains.
To what shall I liken me, Lord?
To a rose that is cut and left to dry up in the hand. It
    loses its perfume; but if it remains on the rosebush,
    it is always fresh and beautiful and keeps all its
    perfume.
Keep me, Lord, to give me life in You.
To what shall I liken You, Lord?
To the dove that feeds its little ones, to a tender mother
    who nourishes her little babe.   (*MLA*)

I invited the whole earth, to bless Thee, to serve
    Thee.
Forever and always, never to end! With Thy love my
    heart made one.
I invited the entire sea, to bless Thee, to serve Thee.
Forever and always, never to end!
I called them, invited them, little birds of the air, to
    bless Thee, to serve Thee.
Forever and always, never to end!
I called, I invited, the star of the morn. Forever and
    always,
never to end!
My Beloved, yes I hear Him, He is very near, Go
    forward!
Forever and always, never to end!
Open, O curtain that hides Him, I want to see Him,
    my Beloved,
to adore and to love.

Forever and always, never to end! With His love my
    heart made one.
I called him, invited ungrateful man, to bless Thee, to
    serve Thee, to praise and to love Thee. Forever and
    always, never to end.   (*MLA*)

Lord, my land is dry and parched:
    Send it your dew.
My flesh is falling off in rottenness,
    My feet can no longer support me,
    Nor my hands move.
My nerves are all on edge;
    My bones are wasted away,
    The marrow of my bones is like rotten smoke.
The hairs of my head are stiff,
    All standing straight up
    And they prick me like needles.
My ears are closed
    And so dull I cannot hear.
My eyes are on fire,
    They no longer see the light.
My nose is all pinched;
My tongue cleaves to my palate
    And can no longer utter a word
    To cry to You.
My teeth are so locked
    The air can no longer pass through
    And I am going to die.
My lips are so tight closed
    That I can no longer move them
    To call You to my aid.
Lord, send Your dew upon this sterile earth,
    And it will return to life.   (*MLA*)

My enraptured spirit contemplates all Thy works.
  Who can speak to Thee, O God so great!
  O Omnipotent One, (it is) my ravished soul!
A nothing, a bit of dust says to You: Come to me.
  Who can say that an Omnipotent One takes notice!
One glance! You who look at me, come to me.
  You alone, my God, my all.
I see Thee, goodness supreme: Thy glance is
  maternal.
  Come quickly, O Sun of justice, arise!
My soul is consumed, I languish while waiting.
  Come quickly!
My soul, fly with wings of the dove to my God:
  He is my All.
Thy glance consoles me, my soul is thrilled.
The nothing, the dust trembles
  In the presence of a God so great.
He has visited His field: fly away O my soul!
My soul sees Thee in the cloud,
  It can no longer remain here below.
Thy glance is enough to draw the nothing from this
  earth.
God is splendid in His power.
  Let all things praise Him, praise Him!
My soul is foolish, it can bear no more, take it!
Who has God, possesses all things.   (*MLA*)

Canticle to the Tree of Life

Hail, hail, Tree of life,
  That gives us the fruit of life!
From the center of this earth
  My heart repines, my heart sighs out.

Oh! Who will give me wings
   To fly to my Beloved!
Hail, hail, Tree of life,
   That gives us the fruit of life!
I see on thy leaves these words are written:
   Have no fear of anything!
Thy verdure says: Have hope.
Thy branches tell me: Charity.
And Thy shade: Humility.
Hail, hail, Tree of life;
   In Thee I find the fruit of life.
From the center of this earth,
   My heart repines, my heart is longing.
Oh! Who will give me wings
   To fly to my Beloved!
Hail, hail, blessed Tree;
   Thou bearest the fruit of life.
Under Thy shade, I wish to sigh;
At Thy feet, I wish to die.   (*MLA*)

At the feet of Mary, my mother dear,
   I came back to life.
O all you who suffer, come to Mary,
   At the feet of Mary I came back to life.
O you who work in this monastery,
   Mary counts your steps and your labors.
   Tell yourselves:
   At the feet of Mary, I came back to life.
You who dwell in this monastery,
   Detach yourselves from things of earth.
Your salvation and your life are at the feet of Mary.

I dwell in the heart of my mother,
   There I find my Beloved.
Am I then an orphan? In the bosom of Mary
   I have found life.
Do not say I am an orphan:
   I have Mary for Mother and God for Father.
The serpent, the dragon wished to catch me
   And take my life;
   But at the feet of Mary, I recovered my life.
Mary called me, and, in this monastery,
   Will I remain forever.
   At the feet of Mary
I came to life again.   (*MLA*)

I unite myself to Jesus when He was carrying His
   cross in the streets
Of Jerusalem. May You be blessed my God.
I unite my voice with that of Jesus in the garden of
   olives. May You be blessed, my God.
I unite my sufferings to those of Jesus betrayed by
   Judas. May You be blessed, my God.
I unite myself to Jesus falling under the weight of the
   cross. May You be blessed, my God.   (*MLA*)

Lord, to suffer or to be despised for Your love.
Lord, I deserve rather to be thrust down, to the
   bottom. Forgive me, forgive me!
Lord, may Your will be done, and not mine.
Ask Jesus to deliver me from the interior joys that I
   experience. They are so great that I do not feel any
   suffering.

Lord, I adore Your word. The earth will pass away,
   but Your word will never pass away.
Mary, my mother, come to my help! Everyone cry
   out with me: Jesus, wake up!
Lord, I accept all that You will.
Love, O love, You are not known!   (*MLA*)

Holy Spirit, inspire me.
Love of God, consume me.
Along the true road, lead me.
Mary, my mother, look upon me.
With Jesus bless me.
From all evil, from all illusion,
From all danger, preserve me.   (*MLA*)

In a vision Blessed Mary saw Jesus holding a three-year-old
girl dressed as a Carmelite. She said to Our Lord: "This little
one is fortunate, You love her so much!" And Jesus replied:
"Yes, I love her, see how I hold her in My arms; but she
doesn't know it."—She doesn't know it! Ah, if I were like
that, I promise You that I would feel it and I would be happy!
O little one, pray for me who am so sinful. You are pure and
I am dung. (The little one didn't see me; she was looking
only at Jesus, and Jesus was looking only at her all the time.)
                                                    (*MLA*)

Finding the milk all curdled one morning, she turned to
God: "You know that I need the milk to feed the sisters. I am
going to use it for cooking. Bless it, and instead of letting it
get more spoiled, make it all good again." (A few minutes
later the milk was good again.)   (*MLA*)

My God, in spite of all my miseries and sins, I will always hope in You. Even if You cast me into hell, I will still hope in You.

I am nothing, I can do nothing, but You can do all. I hope in divine mercy.

I do not know if I will be saved; but I hope, my God, that You will save me. Yes, I have the hope that I will see God.

Hasten, Lord, hasten the time of my departure, I am tired of being on earth! I am like a child that has lost its father and who runs in search of him. You are good, Lord, but You are hard! Ah, if I were Jesus and You were Sister Mary of Jesus Crucified, I would not let You languish so long! I am like a bird imprisoned in its cage: open the door for me, so that I may take my flight toward You!

I can live no longer, O my God, take me away!

I will see my God. Not from afar as I see Him now, but in reality, in truth. I will see the living God! I will hear His voice, my bones and my flesh will be filled with joy. After having been in an abyss, I will be in a palace with Him! O blessed death, bring me quickly to my Beloved!   (MLA)

I offer my sufferings in union with Jesus and with all the martyrs who suffered for the triumph of the Church. I desire to immolate myself, to suffer, to be roasted, broken to pieces, for the triumph of the Church. I unite myself to Jesus on Calvary, immolating myself with Him for the conversion of sinners and for the children of the Church. I offer my sufferings for the blind who do not recognize the Church, that they may know her.   (MLA)

My enraptured spirit contemplates all your works.
Who can speak of You, O God so great!
Omnipotent One, my soul is carried away!
His wonderful beauty delights my soul.
Who can tell what the Almighty looks upon?
One look!
You who gaze at me, come to me, a little nothing.
I cannot remain here on earth, my soul longing.
Call me close to You, awaken me.
You alone, my God, my All.
The heavens, the earth, the sun rejoice at your Name
    so great.
I see You, supreme goodness: Your gaze is maternal.
My Father, my Mother, it is in You that I sleep,
It is in You that I breathe. Awaken!
My soul is mad with yearning, it can do no more,
    take it.
When will we see Him forever world without end!

                                                    (*MLA*)

O You Who are so tender, how is Your heart so hard as not
to compassionate me? I have sinned, it is true, but You see
how all else but You has failed me.   (*LCJ*)

Lord, if You abandon me, I am like a cinder. The cinder will
not produce any fruit. It hinders vegetable growth. But if
You, Lord, look down on me, I become a good earth, a
fertile soil that brings forth good fruits, and plants producing
flowers. O Lord, look down on me always!   (*LCJ*)

O my God, I am blind and without understanding, but I see to follow Thy footprints, in Thy perfume. Lord, I wish to follow You. . . . When I fall You will take me up. If even my whole body were to pass through fire, I would follow the Lord. O God, have pity on a helpless child; on a fly. . . . But I hope in You. I am less than a little *ant*, less than a little nothing; I will follow Your steps and shall gain strength from your shadow, through the fragrance of your shadow. . . . And your odours will satisfy me. How comes it that a little worm that creeps in the shadow of the King is not crushed? I am in the shadow of the King of Kings. (*LCJ*)

In ecstasy:

Yes, if I could don the doctor's hat, I would preach to all the earth. But, alas! my wings are clipped. They are my sins . . . I see all . . . It is that which increases the pain of my sins.

(*LCJ*)

In ecstasy beholding Our Saviour with all of His wounds bleeding:

Oh! How my Father is offended! My Saviour, give me if it is Your Will all these sufferings, but have mercy on sinners.

(*LCJ*)

On Good Friday while suffering the Passion:

My God, do not abandon me; my God I offer it to You, do not abandon me. Pardon, my God; Pardon! Do not reject me in Your anger! Remove Your indignation from me! Have pity on me, call me to-day. (*LCJ*)

My heart with ardent longings
Awaits my Well-Beloved
I ask of heaven and all created things
Where the Loved One dwells.
And all reply: You'll find Him
In the straight and humble heart.
Oh! Thought of Him so strong!
Oh! His looks, all Love and Mercy.   (*TSM*)

Oh! My nature revolts, it does not want to die. And at the same time my heart thrills with joy because my eyes will see my Creator. O my God, what happiness! My eyes will see You, I will go to You! It is true that I have sinned, but I have great confidence. My God, hasten the moment of going to You. Nothing gives me pleasure on earth. Hurry, Hurry, Lord! I am not holding fast to anything now; but if I live, I fear I will attach myself to something. I am afraid of myself.

My heart is worn out, and how do You expect me to live! O blessed Death that will permit me to see my God! My whole being will leap for joy when I see my God.

My flesh loves the Lord; my bones love my God; my soul and all my senses crave my God. Do not delay: listen to my laments, O my God!

When I see You, everything in me will recover life and new strength in You, O my God!

O my God, how blind the world is, when it fears death! This blessed death!   (*MLA*)

As the thirsty stag sighs for the water of the torrent, so my soul sighs for [You], O my God!   (*MLA*)

Oh yes, mercy!   (*MLA*)

Prayers Uttered in Ecstasy

What are You like, my God? The ocean? That comparison is too feeble. One single raindrop is not enough to refresh the whole earth; so too, the love of all hearts is not enough for You, my God.

The drop of water is myself; the ocean is You. I wish to have a heart greater than earth and sea to love You! *(TSM)*

Stop, my God, enough, enough! Soften Your heart, my God. Listen to the cries and lamentations. Look on all the scenes of wretchedness. Stop, my God, enough; soften Your heart; be sympathetic to these cries.

Well I do know, Lord, that You find it no pleasure to strike us; it is Your Justice that forces You, as it were, against Your will. But have pity on us, Lord. It is Your nature to be infinitely compassionate; but Your justice is harder than hell. Do not let Your treatment of us be inspired by Your justice, but by Your mercy. No one but You is holy; no one but You is just.

I prefer my brothers and I appear before Your mercy rather than before Your justice.

Let Your mercy, Lord, rule all Your dealings with us, our injustices can never find acquittal before Your justice. If You use justice in judging me, how deep a hell will be the lot of me and of my brothers!

Because you are just, my God, act with us in mercy.

Have pity on the cries of my brothers.

My God, be our judge, not as man, but as God, as our Father and Creator. *(TSM)*

Lord, I thank You for being my judge. A thousand times better is it that it is You and not myself who is my judge. If I were my own judge, I should condemn myself to hell. But with You as judge, my sentence will be a merciful one.

I judge myself to be worthy of hell. But if You willed to send me there, I should prefer to go to hell by Your will and judgment, rather than to heaven by my own.   (*TSM*)

Lord, I am blacker than soot. But Your mercy, greater than the sea, will wash me clean.

If everyone drank from the sea, the sea would not run dry; if everyone washed in the sea, the sea would not become dirty. Lord, You are that sea. Many there are that desire You, but souls are blind, darkness blinds them and so they cannot look for You, cannot see or find You. And I too, Lord, am one of them.   (*TSM*)

Have pity on my brothers, Lord, have pity. They praise You better than I. I was far below them, and You have drawn me up out of the abyss. My love for You is less than You deserve. Blot out our sins, O God, blot out our sins.

Yes, Lord, You tell my brothers they have not their hearts right; You say to them that: "Those who fear creatures set me aside."   (*TSM*)

Lord, keep me always in Your love, like the child in its mother's womb, where it has no need to eat or drink, where it is sheltered from every danger and has everything necessary.

I, too, Lord, shall want for nothing if You keep me in Your love.   (*TSM*)

Lord, I am like the little chicken that the hawk has caught and stabbed on the head and almost crushed to death and that has fled under its mother's wing for safety.

I, too, have been in anguish, in sadness and in pain, my bones have been dislocated, my flesh has been bruised. I turned my eyes to my Father: He turned His eyes to me, and in that look I found my healing. My bones knit and grew strong again, like those of a fifteen-year-old; my flesh, my whole being, trembled with joy. *(TSM)*

How admirable is Jesus! My God I adore You. You alone are great. I adore Your greatness and Your power. You alone are worthy of admiration. Who is to compare with You? You are the only God there is; no one like You in heaven or on earth.

How happy I am that God has created me to call Him my God! If You had created me without the gift of reason, I could not call You my God. I thank You for giving me a mind; I offer it to You.

How happy I am to have a Father who fills heaven and earth! Let all things echo with the praises of my God! Let the mountains skip with joy; let the earth quiver with gladness!

(TSM)

I said to Jesus: You are an infinite sea. Your waters are whiter than snow, brighter than light. *(TSM)*

Lord, You are a seed, the seed of my soul. And God the Father is the sun warming this poor ground. And You, Holy Spirit, are the rain refreshing its sterility.

You, Jesus, are the seed, for You come every day. This dear seed comes every day. *(TSM)*

I saw a large flowerbed formed of several concentric circles.

The first circle was planted with roses; the rose signifies charity and its thorns vigilance.

The second was covered with vines; the grape signifying love and the leaf mildness.

The third was sown with wheat, which signifies hope and confidence.

The center was all of violets, which signify true humility.

And in the center I make a throne, and set Jesus upon it. And from under His feet comes a spring which says "Everything passes, everything flows by like water."

Beside the throne I plant pansies and ivy. The ivy says to me: "Cling to Jesus unceasingly." And the pansy says to me: "Think only of Jesus."

Lord Jesus, plant all these virtues in the depths of my heart, and by Your own power make them grow.   (*TSM*)

Lord, how good You are to hold a weak reed in Your hand! I am that reed; I am even weaker. But I shall remain always with You, like that reed. If You dropped it, it would get broken. You carry it; it is not the reed that carries You.

(*TSM*)

Oh, my brother, if you want to sell the Beloved, I shall buy Him from you. O Saviour, I shall buy You with my tears and obedience, with humility and charity, with sacrifice and with death, with the purest love of neighbor. And when I do, I shall buy You for those who sell You.   (*TSM*)

The virgin is always singing; she follows the Lamb and never gets tired.

O sight of the Lamb, my Sun, my Life! My soul cannot bear to stay on earth any longer.   (*TSM*)

Forgive, my God! You alone, You alone! Jesus is not known, is not loved. The black bread is taken and the white is left. God left for creatures.

O my God, You alone! I wish I were a bird, to cry through-out the earth: "You alone, my God."   (*TSM*)

Lord, I am an ignorant child, blind and feeble. I come to You for vigor and for life. Have pity on Your child, frail by its fallen nature, but foul by its personal pride. Come; come and give me strength, for fear the lion devour me. Come, Your very look will cure me, for Your look can work miracles, can give life where there was none.

Take my heart and soul; make them one with You and offer them to the Heavenly Father.   (*TSM*)

I have everything. The puppy has asked for a crumb or two, and the Lord has given Himself to it.   (*TSM*)

THE WHEAT OF LIFE

The Bread destined for me has been blessed by the
    Mother of God.
Praise your Creator, my soul, become through love a
    little lamb;
The pure wheat is going to rest within you,
    unfathomable mystery.

The Lord has no use for the wheat of mixture.
Pick your own wheat, Most High, and wash It from
    the dust that hides Its whiteness.   (*TSM*)

I was low in spirits because I did not experience God. My heart seemed to be like iron. I could not think of God. I invoked the Holy Spirit, saying: "It is You who get us to know Jesus. The Apostles spent a long time with Jesus without ever understanding Him; but when You came to them they understood Him then. You can get me too to understand Him.

"Come, my consolation; come, my joy and peace, my strength and light. Come, give me the light to find the spring where I can quench my thirst. One drop of You is enough to show me Jesus as He is.

"Jesus has said that You will come to the ignorant; I am the most ignorant of all. I ask You for no other knowledge than the knowledge of how to find Jesus; I ask You for no other vision than the wisdom of keeping Him."   (*TSM*)

Holy Spirit, enlighten me. To find Jesus, what am I to do, and how am I to do it? The disciples were very ignorant; they were with Jesus yet did not understand Him. I, too, live in the same house with Jesus and do not understand Him. The least thing troubles and upsets me. I am too sensitive; I have not generosity enough to make sacrifices for Jesus.

O Holy Spirit, when You gave them a ray of light, the disciples disappeared; they were no longer what they were before. They found new strength; they found it easy to make sacrifices. They knew Jesus better than they had ever known Him when with them.

Source of peace and light, come and enlighten me. I am

hungry, come and feed me; thirsty, come and refresh me; blind, come and give me sight; poor, come and enrich me; ignorant, come and instruct me.

Holy Spirit, I abandon myself to You. (*TSM*)

Mary, Banquet and Rest

The bread set aside for me, my beautiful Mother has
  blessed it.
Now that my life on earth is drawing to its close, I ask
  you, good Mother, to keep me forever beside you.
My food is the desire I have, dearest Mother, to see
  you;
The water my thirsty soul drinks is my love for you.
My true life, my soul's life, grows more vigorous by
  loving you;
The rest I take is to seek you, restless, day and night.
(*TSM*)

Lord, what could an infant do for itself, if abandoned by its mother and with no one to look after it? It could not protect itself against the bites of the flies and wasps and snakes; and it would die of hunger and thirst.

Lord, my sins are the cause of my miseries. I am like that little infant. But You are my Father. Have pity on me; I am the work of Your hands. (*TSM*)

Thank You, my God, for making me aware of what I am. I prefer to know my weakness than to perform miracles. That is better for me, for when people see me fall I have nothing then to nourish my pride upon. It is better for me because it makes me see You are my only strength; better for me to fall a thousand times if it makes me say to You two thousand times: "I hope in You, O Lord." Thank You, thank You, Lord.   (*TSM*)

I have sinned so much! How can I hope to reach heaven! But, my God, it is because I have sinned so much that I hope much. In heaven the Lord's mercies to me will be seen to have been greater than His mercies to any of my sisters.

(*TSM*)

The Beloved, walks before me; my heart and soul are filled with joy.

O Origin of all that is, Your look reduces me to nothing.

Open, earth, and bury me. My heart yearns to leave this exile, to praise You, Goodness supreme.

Free me from these fetters that shackle me.

The Lord reprimands me for the uprisings of my nature. But I know it is Love reprimanding me.   (*TSM*)

Lord, visit Your house. Look with love upon it. See all these animals entering it, and how they make it shake! Visit, O Lord, Your house.

Jesus, visit Your garden. When You are absent, it is winter there; fruits there are none. Be like the gardener, Lord, who digs the ground and manures it, who sows and weeds and waters. Your garden, Lord, my soul, is dry, with no one to give it a drop of water. Come, Lord Jesus, without You my flowers wither and fall. You alone are my strength; You alone are my joy.

Lord, nothing created can console me, neither heaven nor earth, neither men nor angels. Nothing can give me the joy and peace I lost in losing You, my God. Have pity on Your servant. I hope in Your mercy, Lord; I cannot live without You.   (*TSM*)

My God, no one has sinned as I. And therefore do I rejoice and hope much, for the extent of Your mercy will be all the more clearly seen in me.

Scarcely ever do I feel confidence; I have no conscious perception of having hope, but I hope against hope. What I do feel is that I am not dead to self; and so the only one I fear is myself.   (*TSM*)

You ask from me, Lord, the sacrifice of Your presence; but I cannot consent to it. Send me any suffering You wish, but do not leave me without You. See, Lord, I am on the brink of death. Come quickly, Jesus, I cannot live without You. You are my life. Without You I am a corpse, mouldering, rotting, falling into dust. I am but a little dust; and this little dust is calling to You. Listen to it, Lord. Come and gather it up and give it life.

O my salvation, come and melt the ice that is in my heart. In winter when the sun's rays are feeble, the ice is hard as stone; but when the sun's strong rays appear the ice begins to melt. My soul is like that, Lord; when You forsake it, it becomes thick ice.

When the soul and body separate, the body dies; it becomes cold, turns green, then black; the worms infest it, and finally it is dust. My soul is the same; if You leave it, Lord, it becomes cold, it putrefies and withers.

Come, come, my life. Come quickly and give life back to me. I am on the point of death, I am falling into dust. And dust cannot praise You or serve You. Lord, restore my soul to life, and then it will praise You and serve You. . . .

Everything has its time. There is the time of frost and ice when the sap does not mount in the tree. There is the time of dew and rain and sun when the tree is green with leaves and covered with flowers and fruit. And there is the time for pruning too. At present my soul is like a piece of dry wood; if You leave it there, it will be useless and will eventually rot and vanish into dust. But if You throw this piece of wood into the fire, it will become a little glowing altar burning incense before You.

You ask from me, Lord, three sacrifices? Not only three, but six if You wish. You know I desire to please You in everything. If my eyes can please You, take them; if my ears, my tongue, my mouth, my nose, take all of them; my head, my limbs, my whole body, take all; I give You all. But I cannot consent to have my heart cold for You, Lord. Cast me into Your furnace to burn as incense before You. . . .

I am like a lamp without oil. The wick cannot burn without oil. If you try to light it, the glass breaks and the lamp goes out. You, Lord, are the oil of my soul, with You not present it goes out and cannot be relit. Pour the oil of Your grace into the lamp of my soul and I shall burn before You.

What are You, Lord, like? The dove who feeds her little ones; the tender mother who suckles her child. What are You like, Lord? There is nothing to which You can really be compared.

Show Yourself to me, my God. Draw aside the curtain that conceals You; open this curtain for me to see. Raise the veil that hides You; I cannot live if I cannot see you. Come, Lord, quickly and show Yourself.   (*TSM*)

The soul that hopes in God will be changed by His mercy into a beautiful diamond.   (*TSM*)

I take the wings of my Saviour. I see the whole earth calling me blessed. Oh, how wonderful it is to belong all to You, my Saviour. The greatness of Your name fills the heavens. Every creature praises it and in its presence is filled with joy.

(*TSM*)

O Love, Love, Love! Love is not known, Love is not loved! Let us love Love, let us love Love!, Love alone, Love alone!

(*TSM*)

My Love, where are You? Who has seen my Dearest One? I have searched for Him and cannot find Him.

My Well-Beloved, I walk, I run, I weep, I have found You nowhere. O Jesus, my Love, I cannot live without You. Where are You, my Well-Beloved? Who has seen my Jesus? Who has found my Dearest Friend?

You are aware, my Love, how all the earth means nothing to me without You; all the water in the world would not suffice to slake my heart's thirst.

Who has consoled my heart? Only You, my Well-Beloved. Who has appeased its longings? Only You, my Love.

Enough, Jesus, enough, or I shall die of pain and ecstasy.

(*TSM*)

Canticle to Love

Come, kings of the earth, to Love; come and adore
my Love.

I sing of our Creator's power and glory; come let us
adore Him.

For we are the work of His hands, the price of His
Blood.

There is no one like to God; come let us adore Him.

Stop not at the things of the earth, for they are
nothing; pass to their Maker's praise.

Come, all dwellers on the earth, for they are nothing;
pass by the passing things of earth.

And remembering we are only pilgrims, come in
adoration to our Father and King.

Fall down before the Creator of all and offer Him
your hearts.

Praise and bless Him, sing with lips and heart! There
is no one like You, Lord.

Let us adore the Trinity, One God, mystery
unfathomable;

Three immensities making only one power; come and
adore.

His anger is terrible; come, let us adore Him.

The fiercest of wild beasts tremble before Him; come,
sinners, adore Him.

His tenderest goodness is for souls who seek after
Him; come, you upright, and adore Him.

All creation bows down with rejoicing before Him;
come, all, and adore Him.

(TSM)

O my God, my God! If my eye is going to offend You, pluck it out, or I shall pluck it out myself. If my hands, my feet, my tongue are going to offend You, cut them off. Break my body with pains the most intolerable rather than allow any of my members to offend You.   (*TSM*)

I do not want to die, my God! It is too great a joy.   (*TSM*)

I say every morning to Jesus as I face another day on earth: Lord, how hardhearted You are!

But these words no sooner escape me than I say: Pardon me, my God, for speaking like that.

Come, come and take my place and You will see just how very good it is. Change with me, Lord. My heart can bear no more. And how can You persist in willing me to live?

(*TSM*)

My heart is melting; my heart is mine no more; it has melted into God. All my powers are fixed on God. I shall see my God. I shall see my God.

Like a child that has just fallen on a dunghill and leaves it covered with filth, I cast myself at the merciful feet of Jesus. I shall say to Him: In Your kingdom are many mansions; put me in the one You wish; only let me love You for all eternity.

My heart melts into Jesus. My heart can live no longer here below. My heart I have given to God. O happy death which will bring to me the sight of God. I am going to leap and dance with joy when I shall see my God.   (*TSM*)

O my God, how blind the world is in its fear of death! Death is a happy event, not a frightening one. Dying means going to see God.

O desirable death, bring me quickly to my Beloved; bring me out of prison; bring me out of darkness into day.

I shall see my God; the Lord promised me. (*TSM*)

Once I have reached the vision of You, O God of Light,
It shall be mine unendingly.
When my soul has fed on the eternal banquet
My joy and happiness will have reached their peak.
My death shall strike off a chain that never again will bind me to earth.
My death shall wing me out of darkness to the God of Light, my Lover.
I shall eat a food that shall never fail and drink from a spring eternal. (*TSM*)

I was in the oratory before the Blessed Sacrament. I felt a great desire to do something for Jesus, and I said to Him: "Lord Jesus, what should I do to please and serve You?" And a voice answered: "Serve your neighbor and you will be serving Me."

I asked a second time: "Lord, what should I do to love You?" And the voice replied: "Love your neighbor and you will be loving Me. That is the proof that you really love Me." (*TSM*)

Lord, make them all one, all who live in this monastery. Bring about union and charity. Unite all hearts to You. Get them to think of You; let nothing distract them from You. Let the only bond that ties them be to You. If You see one of them about to stray from You, take her out of this life before she does so. Allow no one to enter the Community who is not entirely Yours. (*TSM*)

I am right in asking for charity—the purest. It is a tree. And a tree so beautiful, so magnificent! That tree is like cedar, with leaves like the banana, with flowers like the violet, with fruit like the olive.

Lord, give my sisters a little grain of charity which the earth does not corrupt, a little grain of charity which the sun does not wither. (*TSM*)

Lord, get everyone to burn like the candles of the sanctuary. Get everyone to melt for You alone and not for the stranger. You see, Lord, how everybody wants to be Your infirmarian; one to see after Your bodily needs, another to comfort Your soul. Everyone is eager to serve You.

My request of You, dear Lord, is that all the sisters in this house, and all those to come after, may love only You, burn only for You and not attach themselves to the stranger.

Take from me every consolation, to give them to my sisters. Let me do all the suffering, and send them none. Do not abandon them.

All of us are weak as worms. Hide us away, O God. We are not able to hide ourselves; we are always coming out into danger. Put all these frail worms down into a humid soil where they may be able to live. They cannot live in this dry soil, but are always coming out of it. Hide them in Your own good soil and keep them there. (*TSM*)

(This prayer, dictated by Sister Mary, was sealed up in the first stone of the Carmel of Bethlehem and placed in the foundations of the monastery):

One grace I ask of You, O good Jesus: that this house shall remain as long as earth lasts and that Carmelites may always occupy it; Carmelites who are charitable, fervent, lovers of Your divine Heart, detached from all that is on earth. Fill this Carmel always with subjects able to praise and serve You. Never allow, good Master, any one to enter or be received if she is not going to be saved.

Give to this Carmel Your peace and Your love. Allow no power, present or to come, to do any evil to it. Be always at its head and make kings tremble before it. Strike terror into those who come to do it harm.

Give peace and union to all who do good to this house.

So long as the world lasts, You are its Master. Make saints of all who will live there. Ensure that they retain Your Spirit and observe Your Commandments.   (*TSM*)

Lord, make the hearts of all my brothers and sisters entirely devoted to You. Take them under Your protection and let no bitterness be found among them. Let each one keep the bitterness for himself and give the sweetness to the others. That is what I ask You, Lord, for them.   (*TSM*)

My God, I keenly regret having ever offended You. Pardon me; I repent with all my heart. Show me mercy.

My God, I hope; I abandon myself to You. Place me where You want me, in hell if it is Your will; I accept. But never allow me to offend You, my God.

Rather to die a thousand times than to displease You.

O my God, so great, so powerful, You are our Father. You

in heaven; and we, little grubs, dust and ashes, on the earth! Today in this world, and dead perhaps tomorrow.

And during the swift moment of our existence we dare to offend You! My God, have pity on us. *(TSM)*

Lord, You are Being and I am nothingness. You are God and I am a mere speck of dust. If this speck of dust, if this nothingness is to survive, You, Eternal God, who are Everything, must have pity and mercy on me. Remember, Lord, the work of Your hands. *(TSM)*

O fraternal charity, O humility, be water to wash me, be light to instruct me. O simplicity, be bread to nourish me. *(TSM)*

You who are so tender, how can You be so hard as not to have compassion on me? True, I have sinned; but look now at the extremity to which I am reduced. *(TSM)*

My God, I too am blind and deaf; but I want to follow Your footprints. Yes, the torments of God are for me delights, and the delights of the wicked are for me torments. Lord, I want to follow You. When I fall You will pick me up. . . . O God, have pity on Your lame child. I hope in You. I am less than a tiny ant, less than nothing. I shall follow in Your steps and shall be healed by Your shadow, by the fragrance of Your shadow. And Your perfumes restore my strength. *(TSM)*

Lord, You who are so pure, how can You endure at Your table Your little servant in dirty clothes. And yet You came to dine with me; You enter into my sullied heart. Have pity on me for having dared to receive You in my own poor home, You who are the great King. And yet, I receive You as a child would its father, as a friend would his friend, at home and very simply.   (*TSM*)

I am a bad fruit, a rotten fruit, a fruit thrown on the dunghill by my sins. Who would think of using this bitter rotten fruit? Nobody would have it on his table. Leave it on the dunghill.

But, Gardener, look. In that fruit the Lord has placed a little seed. Take it. Dig a hole and drop it in, and cover it with earth. Wait, have patience, and it will become a tree. Through Your care it will produce good fruit, and You will serve this fruit at the table of the Lord. Everybody shall see it. People will eat it and will praise the Lord.   (*TSM*)

How feeble I am, my God; the feeblest of all. And I wish everybody knew me as such, and that my feebleness and cowardice were written on the walls and doors of the monastery. Oh, how ashamed I feel about going to receive Jesus in Holy Communion with such miseries!   (*TSM*)

O my God, make me faithful to the little lights, to little inspirations, so as not to fall into hell.   (*TSM*)

O chalice! O sacrifice! O Jesus, have pity on me.   (*TSM*)

My God, provided only that I come to You, I am ready to come through water, through fire, through hell itself, if such be Your will. Only let me find You!   (*TSM*)

Lord, I have need of brothers and sisters. Give me brothers and sisters to adore You. (*TSM*)

My God, I want to suffer all the time, if this is what pleases You.

To suffer to the end of the world, O my God, if this is Your will! To suffer always what You wish. My one desire is to please You, Jesus. Get me to do Your will. (*TSM*)

XIX

Saint Thérèse of the Child Jesus and the Holy Face

(1873–1897)

Thérèse Martin was born into a very loving and pious family at Alençon, France, in 1873. She had four sisters, three of whom would also be her sisters in religion in the Carmel of Lisieux. Thérèse lost her mother at the age of five. She was a very sensitive child, and this only seemed to make matters worse. She suffered from a very serious illness and petitioned our Lady to help her. She saw her statue of our Lady smile a "ravishing smile" and from that moment enjoyed good health.

At the age of fifteen she knew she had been called to Carmel, but she was denied admission because of her age. She even went so far as to petition the Holy Father himself. Soon after, however, her wish was fulfilled, and she entered Carmel in 1888. Thérèse wanted to be a saint, but she knew she could not do great things like other saints. She wished to be prophet, priest, missionary, apostle and to travel on all five continents. One day it came to her that her mission was to be love in the heart of the Church. She devised her little way of spiritual childhood, which involved offering little nothings to Jesus. She offered Him her very weakness. She sought opportunities to do little things that were unnoticed and unappreciated. She served quietly and humbly. Thérèse made an "Act of Oblation to Merciful Love" because she believed that she had to rely on God's mercy and that His mercy would outweigh His justice. She completely abandoned herself like a child in His arms. While filled with tuberculosis, and in obedience to her superiors, she wrote her autobiography, which became the *Story of a Soul*, and she suffered joyfully even though passing through the blackest night of faith until her death in 1897. This "little one" was named Doctor of the Church in 1997.

PRAYERS

O my God! I offer Thee all my actions of this day for the intentions and for the glory of the Sacred Heart of Jesus. I desire to sanctify every beat of my heart, my every thought, my simplest works, by uniting them to Its infinite merits; and I wish to make reparation for my sins by casting them into the furnace of Its merciful love.

O my God! I ask of Thee for myself and for those whom I hold dear, the grace to fulfill perfectly Thy holy will, to accept for love of Thee the joys and sorrows of this passing life, so that we may one day be united together in heaven for all eternity. Amen. (*CD*)

Prayer for the Missions

O most loving Lord Jesus, who hast redeemed the world at the cost of Thine own most precious Blood, look down with Thine eyes of mercy upon our poor humanity, which for the greater part still remains immersed in the darkness of error and in the shadow of death, and grant that the light of Thy truth may shine upon mankind in all its splendor.

Increase, O Lord, the number of the missionaries of Thy gospel; make them fervent, render fruitful and bless with Thy grace their zeal and labors, so that through them all infidels may know and be converted to Thee, their Creator and Redeemer.

Recall to the fold all those who have wandered from it, and bring back to the bosom of Thy true Church all who are in rebellion against her.

Hasten, O most loving Saviour, the joyful establishment of Thy kingdom upon earth. Draw all men to Thy most loving Heart in order that they may partake of the incomparable benefits of Thy Redemption in the everlasting happiness of Paradise. Amen.   (CD)

Saint Joseph, how much I love you! How much good it does me to think of your humble, simple life. Like us you lived by faith. Everything in your life was just as it is in ours.   (GA)

But good Blessed Virgin, it seems to me that I am more fortunate than you, for I have you for Mother and you have no Blessed Virgin to love. Jesus on the Cross gave you to us for our Mother, so we are richer than you, since we possess Jesus and you are ours as well.   (GA)

O Jesus, I know well that You do not look so much at the greatness of my actions, as at the love with which I do them. It is true I am not always faithful, but I shall not lose courage. I desire to make use of every opportunity to please You.

                                                              (GA)

O my Jesus, since You would never put unreasonable desires into my heart, I know that in spite of my littleness I can aspire to sanctity. Come, take possession of all my faculties in such a way that everything I do, from being merely human and personal, may be wholly divine. I long to prove my love in countless ways, to tread in Your footsteps.   (*GA*)

O Jesus, if our sorrows belong to You, so do our joys. It is enough that we are not absorbed in selfish happiness, but that we offer You the smallest pleasures You sow in our life's path to win souls and raise them to You.   (*GA*)

O my God, I ask You for myself and for those whom I hold dear the grace to fulfill perfectly Your holy will, to accept for love of You the joys and sorrows of this passing life, so that we may one day be united together in heaven for all eternity.
                                                                    (*GA*)

O my God, You see how easily I lose heart at the thought of my imperfections. Nevertheless, I shall continue to strive after virtue. Gladly will I forego all consolation in order to offer to You the "fruit" of all my efforts. I wish to make profit out of the smallest actions and do them all for love.
                                                                    (*GA*)

O Jesus, my Divine Spouse! May I never lose the second robe of my baptism! Take me before I can commit the slightest voluntary fault. May I never seek nor find anything but Yourself alone. May creatures be nothing for me and may I be nothing for them, but may You, Jesus, be *everything*! May the things of earth never be able to trouble my soul, and may nothing disturb my peace. Jesus, I ask You for nothing but peace, and also love, infinite love without any limits other than Yourself; love which is no longer I but You, my Jesus. Jesus, may I die a martyr for You. Give me martyrdom of heart or of body, or rather give me both. Give me the grace to fulfill my Vows in all their perfection, and make me understand what a real spouse of Yours should be. Never let me be a burden to the community, let nobody be occupied with me, let me be looked upon as one to be trampled underfoot, forgotten like Your little grain of sand, Jesus. May Your will be done in me perfectly, and may I arrive at the place You have prepared for me. . . .

Jesus, allow me to save very many souls; let no soul be lost today; let all the souls in purgatory be saved. . . . Jesus, pardon me if I say anything I should not say. I want only to give You joy and to console You.   (SS)

Jesus, Your little brides resolve to keep their eyes lowered in the refectory so that they may honor You and imitate the example You gave them when You were in Herod's presence. When that impious ruler mocked You, O Infinite Beauty, not a complaint fell from Your divine lips. You did not even deign to rest Your adorable eyes on him. Oh! Divine Jesus, doubtless Herod did not deserve a look from You, but we, your brides, want to attract Your divine gaze toward us. We ask You to reward us with a *look* of love every time we deprive ourselves of raising our eyes, and we ask You not to refuse us this gentle *look* even when we fall, since we will count our failings. We will form a bouquet that You will not reject; we are confident of it. In these flowers You will see our desire to love You and to resemble You, and You will bless your little children.

O Jesus! *Look* on us with love and give us your sweet kiss.
                                                                          (PST)

Bouquet of Aspirations for a Lay Sister's Clothing Day

White Roses

O Jesus! Purify my soul that it may become worthy to be Your bride!

Daisies

O Jesus! Grant me the grace in all I do to please You alone.

White Violets

Jesus, gentle and humble of Heart, make my heart like Yours! . . .

Lilies of the Valley

Saint Teresa, my Mother, teach me to save souls so that I may become a true Carmelite.

Wild Roses

O Jesus! It is You alone I serve when I serve my Mothers and Sisters.

Tea Roses

Jesus, Mary, Joseph, grant me the grace to make a good retreat and prepare my soul for the beautiful day of my profession.

White Bellflowers

O Saint Mary Magdalene! Obtain for me the grace that my life may be one act of love.

Honeysuckle

O Jesus! Teach me to deny myself always to please my sisters.

White Peonies

O my God, look at the Face of Jesus and count all sinners among the elect.

Jasmine

O Jesus, I want to have joy only in You alone! . . .

White Forget-me-nots

O my Holy Guardian Angel! Cover me always with your wings so that I may never have the misfortune to offend Jesus.

Meadowsweet

O Mary, my dear Mother, grant me the grace never to stain the robe of innocence that you will give me on the day of my profession.

White Verbena

My God, I believe in You, I hope in You, I love You with all my heart.

White Iris

My God, I thank You for all the graces You have given me during my retreat.

The Great Day Has Arrived

Lilies

My Beloved Jesus, You are now all mine and I am Your little Bride forever!!!... (*PST*)

Act of Oblation to Merciful Love

O my God! Most Blessed Trinity, I desire to *Love* You and make You *Loved*, to work for the glory of Holy Church by saving souls on earth and liberating those suffering in purgatory. I desire to accomplish Your will perfectly and to reach the degree of glory You have prepared for me in Your Kingdom. I desire, in a word, to be a saint, but I feel my helplessness and I beg You, O my God! To be Yourself my *Sanctity*!

Since You loved me so much as to give me Your only Son as my Savior and my Spouse, the infinite treasures of His merits are mine. I offer them to You with gladness, begging You to look on me only in the Face of Jesus and in His Heart burning with *Love*.

I offer You, too, all the merits of the saints (in heaven and on earth), their acts of *Love*, and those of the holy angels. Finally, I offer You, *O Blessed Trinity!* the *Love* and merits of the *Blessed Virgin, my dear Mother*. It is to her I abandon my offering, begging her to present it to You. Her Divine Son, my *Beloved* Spouse, told us in the days of His mortal life: *"Whatsoever you ask the Father in My name He will give it to you!*" I am certain, then, that You will grant my desires; I know, O my God! that *the more You want to give, the more You make us desire.* I feel in my heart immense desires and it is with confidence I ask You to come and take possession of my soul. Ah! I cannot receive Holy Communion as often as I desire, but, Lord, are You not *all-powerful*? Remain in me as in a tabernacle and never separate Yourself from Your little victim.

I want to console You for the ingratitude of the wicked, and I beg of You to take away my freedom to displease You. If through weakness I sometimes fall, may Your *Divine Glance* cleanse my soul immediately, consuming all my imperfections like the fire that transforms everything into itself.

I thank You, O my God! For all the graces You have granted me, especially the grace of making me pass through the crucible of suffering. It is with joy I shall contemplate You on the last day carrying the scepter of Your Cross. Since You deigned to give me a share in this very precious Cross, I hope in heaven to resemble You and to see shining in my glorified body the sacred stigmata of Your Passion.

After earth's Exile, I hope to go and enjoy You in the Fatherland, but I do not want to lay up merits for heaven. I want to work for Your *Love alone* with the one purpose of pleasing You, consoling Your Sacred Heart, and saving souls who will love You eternally.

In the evening of this life, I shall appear before You with empty hands, for I do not ask You, Lord, to count my works. All our justice is stained in Your eyes. I wish, then, to be clothed in Your own *Justice* and to receive from Your *Love* the eternal possession of *Yourself.* I want no other *Throne*, no other *Crown* but *You*, my *Beloved*!

Time is nothing in Your eyes, and a single day is like a thousand years. You can, then, in one instant prepare me to appear before You.

In order to live in one single act of perfect Love, I OFFER MYSELF AS A VICTIM OF HOLOCAUST TO YOUR MERCIFUL LOVE, asking You to consume me incessantly, allowing the waves of *infinite tenderness* shut up within You to overflow into my soul, and that thus I may become a *martyr* of Your *Love*, O my God!

May this martyrdom, after having prepared me to appear before You, finally cause me to die and may my soul take its flight without any delay into the eternal embrace of *Your Merciful Love.*

I want, O my *Beloved*, at each beat of my heart to renew this offering to You an infinite number of times, until the shadows having disappeared I may be able to tell You of my Love in an *Eternal Face to Face*! (SS 276–77)

Prayer to Jesus in the Tabernacle

O God hidden in the prison of the tabernacle! I come with joy to You each evening to thank You for the graces You have given me. I ask pardon for the faults I committed today, which has just slipped away like a dream. . . .

O Jesus! How happy I would be if I had been faithful, but alas! Often in the evening I am sad because I feel I could have corresponded better with Your graces. . . . If I were more united to You, more charitable with my sisters, more humble and more mortified, I would feel less sorrow when I talk with You in prayer. And yet, O my God, very far from becoming discouraged at the sight of my miseries, I come to You with confidence, recalling that "those who are well do not need a doctor but the sick do." I beg You, then, to cure me and to pardon me. I will keep in mind, Lord, "that the soul to whom You have forgiven more should also love You more than the others"! . . . I offer You every beat of my heart as so many acts of love and reparation and I unite them to Your infinite merits. I beg You, O my Divine Bridegroom, to be the Restorer of my soul, to act in me despite my resistance; and lastly, I wish to have no other will but Yours. Tomorrow, with the help of Your grace, I will begin a new life in which each moment will be an act of love and renunciation.

Thus, after coming each evening to the foot of Your Altar, I will finally reach the last evening of my life. Then will begin for me the unending day of eternity when I will place in Your Divine Heart the struggles of exile! Amen.   (PST)

Prayer for Abbé Bellière

O my Jesus! I thank You for having fulfilled one of my greatest desires, that of having a brother, a priest, an apostle . . .

I feel very unworthy of this favor. And yet, since You grant Your little spouse the grace of working specially for the sanctification of a soul destined for the priesthood, I offer You joyfully *all* the *prayers* and *sacrifices* at my disposal. I ask You, O my God: not to look at what I am but what I should be and want to be, a religious wholly inflamed with Your love.

You know, Lord, that my only ambition is to make You known and loved. Now my desire will be realized. I can only pray and suffer, but the soul to whom You unite me by the sweet bonds of charity will go and fight in the plain to win hearts for You, while on the mountain of Carmel I will pray that You give him victory.

Divine Jesus, hear the prayer I offer You for him who wants to be Your Missionary.

Keep him safe amid the dangers of the world. Make him

feel increasingly the nothingness and vanity of passing things and the happiness of being able to despise them for love. May he carry out his sublime apostolate on those around him. May he be an apostle worthy of Your Sacred Heart. . . .

O Mary! Gentle Queen of Carmel, it is to you that I entrust the soul of the future priest whose unworthy little sister I am. Teach him even now how lovingly you handled the Divine Child and wrapped Him in swaddling clothes, so that one day he may go up to the Holy Altar and carry in his hands the King of Heaven.

I ask you also to keep him safe beneath the shadow of your virginal mantle until the happy day when he leaves this valley of tears and can contemplate your splendor and enjoy for all eternity the fruits of his glorious apostolate.   (*PST*)

Prayer of Céline and Thérèse

O my God! We ask that Your two lilies never be separated on earth. Together, may they console You for the little love You find in this valley of tears. For all eternity may their corollas shine with the same brilliance and may they shed the same fragrance when they bow before You!   (*PST*)

Morning Offering

My God, I offer You all that I do today for the intentions and the glory of the Sacred Heart of Jesus. I want to sanctify every beat of my heart, my thoughts and my simplest works by uniting them to His infinite merits. I want to repair for my faults by casting them into the furnace of His merciful love.

O my God! I ask You for myself and those dear to me the grace to fulfill perfectly Your holy will and to accept for love of You the joys and sorrows of this passing life so that one day we may be reunited in heaven for all eternity. Amen.

(PST)

Consecration to the Holy Face

O Adorable Face of Jesus! Since You have deigned to choose our souls to be intimately Yours in order to give Yourself to them, we come to consecrate them to You. . . . O *Jesus*, we seem to hear You say to us: "Open to Me my sisters, My beloved brides, for *My Face* is covered with dew and *My hair* with the drops of the night." Our souls understand Your language of *love*; we want to dry Your *gentle Face* and to console You for the forgetfulness of the wicked. In their eyes You are still as one hidden; they look upon You as an object of contempt. . . .

O *Face* more beautiful than the lilies and roses of springtime! You are not hidden from our eyes. . . . The *Tears* that veil Your *divine look* seem to us like *precious Diamonds* which we want to collect to buy the souls of our brothers and sisters with their infinite value.

From Your *Adorable Mouth* we have heard Your *loving complaint*. Since we know that the *thirst* which consumes You is a *thirst for Love*, we would wish to have *an infinite Love to quench Your thirst*. . . . *Beloved Bridegroom* of our souls, if we had the *love* of all hearts, all that *love* would be for you! Then, heedless of our exile on the banks of Babylon, we will sing for your *Ears* the sweetest melodies. Since You are the true, the only Homeland of our hearts, we will not sing our songs in an alien land.

O *Beloved Face of Jesus!* As we await the everlasting day when we will contemplate Your infinite Glory, our one desire is to charm Your *Divine eyes* by hiding our faces too so that here on earth no one can recognize us. . . . *O Jesus!* Your *Veiled Gaze* is our *Heaven*! (*PST*)

To the Child Jesus

O Little Child! My only Treasure. I abandon myself to Your Divine Whims. I want no other joy than that of making You smile. Imprint on me Your childish virtues and graces so that on the day of my birth into heaven, the angels and saints may recognize Your little bride. (*PST*)

Eternal Father, Your Only Son

All that you ask from my Father in my Name, He will give it to you. . . .

Eternal Father, Your only Son, the gentle Child Jesus is mine, since You have given Him to me. I offer You the infinite merits of His divine Childhood and I ask you in His Name to call the joys of heaven a countless host of little children who will follow the Divine Lamb for all eternity.

(*PST*)

Eternal Father, since You have given me for my inheritance the Adorable Face of Your Divine Son, I offer it to You and I ask You, in exchange for this infinitely precious Coin, to forget the ingratitude of souls who are consecrated to You and to pardon poor sinners. (*PST*)

To a novice too attached to sensible consolations she replies:

Ask for consolations! If you really want to be like me you will say: 'Oh! Fear not, Lord, that I'll awaken Thee, I await in peace the shore of heaven!' " (*SR*)

I asked Jesus to draw me into the flames of His love, to unite me so intimately with Him that He will live and act in me.

(SR)

On being delayed for her profession in Carmel she said:

O my God! I do not ask You to let me pronounce my holy vows; I shall wait as long as You wish, only I do not want my union with You to be postponed through my own fault.

(SR)

I run to Jesus and I tell Him that I am ready to shed my blood to the last drop to affirm that there is a Heaven. I tell Him that I am happy not to enjoy this beautiful Heaven on earth. (SR)

To the Holy Face

O Adorable Face of Jesus, the only Beauty that captivates my heart, deign to imprint in me your Divine Likeness so that You may not behold the soul of Your little bride without seeing Yourself in her.

O my Beloved, for love of You, I accept not seeing here below the gentleness of Your Look nor feeling the ineffable kiss of Your Mouth, but I beg You to inflame me with Your love so that it may consume me rapidly and soon bring me into Your presence.   (SR)

Lord God of Hosts

Lord, God of hosts, in the Gospel You told us: "I have not come to bring peace but the sword." Arm me for battle; I burn to fight for Your glory, but I beg You to strengthen my courage. . . . Then with the holy King David I can exclaim:

"You alone are my sword, You, Lord, train my hands for war . . ."

O my Beloved! I know what combat You have in mind for me; the contest will not be on the field of battle . . .

I am a prisoner of Your Love. I have freely forged the chain that binds me to You and separates me forever from that world which You have cursed. . . . My sword is nothing but Love—with it I will chase the foreigner from the kingdom. I will have You proclaimed King in the souls who refuse to submit to Your Divine Power.

Doubtless, Lord, You do not need such a feeble instrument as myself, but Joan, your chaste and courageous bride, said: "We must fight so that God may give the victory." O my Jesus, I will fight then, for Your Love, until the evening of my life. As You did not wish to rest on earth, I want to follow Your example. I hope this promise that fell from Your Divine lips will find fulfillment in me: "If anyone follows Me, where I am, there also will my servant be. Whoever serves Me, my Father will honor."

To be with You, to be in You is my one desire. . . . This assurance that You give me of its fulfillment helps me to bear my exile while awaiting the glorious day of the eternal Face to Face! (PST)

O Holy Innocents, O Saint Sebastian

O Holy Innocents! May my Palm and my Crown resemble yours!

O Saint Sebastian! Obtain for me your love and your courage so that like you, I may be able to fight for the glory of God! . . .

O Glorious Soldier of Christ! You fought victoriously for the honor of the God of hosts and received the palm and crown of Martyrdom. Listen to my secret: "Like the angelic Tarcisius I carry the Lord." I am only a child and yet I must fight each day to preserve the priceless Treasure that is hidden in my soul. . . . Often I must redden the arena of combat with my heart's blood. . . .

O Mighty Warrior! Be my protector, sustain me by your victorious arm and I will not fear my powerful enemies. With your help I will fight until the evening of life, then you will present me to Jesus and from His hand I will receive the palm that you helped me to win!   (PST)

Act of Faith

My God, with the help of Your grace I am ready to shed all my blood to affirm my faith.   (PST)

Prayer for Acquiring Humility

O Jesus! When You were a Pilgrim on earth, You said: "Learn of Me for I am gentle and humble of heart and you will find rest for your souls." O Mighty Monarch of Heaven, yes, my soul finds rest in seeing You, clothed in the form and nature of a slave, humbling Yourself to wash the feet of Your apostles. I recall Your words that teach me how to practice humility: "I have given you an example so that you may do what I have done. The disciple is not greater than the Master. . . . If you understand this, happy are you if you put them into practice." Lord, I do understand these words that came from Your gentle and humble heart and I want to practice them with the help of Your grace.

I want truly to humble myself and to submit my will to that of my sisters. I do not wish to contradict them nor seek to see whether or not they have the right to command me.

O my Beloved, no one had the right over You and yet You obeyed not only the Blessed Virgin and St. Joseph but even Your executioners. Now in the Sacred Host I see You at the height of Your annihilations. How humble You are, O Divine King of Glory, to subject Yourself to all Your priests without making any distinction between those who love You and those who are, alas! lukewarm or cold in Your service. . . . At their word, You come down from heaven. Whether they advance or delay the hour of the Holy Sacrifice, You are always ready . . .

O my Beloved, how gentle and humble of heart You seem under the veil of the white Host! To teach me humility You cannot humble Yourself further. Therefore, to respond to Your love, I desire that my sisters always put me in the lowest place, and I want to convince myself that this place is indeed mine.

I beg You, my Divine Jesus, to send me a humiliation whenever I try to set myself above others.

I know, O my God, that You humble the proud soul but to the one who humbles herself You give an eternity of glory. So I want to put myself in the last rank and to share Your humiliations so as "to have a share with You" in the kingdom of Heaven.

But, You know my weakness, Lord. Every morning I make a resolution to practice humility and in the evening I recognize that I have committed again many faults of pride. At this I am tempted to become discouraged but I know that discouragement is also pride. Therefore, O my God, I want to base my hope in *You alone*. Since You can do everything, deign to bring to birth in my soul the virtue I desire. To obtain this grace of Your infinite mercy I will very often repeat: "O Jesus, gentle and humble of heart, make my heart like Yours!"   (*PST*)

If I Were Queen of Heaven

O Mary, if I were Queen of Heaven and you were Thérèse, I would want to be Thérèse so that you might be Queen of Heaven!!!...   (*PST*)

God cannot inspire unrealizable desires. I can, then, in spite of my littleness, aspire to holiness. It is impossible for me to grow up, and so I must bear with myself such as I am with all my imperfections. But I want to seek out a means of going to heaven by a little way, a way that is very straight, very short, and totally new. We are living now in an age of inventions, and we no longer have to take the trouble of climbing stairs, for . . . an elevator has replaced these very successfully. I wanted to find an elevator which would raise me to Jesus, for I am too small to climb the rough stairway of perfection. I searched, then, in the Scriptures for some sign of this elevator, the object of my desires, and I read these words coming from the mouth of Eternal Wisdom: "*Whoever is a* LITTLE ONE, *let him come to me.*" And so I succeeded. I felt I had found what I was looking for. . . . The elevator which must raise me to heaven is in Your arms, O Jesus! And for this I had no need to grow up, but rather I had to remain *little* and become this more and more. O my God, You surpassed all my expectation. I want only to sing of Your Mercies.   (*SS*)

O Jesus, You offer me a cup so bitter that my feeble nature cannot bear it. But I do not want to draw back my lips from the cup Your hand has prepared. . . . You teach me the secret of suffering in peace. The word peace does not mean joy, at least not felt joy; to suffer in peace, it is enough to will whatever You will. To be Your spouse, Jesus, one must be like You, and You are all bloody, crowned with thorns!

How consoling it is to remember that You, the God of might, knew our weaknesses, that You shuddered at the sight of the bitter cup, the cup that earlier You had so ardently desired to drink.   (*TGC* 63; 184; 59)

With bold surrender, I wish to remain gazing upon You, O Lord, my divine Sun. Nothing will frighten me, neither wind nor rain, and if dark clouds come and hide You from my gaze, I will not change my place because I know that beyond the clouds You still shine on and Your brightness is not eclipsed for a single instant. Even if You remain deaf to the sorrowing of Your creature, even if You remain hidden, I accept being numb with cold and rejoice in this suffering. My heart is at peace and continues its work of love.

(*DI* 2. Paraphrase of *SS*)

O Immaculate Virgin, O tenderest Mother! . . . you rejoiced that Jesus gave us His life and the infinite treasures of His divinity. How can we not love you and bless you, O Mary, for such great generosity.

You love us as Jesus loves us, and for our sake you are willing to live far from Him. To love means to give all, to give one's self, and you wanted to prove that by remaining our support. The Savior knew well the secrets of your Mother's heart, the immensity of your tenderness. . . . Jesus left us to you, O Refuge of Sinners, when He left the cross to wait for us in heaven.

O Mary, I see you on Calvary's height, standing near the cross like a priest at the altar, offering the sweet Emmanuel, your dear Jesus, to appease the Father's justice. O desolate

Mother, a prophet said of you: "There is no sorrow like to your sorrow." O Queen of martyrs, standing there bereft, you pour out all your heart's blood for us.

(DI 2. PST 34:21–23)

O Lord, to me You have granted Your infinite mercy; and through it I contemplate and adore Your other divine perfections! All of these perfections appear to be resplendent with love, even Your justice—and perhaps this even more so than the others—seems to me clothed in love. What a sweet joy to think that You, O God, are just, that is, that You take into account our weakness, that You are perfectly aware of our fragile nature. What should I fear then? Must not You, the infinitely just God who deigned to pardon the faults of the prodigal son with so much kindness, be just also to me who am with You always?

I know one must be most pure to appear before You, God of all holiness, but I know too that You are infinitely just; and it is this justice, which frightens so many souls, that is the basis of my joy and trust. To be just means not only to exercise severity in punishing the guilty, but also to recognize right intentions and to reward virtue.

I hope as much from Your justice, O God, as from Your mercy, because You are compassionate and merciful, long-suffering and plenteous in mercy. For You know our weakness and You remember we are but dust.

(DI 3. Letter of May 9, 1897)

Ah! Lord, I know You don't command the impossible. You know better than I do my weakness and imperfection. You know very well that never would I be able to love my Sisters as You love them, unless *You*, O my Jesus, *loved them in me*. It is because You wanted to give me this grace that You made Your *new* commandment. Oh! How I love this new commandment since it gives me the assurance that Your will is *to love in me* all those you command me to love!   (SS 221)

What a grace, when in the morning we feel no courage or strength for the practice of virtue—then is the moment to put the ax to the root of the tree. . . . Love can do all; "The most impossible things do not seem difficult to it."   (DI 3)

O Jesus, the sight of Your precious blood flowing from Your wounds strikes me deeply, and I feel a great pang of sorrow in thinking that this blood is falling to the ground without anyone's hastening to gather it up. I want to remain here in spirit at the foot of the cross to receive this divine dew and to pour it out upon souls. O Jesus, Your cry sounds continually in my heart: "I thirst!" These words ignite in me an unknown and very living fire. I wish to give You to drink, O my Beloved, and I feel myself consumed with a thirst for souls. It is the souls of great sinners that attract me, and I burn with the desire to snatch them from the eternal flames.

My desire to save souls grows from day to day, and I seem to hear You say to me what You said to the Samaritan woman: "Give me to drink!" What a wonderful interchange of love! To souls I give Your blood, to You I offer these same souls refreshed by Your divine dew. I hope thus to slake Your thirst, and the more I give You to drink, the more the thirst of my poor little soul increases; but truly this ardent thirst You are giving me is the most delightful drink of Your love.   (DI 4. Paraphrase of SS 99, 101)

Draw me, we shall run after you in the odor of your ointments." O Jesus, it is not even necessary to say: "When
drawing me, draw the souls whom I love!" This simple
statement: "Draw me" suffices; I understand, Lord, that
when a soul allows herself to be captivated by the odor of
Your ointments, she cannot run alone, all the souls whom
she loves follow in her train; this is done without constraint,
without effort, it is a natural consequence of her attraction
for You. Just as a torrent, throwing itself with impetuosity
into the ocean, drags after it everything it encounters in its
passage, in the same way, O Jesus, the soul who plunges into
the shoreless ocean of Your love, draws with her all the
treasures she possesses. Lord, You know it, I have no other
treasures than the souls it has pleased You to unite to mine; it
is You who entrusted these treasures to me. . . .

"Draw me, Lord, we shall run." . . . O Jesus, I ask You to
draw me into the flames of Your love, to unite me so closely
to You that You live and act in me. I feel that the more the
fire of love burns within my heart, the more I shall say:
"Draw me", the more the souls who will approach me . . .
will run swiftly in the odor of Your ointments.

(DI 4. SS 254, 257)

My God, "*I choose all!*" I don't want to be a *saint* by *halves*,
I'm not afraid to suffer for You, I fear only one thing: to keep
my *own will*; so take it, for "*I choose all*" that You will!   (*SS*)

O Jesus, unspeakable *sweetness*, change all the consolations
of this earth into *bitterness* for me.   (*SS*)

O my God! I don't ask You to make Profession. *I will wait as
long as You desire*, but what I don't want is to be the cause of

my separation from You through my fault. I will take great care, therefore, to make a beautiful dress enriched with priceless stones, and when You find it sufficiently adorned, I am certain all the creatures in the world will not prevent You from coming down to me to unite me to Yourself forever, O my Beloved!   (SS)

O my God! Will Your Justice alone find souls willing to immolate themselves as victims? Does not Your *Merciful Love* need them too? On every side this love is unknown, rejected; those hearts upon whom You would lavish it turn to creatures seeking happiness from them with their miserable affection; they do this instead of throwing themselves into Your arms and of accepting Your infinite *Love*. O my God! Is your disdained Love going to remain closed up within Your Heart? It seems to me that if You were to find souls offering themselves as victims of holocaust to Your Love, You would consume them rapidly; it seems to me, too, that You would be happy not to hold back the waves of infinite tenderness within You. If Your Justice loves to release itself, this Justice *which extends only over the whole earth*, how much more does Your Merciful Love desire to *set souls on fire* since Your Mercy *reaches to the heavens*. O my Jesus, let me be this happy victim; consume Your holocaust with the fire of Your Divine Love!
                                                                 (SS)

O Jesus, my Beloved, who could express the tenderness and sweetness with which You are guiding my soul! It pleases You to cause the rays of Your grace to shine through even in the midst of the darkest storm!   (SS)

O Jesus, the storm was no longer raging, heaven was calm and serene. I believed, I *felt* there was a *heaven* and that this *heaven* is peopled with souls who actually love me, who consider me their child. This impression remains in my heart. . . .

O my Beloved! This grace was only the prelude to the greatest graces You wished to bestow upon me. Allow me, my only Love, to recall them to You today, *today* which is the sixth anniversary of *our union*. Ah! My Jesus, pardon me if I am unreasonable in wishing to express my desires and longings which reach even unto infinity. Pardon me and heal my soul by giving her what she longs for so much! (SS)

I feel in me the *vocation of* the PRIEST. With what love, O Jesus, I would carry You in my hands when, at my voice, You would come down from heaven. And with what love would I give You to souls! But alas! while desiring to be a *Priest*, I admire and envy the humility of St. Francis of Assisi and I feel the *vocation* of imitating him in refusing the sublime dignity of the *Priesthood*.

O Jesus, my Love, my Life, how can I realize the desires of my poor *little soul*?

Ah! In spite of my littleness, I would like to enlighten souls as did the *Prophets* and the *Doctors*. I have the *vocation of the Apostle*. I would like to travel over the whole earth to preach Your Name and to plant Your Glorious Cross on infidel soil. But *O my Beloved*, one mission alone would not be sufficient for me, I would want to preach the Gospel on all the five continents simultaneously and even to the most remote isles. I would be a missionary, not for a few years only but from the beginning of creation until the consummation of the ages. But above all, O my Beloved Savior, I would shed my blood for You even to the very last drop.

Martyrdom was the dream of my youth and this dream has grown with me within Carmel's cloisters. But here again, I feel that my dream is a folly, for I cannot confine myself to desiring *one kind* of martyrdom. To satisfy me I need *all*. Like You, my Adorable Spouse, I would be scourged and crucified. I would die flayed like St. Bartholomew. I would be plunged into boiling oil like St. John; I would undergo all the tortures inflicted upon the martyrs. With St. Agnes and St. Cecilia, I would present my neck to the sword, and like Joan of Arc, my dear sister, I would whisper at the stake Your Name, O JESUS. . . . Jesus, Jesus, if I wanted to write all my desires, I would have to borrow Your *Book of Life*, for in it are reported all the actions of all the saints, and I would accomplish all of them for You.

O my Jesus! what is your answer to all my follies? Is there a soul more *little*, more powerless than mine? Nevertheless even because of my weakness, it has pleased You, O Lord, to grant my *little childish desires* and You desire, today, to grant other desires that are *greater* than the universe.   (SS)

I understood that the Church *had a Heart and that this Heart* WAS BURNING WITH LOVE. *I understood it was Love alone* that made the Church's members act, that if Love ever became extinct, apostles would not preach the Gospel and martyrs would not shed their blood. I understood that LOVE COMPRISED ALL VOCATIONS, THAT LOVE WAS EVERYTHING, THAT IT EMBRACED ALL TIMES AND PLACES. . . . IN A WORD, THAT IT WAS ETERNAL!

Then in the excess of my delirious joy, I cried out: O Jesus, my Love . . . my *vocation*, at last I have found it. . . . MY VOCATION IS LOVE!

Yes, I have found my place in the Church and it is You, O

my God, who have given me this place; in the heart of the Church, my Mother, I shall be *Love*. Thus I shall be everything, and thus my dream will be realized.

Why speak of a delirious joy? No, this expression is not exact, for it was rather the calm and serene peace of the navigator perceiving the beacon which must lead him to the port. . . . O luminous Beacon of love, I know how to reach You, I have found the secret of possessing Your flame.

I am only a child, powerless and weak, and yet it is my weakness that gives me the boldness of offering myself as VICTIM *of Your Love, O Jesus!* . . .

O Jesus, I know it, love is repaid by love alone, and so I searched and I found the way to solace my heart by giving You Love for Love. . . . I presented myself before the angels and saints and I said to them: "I am the smallest of creatures; I know my misery and my feebleness, but I know also how much noble and generous hearts love to do good. I beg you then, O Blessed Inhabitants of heaven, I beg you to ADOPT ME AS YOUR CHILD. *To You alone will be the glory* which You will make me merit, but deign to answer my prayer. It is bold, I know; however, I dare to ask You to obtain for me YOUR TWOFOLD SPIRIT.

Jesus, I cannot fathom the depths of my request; I would be afraid to find myself overwhelmed under the weight of my bold desires. . . . Well, I am the *Child of the Church* and the Church is a Queen since she is Your Spouse, O divine King of kings. . . . What this child asks for is Love. She knows only one thing: to love You, O Jesus. Astounding works are forbidden to her; she cannot preach the Gospel, shed her blood; but what does it matter since her brothers work in her stead and she, *a little child*, stays very close to the *throne* of the King and Queen. She *loves* in her brothers' place while they do the fighting. But how will she prove her *love* since *love* is proved by works? Well, the little child *will strew flowers*, she will perfume the royal throne with their *sweet scents*, and she will sing in her silvery tones the canticle of *Love*.

Yes, my Beloved, this is how my life will be consumed. I have no other means of proving my love for You other than that of strewing flowers, that is, not allowing one little sacrifice to escape, not one look, one word, profiting by all the smallest things and doing them through love; and in this way I shall strew flowers before Your throne. I shall not come upon one without *unpetalling* it for You. While I am strewing my flowers, I shall sing, for could one cry while doing such a joyous action? I shall sing even when I must gather my flowers in the midst of thorns, and my song will be all the more melodious in proportion to the length and the sharpness of the thorns.

O Jesus, of what use will my flowers be to You? Ah! I know very well that this fragrant shower, these fragile, worthless petals, these songs of love from the littlest of hearts will charm You. Yes, these nothings will please You. They will bring a smile to the Church Triumphant. She will gather up my flowers unpetalled *through love* and have them pass through Your own divine hands, O Jesus. And this Church in heaven, desirous of playing with her little child, will cast these flowers, which are now infinitely valuable because of Your divine touch, upon the Church Suffering in order to extinguish its flames and upon the Church Militant in order to gain the victory for it!

O my Jesus! I love You! I love the Church, my Mother! I recall that "*the smallest act of* PURE LOVE *is of more value to her than all other works together.*" But is PURE LOVE in my heart? Are my measureless desires only but a dream, a folly? Ah! If this be so, Jesus, then enlighten me, for You know I am seeking only the truth. If my desires are rash, then make them disappear, for these desires are the greatest martyrdom to me. However, I feel, O Jesus, that after having aspired to the most lofty heights of Love, if one day I am not to attain them, I feel that I shall have tasted *more sweetness in my martyrdom and my folly* than I shall taste in the bosom of the *joy of the Fatherland*, unless You take away the memory of these earthly hopes through a miracle. Allow me to taste the sweet bitterness of my martyrdom.

Jesus, O Jesus, if the *desire of loving You* is so delightful, what will it be to possess and enjoy this Love?

How can a soul as imperfect as mine aspire to the possession of the plenitude of *Love*? O Jesus, *my first and only Friend,* You whom I *love* UNIQUELY, explain this mystery to me! Why do You not reserve these great aspirations for great souls, for the *Eagles* that soar in the heights?

I look upon myself as a *weak little bird*, with only a light down as covering. I am not an *eagle*, but I have only an eagle's EYES AND HEART. In spite of my extreme littleness I still gaze upon the Divine Sun, the Sun of Love, and my heart feels within it all the aspirations of an *Eagle*. . . .

O Jesus, up until the present moment I can understand Your love for the little bird because it has not strayed far from You. But I know and so do You that very often the imperfect little creature, while remaining in its place (that is, under the Sun's rays), allows itself to be somewhat distracted from its sole occupation. It picks up a piece of grain on the right or on the left; it chases after a little worm; then coming upon a little pool of water, it wets its feathers still hardly formed. It sees an attractive flower and its little mind is occupied with this flower. In a word, being unable to soar like the eagles, the poor little bird is taken up with the trifles of earth.

And yet after all these misdeeds, instead of going and

hiding away in a corner, to weep over its misery and to die of sorrow, the little bird turns towards its beloved Sun, presenting its wet wings to its beneficent rays. It cries like a swallow and in its sweet song it recounts in detail all its infidelities, thinking in the boldness of its full trust that it will acquire in even greater fullness the love of *Him* Who came to call not the just but sinners (Mt 9:11). And even if the Adorable Star remains deaf to the plaintive chirping of the little creature, even if it remains hidden, well, the little one will remain *wet*, accepting its numbness from the cold and rejoicing in its suffering which it knows it deserves.

O Jesus, Your *little bird* is happy to be *weak and little*. What would become of it if it were big? Never would it have the boldness to appear in Your presence, *to fall asleep* in front of You. Yes, this is still one of the weaknesses of the little bird. . . .

O Divine Word! You are the Adored Eagle whom I love and who alone *attracts me*! Coming into this land of exile, You willed to suffer and to die in order *to draw* souls to the bosom of the Eternal Fire of the Blessed Trinity. Ascending once again to the Inaccessible Light, henceforth Your abode, You remain still in this "valley of tears", hidden beneath the appearances of a white host. Eternal Eagle, You desire to nourish me with Your divine substance and yet I am but a poor little thing who would return to nothingness if Your divine glance did not give me life from one moment to the next.

O Jesus, allow me in my boundless gratitude to say to You that Your *love reaches unto folly*. In the presence of this folly, how can You not desire that my heart leap towards You? How can my confidence, then, have any limits? Ah! The saints have committed their *follies* for You, and they have done great things because they are eagles.

Jesus, I am too little to perform great actions, and my own

folly is this: to trust that Your Love will accept me as a victim. My *folly* consists in begging the eagles, my brothers, to obtain for me the favor of flying towards the Sun of Love with the *Divine Eagle's own wings!* (Deut 32:11).

As long as You desire it, O my Beloved, Your little bird will remain without strength and without wings and will always stay with its gaze fixed upon You. It wants to become the *prey* of Your Love. One day, I hope that You, the Adorable Eagle, will come to fetch me, Your little bird; and ascending with it to the Furnace of Love, You will plunge it for all eternity into the burning Abyss of this Love to which it has offered itself as victim.

O Jesus! Why can't I tell all *little souls* how unspeakable is Your condescension? I feel that if You found a soul weaker and littler than mine, which is impossible, You would be pleased to grant it still greater favors, provided it abandoned itself with total confidence to Your Infinite Mercy. But why do I desire to communicate Your secrets of Love, O Jesus, for was it not You alone who taught them to me, and can You not reveal them to others? Yes, I know it, and I beg You to do it. I beg You to cast Your Divine Glance upon a great number of *little* souls. I beg You to choose a legion of *little* Victims worthy of Your LOVE!   (SS)

For a long time You permitted me to be bold with You. You have said to me as the father of the prodigal son said to his older son: "EVERYTHING *that is mine is yours*" (Lk 15:31). Your words, O Jesus, are mine, then, and I can make use of them to draw upon the souls united to me the favor of the heavenly Father. But, Lord, when I say: "I will that where I am, these also whom you have given me may be with me," I do not mean that these cannot attain a higher glory than the one

You will be pleased to give me, but I simply ask that we all be one day united in Your beautiful heaven. You know, O my God, I have never desired anything but to *love* You, and I am ambitious for no other glory. Your Love has gone before me, and it has grown with me, and now it is an abyss whose depths I cannot fathom. Love attracts love, and, my Jesus, my love leaps towards Yours; it would like to fill the abyss which attracts it, but alas! it is not even like a drop of dew lost in the ocean! For me to love You as You love me, I would have to borrow Your own Love, and then only would I be at rest. O my Jesus, it is perhaps an illusion but it seems to me that You cannot fill a soul with more love than the love with which You have filled mine; it is for this reason that I dare to ask You "*to love those whom you have given me with the love with which You loved me*" (Jn 17:23). One day, in heaven, if I discover You love them more than me, I shall rejoice at this, recognizing that these souls merit Your Love much more than I do; but here on earth, I cannot conceive a greater immensity of love than the one which it has pleased You to give me freely, *without any merit on my part.* (SS)

So I kiss my crucifix and lay it gently on the pillow whilst I am dressing, saying: My Jesus, You wept and laboured for thirty-three years upon earth. Today You must rest . . . it is my turn to fight and suffer. (*JFT*)

All that I desire is contained in the following little prayer, which I beg of you to say every day for me: *Most merciful Father, I beseech Thee in the name of Thy beloved Son, of the Virgin Mary and all the Saints, to enkindle my sister's heart with Thy Holy Spirit of Love, that she may by Thy grace draw many souls to love Thee.* (*JFT*)

A few nights before her death Soeur Geneviève came into the infirmary, and found her with eyes raised to heaven and hands joined in prayer: "What are you doing? You ought to be trying to sleep."

"I cannot, so I am praying."

"What do you say to Our Lord?"

"Nothing; I am just loving Him."   (*JFT*)

O Heart of Jesus

O Heart of Jesus, treasured tenderness,
Thou art my joy supreme, my hope, my all!
Thou who didst charm my youth and sweetly bless,
Stay with me now till twilight shadows fall.
Master, to Thee alone my life I give,
To Thee the longings of my heart are known.
Lost in Thy goodness infinite, I live,
O Heart of Jesus, lost in Thee alone!

Thy Heart is all my need and it will be
My strength abiding, my unfailing stay,
I need a love that takes my frailty
And holds me in its keeping night and day.
No creature heart I find whose love is mine
Ever and always with undying power.
Jesus, Thy love must make my nature Thine.
Be Thou my Brother in each suff'ring hour.

If I to see Thy glory would aspire
Then I must know Thy crucible of flame,
But here I choose my purgatory's fire:
Thy burning love, Heart of my God, I claim.
Then when my soul wings upward like a dove
Called from the earth to heaven's home of light,

May it go forth in one pure act of love,
Plunge to Thy Heart in one unswerving flight.　　　(*CP*)

Thy Bethany

The fox goes somewhere safe to earth,
　　The linnet has her nest,
The Son of Man can find nowhere
　　To lay His head and rest:
My heart shall be Thy resting-place,
　　My love shall welcome Thee,
Thou shalt forget man's cold neglect
　　In me, Thy Bethany.　　　(*JFT*)

Near to Heaven

Above the curtain of the clouds
　　Are skies serenely blue,
And thither, like the lark, I rise
　　where no care can pursue,
So near, so near to Heaven's gate!
　　Then to the earth return,
Where to the hidden Fruit of Love
　　With longing eyes I turn.　　　(*JFT*)

Brevity of Life

Oh! What is my life but a passing hour,
　　So brief I can scarce call it mine!
Then just for to-day I will love Thee, Lord,
　　That each moment of it may be Thine!　　　(*JFT*)

I do not lift my eyes to see
   The clouds next day may bring;
From stain of sin, Lord, keep me free
   This day, beneath Thy wing!

I can endure just for today
   The cross that Thou wilt send;
The daily grace, for which I pray,
   Will help me to the end.   (*JFT*)

Make of my soul a sanctuary,
   Thy holy dwelling-place;
Make it a garden of delight
Where every flower seeks the Light:
   The glory of Thy face.   (*JFT*)

My heaven is in the smile of this God Whom I
   adore . . .
When, He hides Himself to test my faith;
To smile while waiting for His gaze once more,
That is my heaven! . . .   (*SR*)

Living Bread

Living Bread, Bread of Heaven, Divine Eucharist,
O touching Mystery produced by Love,
Come dwell within my heart, Jesus, my white
   Host . . .
Deign to unite me unto Thee, O holy and sacred
   Vine,
That my feeble branch may yield its fruit to Thee;
And I will offer Thee a gilded cluster . . .
This cluster of love of which the grapes are souls.   (*SR*)

My Heaven Is Hidden

My heaven is hidden in the little Host
Where Jesus, my Spouse, hides Himself through love.

Thou, the great God Whom the universe adores,
In me Thou liv'st, a prisoner night and day.
Thou liv'st, for me, hidden in a Host,
For Thee I wish to hide myself, O Jesus.
Lovers need solitude,
A heart-to-heart which lasts night and day.   (*SR*)

I am Thy cherished spouse,
Come, my beloved, live in me.
O come, Thy beauty has ravished me,
Deign *to transform me into Thee.*   (*SR*)

Jesus, O holy and sacred vine . . .
I am a gilded cluster
Who for Thee must disappear.
Under the winepress of suffering
I shall prove my love for Thee,
I desire no other joy
Than to immolate myself each day.   (*SR*)

Abandonment alone delivers me
Into Thy arms, O Jesus!
It makes me live
On the bread of the elect . . .
My sweet sun of life . . .
'Tis Thy divine Host,
Small like me . . .

Of its celestial flame,
The luminous ray
Brings to birth in my soul
Perfect abandonment.   (*SR*)

I await in peace the glory
Of the heavenly abode,
For I find in the ciborium
The sweet fruit of love.   (*SR*)

O Tender Mother

O tender Mother! Thy pure heart,
  When Christ thy Son was slain,
Knew the dark night of anguish, the
  Extremity of pain.
God asks our all, and we must give
  What He did first bestow;
To love and suffer is our joy,
  As thine was, here below.   (*JFT*)

To Our Lady of Victories

You who fulfill my hope,
O Mother, hear the humble song
Of love and gratitude
That comes from the heart of your child . . .

You have united me forever
With the works of a Missionary,
By the bonds of prayer,
Suffering and love.

He will cross the earth
To preach the name of Jesus.
I will practice humble virtues
In the background and in mystery.

I crave suffering
I love and desire the Cross . . .
To save one soul,
I would die a thousand times . . .

Ah! For the Conqueror of souls
I want to sacrifice myself in Carmel.
And through Him to spread the fire
That Jesus brought down from Heaven.

Through Him, what a ravishing mystery,
Even as far as East Szechuan
I shall be able to make loved
The virginal name of my tender Mother! . . .

In my deep solitude,
Mary . . . I want to win hearts.
Through your Apostle, I shall convert sinners
As far as the ends of the earth.

Through Him, the holy waters of Baptism
Will make of the tiny newborn babe
The temple where God Himself
Deigns to dwell in His love.

I want to fill with little angels
The brilliant eternal abode . . .
Through Him hosts of children
Will take flight to heaven! . . .

Through Him, I'll be able to gather
The palm for which my soul yearns.

Oh what hope! Dear Mother,
I shall be the sister of a Martyr!!!

After this life's exile,
On the evening of the glorious fight,
We shall enjoy the fruits of our apostolate
In our Homeland.
For Him, Victory's honor
Before the army of the Blessed.
For me . . . the reflection of His Glory
For all eternity in the Heavens! . . .
The little sister of a Missionary.   (LHC)

Why I Love You, O Mary!

Oh! I would like to sing, *Mary, why I love you*,
Why your sweet name thrills my heart,
And why the thought of your supreme greatness
Could not bring fear to my soul.
If I gazed upon you in your sublime glory,
Surpassing the splendor of all the blessed,
I could not believe that I am your child.
O Mary, before you I would lower my eyes! . . .

If a child is to cherish his mother,
She has to cry with him and share his sorrows.
O my dearest Mother, on this foreign shore
How many tears you shed to draw me to you! . . .
In pondering *your life in the holy Gospels*,
I dare look at you and come near you.
It's not difficult for me to believe I'm your child,
For I see you human and suffering like me. . . .

When an angel from Heaven bids you be *the Mother*
Of the God who is to reign for all eternity,
I see you prefer, O Mary, what a mystery!
The ineffable treasure of *virginity*.
O Immaculate Virgin, I understand how your soul
Is dearer to the Lord than his heavenly dwelling.
I understand how your soul, *Humble and Sweet Valley*,
Can contain Jesus, the Ocean of Love! . . .

Oh! I love you, Mary, saying you are the servant
Of the God whom you charm by your humility.
This hidden virtue makes you all-powerful.
It attracts *the Holy Trinity* into your heart.
Then *the Spirit of Love covering you with his shadow*,
The Son equal to the Father became incarnate in you,
There will be a great many of his sinner brothers,
Since he will be called: Jesus, your first-born! . . .

At last you find him and you are overcome with joy,
You say to the fair Child captivating the doctors:
"O my Son, why have you done this?
Your father and I have been searching for you in tears."
And the Child God replies (O what a deep mystery!)
To his dearest Mother holding out her arms to him:
"Why were you searching for me? I must be about
My Father's business. Didn't you know?"

The Gospel tells me that, growing in wisdom,
Jesus remains subject to Joseph and Mary,
And my heart reveals to me with what tenderness
He always obeys his dear parents.
Now I understand the mystery of the temple,
The hidden words of my Lovable King.

Mother, your sweet Child wants you to be the
   example
Of the soul searching for Him in the night of faith.

Since the King of Heaven wanted his Mother
To be plunged into the night, in anguish of heart,
Mary, is it thus a blessing to suffer on earth?
Yes, *to suffer while loving is the purest happiness!* . . .
All that He has given me, Jesus can take back.
Tell him not to bother with me. . . .
He can indeed hide from me, I'm willing to wait for
   him
Till the day without sunset when my faith will fade
   away. . . .

Mother full of grace, I know that in Nazareth
You live in poverty, wanting nothing more.
No rapture, miracle, or ecstasy
Embellish your life, O Queen of the Elect! . . .
The number of little ones on earth is truly great.
They can raise their eyes to you without trembling.
It's by *the ordinary way*, incomparable Mother,
That you like to walk to guide them to Heaven.

While waiting for Heaven, O my dear Mother,
I want to live with you, to follow you each day.
Mother, contemplating you, I joyfully immerse
   myself,
Discovering in your heart *abysses of love*.
Your motherly gaze banishes all my fears.
It teaches me *to cry*, it teaches me *to rejoice*.
Instead of scorning pure and simple joys,
You want to share in them, you deign to bless them.

At Cana, seeing the married couple's anxiety
Which they cannot hide, for they have run out of
   wine,
In your concern you tell the Savior,
Hoping for the help of his divine power.
Jesus seems at first to reject your prayer:
"Woman, what does this matter," he answers, "to you
   and to me?"
But in the depths of his heart, He calls you his
   Mother,
And he works his first miracle for you. . . .

One day when sinners are listening to the doctrine
Of Him who would like to welcome them in
   Heaven,
Mary, I find you with them on the hill.
Someone says to Jesus that you wish to see him.
Then, before the whole multitude, your Divine Son
Shows us the immensity of his love for us.
He says: "Who is my brother and my sister and my
   Mother,
If not the one who does my will?"

O Immaculate Virgin, most tender of Mothers,
In listening to Jesus, you are not saddened.
But you rejoice that He makes us understand
How our souls become *his family* here below.
Yes, you rejoice that He gives us his life,
The infinite treasures of his divinity! . . .
How can we not love you, O my dear Mother,
On seeing so much love and so much humility?

You love us, Mary, as Jesus loves us,
And for us you accept being separated from Him.
To love is to give everything. It's to give oneself.
You wanted to prove this by remaining our support.
The Savior knew your immense tenderness.
He knew the secrets of your maternal heart.
Refuge of sinners, He leaves us to you
When He leaves the Cross to wait for us in Heaven.

Mary, at the top of Calvary standing beside the Cross
To me you seem like a priest at the altar,
Offering your beloved Jesus, the sweet Emmanuel,
To appease the Father's justice . . .
A prophet said, O afflicted Mother,
"There is no sorrow like your sorrow!"
O Queen of Martyrs, while remaining in exile
You lavish on us all the blood of your heart!

Saint John's home becomes your only refuge.
Zebedee's son is to replace Jesus. . . .
That is the last detail the Gospel gives.
It tells me nothing more of the Queen of Heaven.
But, O my dear Mother, doesn't its profound silence
Reveal that *The Eternal Word Himself*
Wants to sing the secrets of your life
To charm *your children*, all the Elect of Heaven?

Soon I'll hear that sweet harmony.
Soon I'll go to beautiful Heaven to see you.
You who came *to smile at me* in the morning of my
    life,
Come smile at me again . . . Mother. . . . It's evening
    now! . . .
I no longer fear the splendor of your supreme glory.

With you I've suffered, and now I want
To sing on your lap, Mary, why I love you,
And to go on saying that I am your child! . . .

(PSTL, PN 54)

Virgin Full of Grace

Now 'tis at Nazareth, O Virgin full of grace,
   In poverty abiding, you never knew desire;
Now ecstasy nor miracle nor rapture there had place,
    To fill your life with splendor, O Queen of
       heavenly choir!
Ah! Countless are the little ones that throng the earth
   today,
    Unfearing, without tremor, to you they lift their
      eyes,
Incomparable Mother, 'tis by the common way
   It pleases you to go, that you may lead them to the
     skies.
Throughout this exile sad I long, O mother mine,
    To dwell with you, to follow each day your path
     above.
In contemplating you, enraptured, I divine
    In your pure, gentle heart the deep abyss of love;
Your gentle gaze maternal will banish all of fear;
    It teaches me to weep, it teaches happiness.   (DI 2)

A Mother's Smile

Oh! That I might wing my way
   To Him, who stands upon the shore
Where breaks the dawn of endless day,
   And life's dark shadows are no more!

There shall I find a Mother's smile,
Safe in the haven of her arms
   My weary spirit fain would be.   (*JFT*)

Humility

No sudden splendor broke the grey
   And even tenor of your days,
No ecstasy made you forget
   Your poverty in its bright rays.

Mary, the lowliest can tread
   With confidence the path you trod,
Your life the bright and shining star
   That leads the wayfarer to God.   (*JFT*)

Pain

Pain, lifted up to Thee,
   Is Pain no more:
Joy casts aside the weeds
   That Sorrow wore.   (*JFT*)

Strewing Flowers

Jesus, my only Love, how I love to strew Flowers
Each evening at the foot of your Crucifix! . . .
In unpetalling the springtime rose for you,
   I would like to dry your tears. . . .

   Strewing Flowers is offering you as first fruits
My slightest sighs, my greatest sufferings.
My sorrows and my joys, my little sacrifices,
   Those are my flowers! . . .

Lord, my soul is in love with your beauty.
I want to squander my perfumes and my flowers on
    you.
In strewing them for you on the wings of the breeze,
    I would like to inflame hearts! . . .

    Strewing flowers, Jesus, is my weapon
When I want to fight to save sinners.
The victory is mine. . . . I always disarm you
    With my flowers! ! !

The flower petals, caressing your Face,
Tell you that my heart is yours forever.
You understand the language of my unpetalled rose,
    And you smile at my love.

    Strewing Flowers, repeating your praise,
That is my only delight in this valley of tears.
Soon I shall go to Heaven with the little angels
    To strew Flowers! . . .   (*PSTL*, PN 34)

An Unpetalled Rose

Jesus, when I see you held by your Mother,
        Leaving her arms
Trying, trembling, *your first steps*
        On our sad earth,
Before you I'd like *to unpetal a rose*
        In its freshness
So that your little foot might rest ever so softly
        On a flower! . . .

This unpetalled rose is the faithful image,
        Divine Child,

Of the heart that wants to sacrifice itself for you
    unreservedly
        At each moment.
Lord, on your altars more than one new rose
        Likes to shine.
It gives itself to you . . . but I dream of something else:
        To be unpetalled! . . .

The rose in its splendor can adorn your feast,
        Lovable child,
But *the unpetalled rose* is just flung out
        To blow away.
An unpetalled rose gives itself unaffectedly
        To be no more.
Like it, with joy I abandon myself to you,
        Little Jesus.

One walks *on rose petals* with no regrets,
        And this debris
Is a simple ornament that one disposes of artlessly,
        That I've understood.
Jesus, for your love I've squandered my life,
        My future.
In the eyes of men, a rose forever *withered*,
        I must *die!* . . .

For you, I must *die*, Child, Beauty Supreme,
        What a blessed fate!
In *being unpetalled*, I want to prove to you that I love you,
        O my Treasure! . . .
Under your *baby steps*, I want to live here below
        With mystery,
And I'd like to soften once more on Calvary
        Your last steps! . . .   (*PSTL*, PN 51)

My Song for Today

My life is but an instant, a passing hour.
My life is but a day that escapes and flies away.
O my God! You know that to love you on earth
        I only have today! . . .

Oh, I love you, Jesus! My soul yearns for you.
For just one day remain my sweet support.
Come reign in my heart, give me your smile
        Just for today!

Lord, what does it matter if the future is gloomy?
To pray for tomorrow, oh no, I cannot! . . .
Keep my heart pure, cover me with your shadow
        Just for today!

If I think about tomorrow, I fear my fickleness.
I feel sadness and worry rising up in my heart.
But I'm willing, my God, to accept trial and suffering
        Just for today!

O Divine Pilot! whose hand guides me,
I'm soon to see you on the eternal shore.
Guide my little boat over the stormy waves in peace
        Just for today!

Ah! Lord, let me hide in your Face.
There I'll no longer hear the world's vain noise.
Give me your love, keep me in your grace
        Just for today!

Near your divine Heart, I forget all passing things.
I no longer dread the fears of the night.
Ah! Jesus, give me a place in your Heart
        Just for today!

Living Bread, Bread of Heaven, divine Eucharist,
O sacred Mystery! that Love has brought forth. . . .
Come live in my heart, Jesus, my white Host,
      Just for today!

Deign to unite me to you, Holy and sacred Vine,
And my weak branch will give you its fruit,
And I'll be able to offer you a cluster of golden grapes
      Lord, from today on.

I've just this fleeting day to form
This cluster of love, whose seeds are souls.
Ah! give me, Jesus, the fire of an Apostle
      Just for today!

O Immaculate Virgin! You are my Sweet Star
Giving Jesus to me and uniting me to Him.
O Mother! Let me rest under your veil
      Just for today!

My Holy Guardian Angel, cover me with your wing.
With your fire light the road that I'm taking.
Come direct my steps . . . help me, I call upon you
      Just for today!

Lord, I want to see you without veils, without clouds,
But still exiled, far from you, I languish.
May your lovable face not be hidden from me
      Just for today!

Soon I'll fly away to speak your praises
When the day without sunset will dawn on my soul.
Then I'll sing on the Angels' lyre
      The Eternal Today! . . .

                        (*PSTL*, PN 5)

Love

There is a tree whose roots are fast
   In Heaven's soil; but see,
Its leafy canopy is spread
   On earth! Love is the tree,
And self-surrender is its fruit.
   O loving soul, draw near!
Beneath its shade true peace is found,
   When love has cast out fear.   (*JFT*)

Song of Love

Oh! Would that all this world doth hold
   Might, as the ebbing tide,
Depart from me! I need it not,
   For Thou art at my side.
If Thou shouldst leave me, Lord, and hide
   Thy face from me awhile,
My song of love shall not be stilled,
   Nor lips forbear to smile.   (*JFT*)

Living on Love! . . .

On the evening of Love, speaking without parable,
Jesus said: "If anyone wishes to love me
All his life, let him keep my Word.
My Father and I will come to visit him.
And we will make his heart our dwelling.
Coming to him, we shall love him always.
We want him to remain, filled with peace,
     In our Love! . . ."

Living on Love is holding You Yourself.
Uncreated Word, Word of my God,
Ah! Divine Jesus, you know I love you.
The Spirit of Love sets me aflame with his fire.
In loving you I attract the Father.
My weak heart holds him forever.
O Trinity! You are Prisoner
        Of my Love! . . .

Living on Love is living on your life,
Glorious King, delight of the elect.
You live for me, hidden in a host.
I want to hide myself for you, O Jesus!
Lovers must have solitude,
A heart-to-heart lasting night and day.
Just one glance of yours makes my beatitude.
        I live on Love! . . .

Living on Love is not setting up one's tent
At the top of Tabor.
It's climbing Calvary with Jesus,
It's looking at the Cross as a treasure! . . .
In Heaven I'm to live on joy.
Then trials will have fled forever,
But in exile, in suffering I want
        To live on Love.

Living on Love is giving without limit
Without claiming any wages here below.
Ah! I give without counting, truly sure
That when one loves, one does not keep count! . . .
Overflowing with tenderness, I have given everything,
To his Divine Heart . . . lightly I run.
I have nothing left but my only wealth:
        Living on Love.

Living on Love is banishing every fear,
Every memory of past faults.
I see no imprint of my sins.
In a moment love has burned everything. . . .
Divine Flame, O very sweet Blaze!
I make my home in your hearth.
In your fire I gladly sing:
          "I live on Love! . . ."

Living on Love is keeping within oneself
A great treasure in an earthen vase.
My Beloved, my weakness is extreme.
Ah, I'm far from being an angel from heaven! . . .
But if I fall with each passing hour,
You come to my aid, lifting me up.
At each moment you give me your grace:
          I live on Love.

Living on Love is sailing unceasingly,
Sowing peace and joy in every heart.
Beloved Pilot, Charity impels me,
For I see you in my sister souls.
Charity is my only star.
In its brightness I sail straight ahead.
I've my motto written on my sail:
          "Living on Love."

Living on Love, when Jesus is sleeping,
Is rest on stormy seas.
Oh! Lord, don't fear that I'll wake you.
I'm waiting in peace for Heaven's shore. . . .
Faith will soon tear its veil.
My hope is to see you one day.
Charity swells and pushes my sail:
          I live on Love! . . .

Living on Love, O my Divine Master,
Is begging you to spread your Fire
In the holy, sacred soul of your Priest.
May he be purer than a seraphim in Heaven! . . .
Ah! glorify your Immortal Church!
Jesus, do not be deaf to my sighs.
I, her child, sacrifice myself for her,
       I live on Love.

Living on Love is wiping your Face,
It's obtaining the pardon of sinners.
O God of Love! may they return to your grace,
And may they forever bless your Name. . . .
Even in my heart the blasphemy resounds.
To efface it, I always want to sing:
"I adore and love your Sacred Name.
       I live on Love! . . ."

Living on Love is imitating Mary,
Bathing your divine feet that she kisses, transported.
With tears, with precious perfume,
She dries them with her long hair . . .
Then standing up, she shatters the vase,
And in turn she anoints your Sweet Face.
As for me, the perfume with which I anoint your Face
      Is my Love! . . .

"Living on Love, what strange folly!"
The world says to me, "Ah! stop your singing,
Don't waste your perfumes, your life.
Learn to use them well . . ."
Loving you, Jesus, is such a fruitful loss! . . .
All my perfumes are yours forever.
I want to sing on leaving this world:
      "I'm dying of Love!"

Dying of Love is a truly sweet martyrdom,
And that is the one I wish to suffer.
O Cherubim! Tune your lyre,
For I sense my exile is about to end! . . .
Flame of Love, consume me unceasingly.
Life of an instant, your burden is so heavy to me!
Divine Jesus, make my dream come true:
       To die of Love! . . .

Dying of Love is what I hope for.
When I shall see my bonds broken,
My God will be my Great Reward.
I don't desire to possess other goods.
I want to be set on fire with his Love.
I want to see Him, to unite myself to Him forever.
That is my Heaven . . . that is my destiny:
       Living on Love!!! . . .

                              (*PSTL*, PN 17)

I Live by Love

I live by love, and so I guard
  A precious treasure rare
Within an earthen vessel frail,
  And cherish it with care.
No angel, I, but Eve's poor child,
  Who hourly fail and fall;
O everlasting arms uphold!
  Love, answer Thou my call!   (*JFT*)

Handmaid

I do not serve Thee, Lord, for gain,
　　That were a hireling's way!
Love does not wait with outstretched hand
　　For payment day by day.
My heart's love is my only wealth,
　　And this I bring to Thee;
I only ask that to the end
　　Thy handmaid I may be.   (*JFT*)

The Priest

Pure as the angel at his side,
　　A soul newborn My priest must be;
A sister, hidden and unknown,
　　Obtains for him this grace from Me.   (*JFT*)

Guardian Angel

Dear Angel, given by God to be
　　My brother and my friend,
Beneath the shadow of your wings
　　May I reach journey's end.
I too shall sing, when breaks the dawn,
　　—Eternity's bright day—
With angel choirs the song of praise
　　You taught me in the way.   (*JFT*)

Echo of Jesus

How sweetly doth mine own soul echo,
  Jesus, those brave words of Thine
Full of longing for Thy Passion,
  All on fire with love divine!   (*JFT*)

Detachment

No charm I find, nor happiness,
  Upon this earth, so bleak and drear.
Jesus! To Thee I lift mine eyes,
  And to my only Joy draw near.   (*JFT*)

Into Thy Hands

My will, my all, I do resign
  Into Thy hands, which feed
My soul with hidden manna sweet,
  Fulfilling all my need.
One look from Thee is my reward,
  Thou knowest what is best;
And, safe within Thy arms, my soul
  Shall sleep and take her rest.   (*JFT*)

Obedience

He speaketh victory who seeks
  In all things to obey;
O God of victories, my will
  Here at Thy feet I lay!

I face undaunted shot and shell,
My weapon in my hand,
And singing go to meet my death,
For at Thy side I stand. (*JFT*)

Her Last Words

My God . . . I love Thee! (*LC*)

XX

Blessed Elizabeth of the Trinity

(1880–1906)

Elizabeth Catez was born in 1880 at Avor, France. Her father was an army captain and died when she was seven. She had a younger sister, Guite, and they were very close to each other and their mother. At the age of seven, Elizabeth told a friend of the family, Canon Angles, that she would be a religious. She was a precocious child with a flashing temper until she made her First Confession. From that time on she was noticeably calm in temperament. She was an accomplished pianist. Her family was middle class, and they enjoyed parties and other social activities. From the time of her First Communion in 1891, she "wanted to give her life and to return a little of His great love". At the age of thirteen she bound herself to Jesus with a vow of virginity. Elizabeth's heart had been captured, and now she could think only of Him. On her twenty-first birthday she had her mother's blessing at last to enter the Carmel in Dijon, close to her home. Elizabeth expresses in her letters a deep joy at being in Carmel. Everything led her to her "Three", the Trinity. She offered herself unconditionally to "Him"; He accepted. Elizabeth became ill shortly after entering Carmel and suffered for five years from a stomach ailment, now thought to have been Addison's disease. Her suffering was intense both spiritually and physically; this caused her love for Jesus to increase, and also her desire to offer these sufferings to Him.

In her writings Elizabeth refers often to the words of Saint

Paul. She speaks of her vocation: "To be a bride, a bride of Carmel", means to have the flaming heart of Elijah, the transpierced heart of Teresa, to be His "true bride", because she was "zealous for His honor". Blessed Elizabeth of the Trinity had true depth of prayer, was a mystic, a great lover of Jesus, and a real friend to her sisters in Carmel and her family. She referred to herself as *Laudem Gloriae*, Praise of Glory. She died November 9, 1906. Her last words were: "I am going to Light, to Love, to Life!"

PRAYERS

O Mary, you are the one created being who knew the gift of God, and lost no particle of it; a creature so pure and luminous that you seemed to be the light itself. "Mirror of justice": your life was so simple, so lost in God, that there is but little to say of it; "faithful virgin": who kept all these things . . . in your heart." You were so lowly, so hidden in God in the seclusion of the temple that you drew upon yourself the complacent regard of the Holy Trinity. "For he has regarded the low estate of his handmaid, for behold, henceforth all generations will call me blessed."

The Father, bending down to you, a creature so lovely, so unaware of your own beauty, chose you for the Mother in time of him whose Father he is in eternity. Then the Spirit of love, who presides over all the works of God, overshadowed you, and, O Virgin, you uttered your "Fiat": "Behold the handmaid of the Lord; be it done to me according to your word," and the greatest of all mysteries was accomplished. By the descent of the Word into your womb, you became God's own for ever and ever.

(*DI* 4. *CWET* 1, "Heaven in Faith", Tenth Day)

In the heaven of her soul, the praise of glory has already begun her work of eternity. Her song is uninterrupted, for she is under the action of the Holy Spirit, who effects everything in her; and although she is not always aware of it, for the weakness of nature does not allow her to be established in God without distractions, she always sings, she always adores, for she has so to speak, wholly passed into praise and love in her passion for the glory of her God. In the heaven of our soul let us be praises of love of our Immaculate Mother. One day the veil will fall, we will be introduced into the eternal courts, and there we will sing in the bosom of infinite Love. And God will give us "the new name promised to the Victor." What will it be?

Laudem Gloriae

(CWET 1, "Heaven in Faith", Tenth Day)

O Lord, what does it matter, when I can retire within myself, enlightened by faith, whether I feel or don't feel, whether I am in light or darkness, enjoy or do not enjoy? I am struck by a kind of shame at making any distinction between such things and, despising myself utterly for such want of love, I turn at once to You, my divine Master, for deliverance. Help me to exalt You . . . above the sweetness and consolations which flow from You, because I have resolved to pass by all else in order to be united with You.

(DI 2. CWET 1, Last Retreat, Fourth Day, paraphrased)

It is one of the redeemed who in its turn must redeem other souls, and for that reason it will sing on its lyre: "I glory in the Cross of Jesus Christ." "With Christ I am nailed to the Cross. . . ." And again, "I suffer in my body what is lacking in the passion of Christ for the sake of his body, which is the Church."

"The queen stood at your right hand": such is the attitude of this soul; she walks the way of Calvary at the right of her crucified, annihilated, humiliated King, yet always so strong, so calm, so full of majesty as He goes to His passion "to make the glory of His grace blaze forth" according to that so strong expression of St. Paul. He wants to associate His Bride in His work of redemption and this sorrowful way which she follows seems like the path of Beatitude to her, not only because it leads there but also because her holy Master makes her realize that she must go beyond the bitterness in suffering to find in it, as He did, her rest.

Then she can serve God *"day and night in His temple"*! Neither trials from without nor from within can make her leave the holy fortress in which the Master has enclosed her. She no longer feels *"hunger or thirst,"* for in spite of her consuming desire for Beatitude, she is satisfied by this food which was her Master's: "the will of the Father." *"She no longer feels the heat of the sun,"* that is, she no longer suffers from suffering. Then the Lamb can *"lead her to the fountain of life,"* where He wills, as He wills, for she does not look at the paths on which she is walking; she simply gazes at the Shepherd who is leading her. God bends lovingly over this soul, His adopted daughter, who is so conformed to the image of His Son, the "firstborn among all creatures," and recognizes her as one of those whom He has "predestined, called, justified." And his fatherly heart thrills as He thinks of consummating His work, that is, of "glorifying" her by bringing her into His kingdom, there to sing for ages unending "the praise of His glory."   (*CWET* I, Last Retreat, Fifth Day)

Coeli enarrant gloriam Dei." This is what the heavens are telling: the glory of God.

Since my soul is a heaven in which I live while awaiting the heavenly Jerusalem, "this heaven too must sing the glory of the Eternal, *nothing* but the glory of the Eternal.

"Day to day passes on this message." All God's lights, all His communications to my soul are this "day which passes on to day the message of His glory." "The command of the Lord is clear," sings the psalmist, "enlightening the eye. . . ." Consequently, my fidelity in corresponding with each of His decrees, with each of His interior commands, makes me live in His light; it too is a "message which passes on His glory." But this is the sweet wonder: "Yahweh, he who looks at You is radiant! ", the prophet exclaims. The soul that by the depth of its interior gaze contemplates its God through everything in that simplicity which sets it apart from all else is a "*radiant*" soul: it is "a day that passes on to day the message of His glory."   (*CWET* I, Last Retreat, Seventh Day)

The soul that penetrates and dwells in these "depths of God" of which the royal prophet sings, and thus does everything "in Him, with Him, by Him and for Him" with that limpid gaze which gives it a certain resemblance to the simple Being, this soul, by each of its movements, its aspirations, as well as by each of its acts, however ordinary they may be, "is rooted" more deeply in Him whom it loves. Everything within it pays homage to the thrice-holy God: it is so to speak a perpetual Sanctus, an unceasing praise of glory!   (*CWET* I, Last Retreat, Eighth Day)

I am praying fervently for you, that God may invade all the powers of your soul, that He may make you live in communion with His whole mystery, that everything in you may be divine and marked with His seal, so that you may be another Christ working for the glory of the Father! ... I want to work for the glory of God, and for that I must be wholly filled with Him; then I will be all-powerful: one look, one desire [will] become an irresistible prayer that can obtain everything, since it is, so to speak, God whom we are offering to God. May our souls be one in Him, and while you bring Him to souls, I will remain like Mary Magdalene, silent and adoring, close to the Master, asking Him to make your word fruitful in souls.   (*CWET* 2, Letter 124)

O faithful Virgin, when you uttered your "fiat", the greatest of all mysteries was accomplished in you. In what peace and recollection did you live and act! Teach me to sanctify my most trivial actions and to spend myself for others when charity requires it, yet all the while to remain like you the constant adorer of God within me.   (*GA*)

O my Guiding Star, the fair light of faith enlightens me to see Thee. What does it matter if I feel or do not feel, if I am in the light or darkness, if I enjoy or do not enjoy. Only let me so fix my gaze on Thee, that I may never wander from Thy light.   (*GA*)

O my God, I want to work for Your glory and for that I must be wholly filled with You and You are love. Then I shall be all-powerful. A look, a desire will become a prayer that cannot be resisted and that can obtain everything. Apostle, Carmelite, it is all one!   (*GA*)

O my God, I ask You to make us genuine in our love, that is, men and women of sacrifice. It is our mission to prepare the ways of the Lord by our union with Him. In contact with Him our soul will become like a flame of love, spreading through all the members of the body of Christ which is the Church. *(GA)*

Ah, my heart is not at all free; I can no longer dispose of it for I have given it to the King of kings. I hear the voice of my Beloved in the depths of my heart: "If you follow Me you will have suffering, and the Cross. But also what joys, what sweetness I will make you taste in these tribulations. Do you feel enough love for your Jesus? I want your heart. I love it. I have chosen it for Me. Keep your heart for Me!" Yes, my Love, my Life, Beloved Spouse whom I adore, yes, be assured I am ready to follow You along this way of sacrifices. Oh, You want to show me all the thorns that I will find. Good Jesus, we will pass through them together; following You, and with You, I will be strong. *(LLL* March 31, 1899, Diary)

Pentecost

With your pure and burning flames,
Holy Spirit, deign to enkindle my soul;
Consume it with divine love,
O you whom I invoke each day!

Spirit of God, brilliant light,
You fill me with your favors,
You inundate me with your sweetness
Burn, annihilate me completely!

You give me my vocation,
Oh, lead me then to this intimate,
Interior union, to this life
Wholly in God, which is my desire.

May my hope be in Jesus alone,
And while living in the midst of this world,
May I long for, may I see only Him,
Him, my Love, my divine Friend!

Holy Spirit, Goodness, supreme Beauty!
O you whom I adore, you whom I love!
Consume with your divine flames,
This body and this heart and this soul!
This bride of the Trinity
Who desires only to do your will!

(*LLL* May 29, 1898, Poems)

May my life be a continual prayer, a long act of love. May nothing distract me from You, neither noise nor diversions, nothing. O my Master, I would so love to live with You in silence. But what I love above all is to do Your will, and since You want me to still remain in the world, I submit with all my heart for love of You. I offer You the cell of my heart; may it be Your little Bethany. Come rest there; I love You so.

(*LLL* January 23, 1900, Personal Notes 5)

I want to leave all, I long to give You my life and to share Your agony. May I die crucified. (*LLL* September 1897, Poems)

Soon I will answer Your call; soon I will belong wholly to You; soon I will have said good-bye to all that I love. Ah, the

sacrifice is already made, my heart is detached from all things;
it costs [the soul] hardly anything when it is for You.

(*LLL* April 2, 1899, Diary 133)

Oh, how good it is in silence
To listen to Him over and over,
To enjoy the peace of His presence,
And then to surrender wholly to His love.

O Lamb, so pure and so meek,
You my All, my only One;
How well You know that Your fiancée,
Your little one, hungers greatly for You.

She hungers to feed upon her Master,
Above all to be consumed by Him,
To surrender fully to Him her whole being
So she may be totally taken.

Oh, that I may be possessed by You;
One who lives by You alone,
Yours, Your living host,
Consumed by You on the Cross.

(*LLL* December 25, 1901, Poems 75)

It seems to me that I have found my Heaven on earth, since
Heaven is God and God is in my soul.

The day I understood that, everything became clear to me.
I wish to tell this secret very softly to those whom I love so
that they also, through everything, may always cling to God.

(*LLL* June 1902, Letter 122)

Amo Christum

House of God," I have within me the prayer
Of Jesus Christ, the divine adorer,
It takes me to souls and to the Father,
As that is its double movement.
   To be savior with my Master,
   That is also my mission.
   So I must disappear,
   Lose myself in Him through union.
      Jesus, Word of life,
      United to You forever,
      Your virgin and Your victim
      Will radiate Your love:
      "Amo Christum."

Mother of the Word, oh, tell me your mystery.
After the moment of the Incarnation,
Tell me how you spent your life
Buried in adoration.
   In a peace wholly ineffable,
   A mysterious silence,
   You entered the Unfathomable Being,
   Bearing within you "the gift of God."
      Oh, keep me always
      In the divine embrace.
      May I bear the imprint
      Of this God of all Love:
      "Amo Christum."

(*LLL* December 25, 1903, Poems 88)

O My God, Trinity Whom I Adore

O my God, Trinity whom I adore, help me to forget myself entirely that I may be established in You as still and as peaceful as if my soul were already in eternity. May nothing trouble my peace or make me leave You, O my Unchanging One, but may each minute carry me further into the depths of Your Mystery. Give peace to my soul; make it Your heaven, Your beloved dwelling place. May I never leave You there alone but be wholly present, my faith wholly vigilant, wholly adoring, and wholly surrendered to Your creative Action.

O my Beloved Christ, crucified by love, I wish to be a bride for Your Heart; I wish to cover You with glory; I wish to love You . . . even to dying of it! But I feel my weakness, and I ask You "to clothe me with Yourself," to identify my soul with all the movements of Your soul, to overwhelm me, to possess me, to substitute Yourself for me that my life may be but a radiance of Your Life. Come into me as Adorer, as Restorer, as Savior.

O Eternal Word, Word of my God, I want to spend my life in listening to You, to become wholly teachable that I may learn all from You. Then, through all nights, all voids, all helplessness, I want to gaze on You always and remain in Your great light. O my Beloved Star, so fascinate me that I may not withdraw from Your radiance.

O consuming Fire, Spirit of Love, "come upon me," and create in my soul a kind of incarnation of the Word: that I may be another humanity for Him in which He can renew His whole Mystery. And You, O Father, bend lovingly over Your poor little creature; "cover her with Your shadow," seeing in her only the "Beloved in whom You are well pleased."

O my Three, my All, my Beatitude, Infinite Solitude, Immensity in which I lose myself, I surrender myself to You as Your prey. Bury Yourself in me that I may bury myself in You until I depart to contemplate in Your light the abyss of Your greatness.   (*LLL* November 21, 1904, Personal Notes 15)

O Love, Love!
You know how I love You, how I desire
      To contemplate You!
   You know also how I suffer . . .
And yet, thirty, forty years more if You like,
      I am ready.
Consume my whole substance for Your glory.
      Let it be distilled
         Drop by drop
      For Your Church.   (*LLL*)

Dear Antoinette, I am offering a prayer for you that Saint Paul made for his followers: he asked that "Jesus dwell through faith in their hearts so they might be rooted in love." That thought is so profound, so mysterious. . . . Oh, yes, may the God who is all love be your unchanging dwelling place, your cell, and your cloister in the midst of the world; remember that He dwells in the deepest center of your soul as if in a sanctuary where He wants always to be loved to the point of adoration.   (*DI* 1, *CW* V 2, Letter 261)

O Virgin most faithful, you remain night and day in profound silence, in ineffable peace, in a divine prayer that never ceases, your soul ever inundated with heavenly light. Your heart is like a crystal that reflects the divine One, the Guest who dwells in you, the Beauty that knows no setting. O Mary, you draw heaven down to you: see, the Father commits His Son to you that you may be His mother, and the Spirit of love overshadows you. The Blessed Three come to you, and all heaven is opened and abases itself before you. . . . I adore the mystery of this God who is made flesh in you, O Virgin Mary.

Mother of the Word, show me your mystery after the incarnation of the Lord; how you lived buried in adoration. . . . Keep me ever in a divine embrace. Let me carry upon me the stamp of this God of love.

(*DI* 2. *Poetical Compositions* 79, 88, paraphrased)

O Lord, it is no longer just a veil that hides You from me, but a thick high wall. . . . It is hard, after having felt so near You! But I am ready to remain in this state for as long as it pleases You to leave me in it, my Beloved, for faith tells me that You are still close at hand, and always will be. . . . I am looking only for You. . . . Help me come to You through pure faith. . . . Never have I so felt my misery, never seen myself so miserable, yet this misery does not completely overwhelm me, for I make use of it to approach You and think now that it is just because of my weakness that You love me so much and have given me so much! . . . I beg You to give other souls all Your graces and consolations in order to draw them to You. For me it is this darkness that brings me close to You. (*DI* 4, Letter 47, paraphrased)

The martyrs of Guadalajara:
Teresa of the Child Jesus, María Pilar, and María Angeles

XXI

The Three Martyred Carmelites of Guadalajara

(D. 1936)

Blessed María Pilar
Blessed María Angeles
Blessed Teresa of the Child Jesus

There were three Carmelite nuns living in Guadalajara at the time a revolution broke out. They were: Sister María Pilar of Saint Francis Borgia, Sister María Angeles of Saint Joseph, and Sister Teresa of the Child Jesus. They were living at the monastery of Saint Joseph of Guadalajara until they were forced out.

Sister María Pilar was the oldest, being fifty-eight at the time of her martyrdom. She had entered Carmel at the age of twenty and was known for her love of the Blessed Sacrament and her skill at making lace. Sister María Pilar had offered herself as a victim, thus sparing her sisters if the occasion arose. She had an older sister at the monastery, Sister Araceli of the Blessed Sacrament, who was able to give a firsthand account of the events.

Sister María Angeles was to live only thirty-one years; details of her life were supplied by her two sisters who survived. She was noted to be pious and full of apostolic zeal even as a youth. The life of Saint Thérèse of Lisieux greatly influenced her decision to become a Carmelite. After caring for her widowed father and an invalid aunt, she was able to enter Carmel at the age of twenty-four. She greatly desired martyrdom and the chance to shed her blood for our Lord, but felt unworthy of that grace. She was the first to die on the afternoon of July 24, 1936.

Sister Teresa of the Child Jesus was a very young martyr. She was born in 1909 and lived only twenty-seven years. After her death, witnesses said that they had never seen a more valiant nun. She resisted the soldiers as well as she could and refused their advances even to death.

From the decree of the Sacred Congregation for the Causes of Saints: "Taught by this great spiritual Mother [Saint Teresa of Avila], the servants of God, María of the Pillar of St. Francis Borgia, María of the Angels of St. Joseph, and María Teresa of the Child Jesus, Discalced Carmelites of the Monastery of Saint Joseph of Guadalajara, not only joyfully embraced the way of Carmel but also that of Calvary, crowning the perfect accomplishment of the evangelical counsels, penance and contemplation with the outstanding witness of martyrdom."

PRAYERS

SISTER MARÍA PILAR

(Preparing adornments for the Blessed Sacrament) It is for the Living One, the Living One. (DCC)

(In the midst of the atrocious sufferings of her martyrdom, she said:) Father, forgive them, they know not what they do. (DCC)

Sister María Angeles

Oh, sweetest Jesus, we would follow You always like faithful lambs, even if necessary, to the giving of our life for Thee.

(DCC)

My God, receive my life in the pains of martyrdom as witness to my love for You, as You have received that of so many souls who love You and died for Your love.   *(DCC)*

Sister Teresa of the Child Jesus

(Sister Teresa died crying out:)

Long live Christ the King!   *(DCC)*

Saint Teresa Benedicta of the Cross (Edith Stein).
Passport photograph from the time of
her deportation

XXII

Saint Teresa Benedicta of the Cross

(1891–1942)

Born into a religious Jewish family in 1891 at Breslau, Germany, Edith Stein became an agnostic in her teen years. She was a very brilliant student and was able to study philosophy under the renowned Husserl. She became a phenomenologist, writing a dissertation entitled *On Empathy*. While staying with friends she picked up a book and began to read. She read all night until she finished it. The book was the life of Saint Teresa of Avila, and as she read she found it to be truth. She was baptized in 1922 and entered the Carmel of Cologne in 1933. She would have liked to enter at the time she was baptized, but she deferred it because of her mother's sorrow. She wrote many profound texts, and some of them continue to be translated.

She was transferred to the Carmel of Echt in the Netherlands because of the persecution of the Jews. She did not want to endanger her sisters. However, she was taken from that Carmel along with her sister Rosa, who also had been baptized Catholic, and was martyred at Auschwitz in August 1942. People who witnessed Sister Teresa Benedicta on the train and in the camp declared that she was calm and went about caring for the children and bringing a sense of peace. In October 1998 this extraordinary woman was declared a saint.

PRAYERS

O Prince of Peace, to all who receive You, You bring light and peace. Help me to live in daily contact with You, listening to the words You have spoken and obeying them. O Divine Child, I place my hands in Yours; I shall follow You. Oh, let Your divine life flow into me.   (GA)

I will go unto the altar of God. It is not myself and my tiny little affairs that matter here, but the great sacrifice of atonement. I surrender myself entirely to Your divine will, O Lord. Make my heart grow greater and wider, out of itself into the Divine Life.   (GA)

O my God, fill my soul with holy joy, courage and strength to serve You. Enkindle Your love in me and then walk with me along the next stretch of road before me. I do not see very far ahead, but when I have arrived where the horizon now closes down, a new prospect will open before me and I shall meet with peace.   (GA)

How wondrous are the marvels of your love,
We are amazed, we stammer and grow dumb,
For word and spirit fail us.   (ESD)

In the morning we will go to the vineyards.
We will see if the vines are budding. Song of Songs 7:13
     (ESD)

Song

My heart is stirred by a noble theme;
I address my poem to the king. Psalm 45:1

[1]   A festive song streams from my heart,
        Which to the King I dedicate
        My tongue shall take the pen's swift part
        His praises duly to relate.
        He is most glorious to behold
        His arm is powerful and bold.

[2]   The Queen stands ever by His side
        In splendid gold-brocaded gown;
        Demure young maidens with her stride
        Whom He has raised to high renown.
        A joyous chorus, sweet they sing,
        Entering the palace of the King.

                                        (ESD)

Vineyard of Carmel

        Come, Love, to the vineyard
        In the morning dew,
        There we'll watch in silence,
        If vineyards bloom anew,
        If the grapes are growing,
        Life with vigor glowing,
        Fresh the vine and true.

        From the heights of Heaven
        Holy Mother descend,
        Lead unto your vineyard
        Our beloved friend.
        Dew and rain let gently

Drop from His kind hand
And the balm of sunshine
Fall on Carmel's land.

Young vines, newly planted,
Tiny though they be,
Grant them life eternal
A gift of grace from Thee.
Trusted vintners strengthen
Their frail and feeble powers,
Shield them from the enemy
Who in darkness cowers.

Holy Mother grant reward
For your vintners' care
Give them, I beseech you,
Crown of Heaven fair.
Don't let raging fire
Kill these vines, we pray,
And grant your life eternal
To each young shoot some day.

(*SW*)

"I Shall Stay with You . . ."

Your throne is at the Lord's right hand,
Within the realm of His eternal glory,
God's word from when the world began.

You reign upon the highest throne of all,
Even in transfigured form,
Since You fulfilled Your task on earth.

So I believe, because Your word has taught me,
And, thus believing, know that this delights me,
And blessed hope blooms out of it.

For where You are, there also are Your dear ones.
And Heaven is my glorious fatherland,
With You I share the Father's throne.

The Eternal One, creator of all being,
Who, holy thrice, encompasses all life,
Retains a quiet realm all to Himself.

The inmost chamber of the human soul
Is favorite dwelling to the Trinity,
His heavenly throne right here on earth.

To free this heav'nly realm from hostile hand,
God's Son descended as the Son of Man.
He gave His blood as ransom.

Within the heart of Jesus pierced with lances,
The realms of Heaven and earth become united.
And here we find the spring of life itself.

This is the heart of Trinity divine,
The center also of all human hearts.
Source of our life from God.

It draws us close with its mysterious might,
It keeps us safe within the Father's lap
And floods us with the Holy Spirit.

This heart beats in a tiny tabernacle
Where it remains in hidden mystery,
Within that orbit, silent, white.

That is Your royal throne, O Lord, on earth,
Which You have built for us, plainly to see.
It pleases You when I draw near.

Your eyes look deeply into mine with love,
And to my whispered words You bend Your ear.
You fill my heart with deepest peace.

And yet Your love cannot be satisfied
By this exchange, for there remains a gap,
Your heart still asks for more.

Each morn You come to me at early Mass,
Your flesh and blood become my food and drink;
And wonders are accomplished.

Your body permeates mine mysteriously,
I feel Your soul becoming one with mine:
I am no longer what I used to be.

You come and go, but still the seed remains
Which You have sown for future splendor,
Hid in the body made from dust.

A heavenly radiance lingers in the soul,
And deeply shines a light within the eye,
A vibrant music in the voice.

The tie remains connecting heart to heart,
The stream of life which wells from You and gives
Life to each limb.

How wondrous are the marvels of Your love,
We are amazed, we stammer and grow dumb,
For word and spirit fail us.

(*SW*)

Edith Stein

For Rosa's Baptism

DECEMBER 24, 1936

My Lord, God,
You have led me by a long, dark path,
Rocky and hard.
Often my strength threatened to fail me.
I almost lost all hope of seeing the light.
But when my heart grew numb with deepest grief,
A clear star rose for me.
Steadfast it guided me—I followed,
At first reluctant, but more confidently later.

At last I stood at Church's gate.
It opened. I sought admission.
From Your priest's mouth Your blessing greets me.
Within me stars are strung like pearls.
Red blossom stars show me the path to You.
They wait for You at holy Night.
But Your goodness
Allows them to illuminate my path to You.
They lead me on.
The secret which I had to keep in hiding
Deep in my heart,
Now I can shout it out:
I believe—I profess!
The priest accompanies me to the altar:
I bend my face—
Holy water flows over my head,
Lord, is it possible that someone who is past
Midlife can be reborn?
You said so, and for me it was fulfilled,
A long life's burden of guilt and suffering

Fell away from me.
Erect I receive the white cloak,
Which they place round my shoulders,
Radiant image of purity!
In my hand I hold a candle.
Its flame makes known
That deep within me glows Your holy life.

My heart has become Your manger,
Awaiting You,
But not for long!
Maria, Your mother and also mine,
Has given me her name.
At midnight she will place her newborn child
Into my heart.

Ah, no one's heart can fathom,
What You've in store for those who love You.
Now You are mine, and I won't let You go.
Wherever my life's road may lead,
You are with me.
Nothing can ever part me from Your love.

(SW)

[1] God, hear me, I implore You,
     And listen to my prayer.
     You saw me stand before You
     In darkness and despair.
     O lift me, gracious Ruler,
     Upon a rocky peak.
     With hope I look to see You, God,
     Your guiding hand I seek.

[2] You are a sturdy tower
     Resisting every foe.

I fear no stormy weather,
With You I have no woe.
You'll offer me safekeeping
Within Your tent of love,
From danger I'm protected
By sheltering wings above.

[3]   My prayers You have heeded,
Your grace bestowed on me.
Who holds Your name in honor
Receives Your legacy.
So grant long life to those who
Devote themselves to You,
Year after year preserve them
And send Your blessings too.

[4]   Before the face of Heaven
Let them forever be!
For God's unending mercy
Lasts to eternity.
And so I'll sing a melody
Just as I promised You,
My praise a gift to You shall be
Day after day anew.

                                        (*SW*)

At the Helm

Fierce are the waves, Lord, rough the seas,
And dark, so dark the night.
I beg of You to grant me, please,
On lonely vigil, light.

Then steer your ship with steady arm,
Trust me and rest your soul.

Your little boat I'll keep from harm,
I'll guide it toward its goal.

Be firm of purpose as you keep
The compass e'er in view.
Through stormy night you'll cross the deep,
'Twill help you to steer true.

The needle trembles faintly, then
Holds steady and prevails,
It points your way and guides you when
I, God, direct your sails.

Be therefore steadfast, calm and true,
Your God is at your side.
Through storm and night He'll see you through
With conscience as your guide.

(SW)

[1]   **W**henever storms are roaring,
You, Lord, are our support.
We praise You, God, imploring,
You guide us safe to port.
Safe, secure we stand,
Trusting hold Your hand,
Mighty oceans break.

[2]   When swelling waters frighten
When solid mountains sway,
Joy comes to our life to lighten.
Our thanks to You, we say,
In Your city dwell,
Keep her safe and well.
A mighty river shelters
God's lofty citadel.

[3]   The nations rage in frenzy,
             The splendor of the proud
             Falls when God speaks with mighty voice
             No thunder is so loud.
             God is with us here.
             Lord of hosts, You're near,
             Our light and our salvation.
             Therefore we have no fear.

[4]   Come here, that you may see them,
             The wonders of His might
             Discord must surely vanish
             Where He brings peace and light.
             Spear and mighty shield
             To His light must yield
             The Lord God indeed
             Rescues all in need.

                                                              (SW)

                          To God, the Father

Bless the mind deeply troubled
Of the sufferers,
The heavy loneliness of profound souls,
The restlessness of human beings,
The sorrow which no soul ever confides
To a sister soul.

And bless the passage of moths at night,
Who do not shun spectres on paths unknown.
Bless the distress of men
Who die within the hour,
Grant them, loving God, a peaceful, blessed end.

Bless all the hearts, the clouded ones, Lord, above all,
Bring healing to the sick.
To those in torture, peace.
Teach those who had to carry their beloved to the
    grave, to forget.
Leave none in agony of guilt on all the earth.

Bless the joyous ones, O Lord, and keep them under
    Your Wing.—
My mourning clothes You never yet removed.
At times my tired shoulders bear a heavy burden.
But give me strength, and I'll bear it
In penitence to the grave.

Then bless my sleep, the sleep of all the dead.
Remember what Your Son suffered for me in agony
    of death.
Your great mercy for all human needs
Give rest to all the dead in Your eternal peace.

(SW)

Seven Beams from a Pentecost Novena

I

Who are You, sweet light that fills me
And illumines the darkness of my heart?
You guide me like a mother's hand,
And if You let me go, I could not take
Another step.
You are the space
That surrounds and contains my being.
Without You it would sink into the abyss
Of nothingness from which You raised it into being.

You, closer to me than I to myself,
More inward than my innermost being—
And yet unreachable, untouchable,
And bursting the confines of any name:
    Holy Spirit—
        Eternal love!

II

Are You not the sweet manna
Which flows from the heart of the Son
Into mine,
Food for angels and for the blessed?
He who from death to life arose,
Has awakened me, too, to new life,
From the sleep of death,
New life He gives me day by day.
Some day His abundance will completely flow
   through me,
Life of Your life—yes, You Yourself:
    Holy Spirit—
        Eternal life!

III

Are You the ray
That flashes from the Eternal Judge's throne
To pierce into the night of my soul,
Which never knew itself?
Merciful, yet unrelenting, it penetrates the hidden
   crevices.
The soul takes fright at sight of her own self,
Makes room for holy awe,

For the beginning of that wisdom
Descending from on high,
And anchoring us securely in the heights,—
For Your workings, which create us anew:
    Holy Spirit—
        All-penetrating ray!

IV

Are You the wealth of spirit and of power
By which the Lamb loosens the seals
From God's eternal decree?
Driven by You the messengers of judgment
Ride through the world
And with sharp sword divide
The reign of light from the reign of night.
Then the Heavens are renewed, and new the earth,
And through Your breath
Everything finds its rightful place:
    Holy Spirit—
        Conquering power!

V

Are You the master who builds the eternal dome
Rising from earth and through to very Heaven?
The columns, enlivened by You, rise high
And stand firm, immovable.
Marked with the eternal name of God,
They reach high up into the light,
Bearing the cupola, which crowns the holy dome,
Your work encompassing the universe,
    Holy Spirit—
        God's shaping hand.

VI

Are You the one who made the mirror bright,
Which stands beside the throne of the Almighty
Just like a sea of crystal
Wherein the Godhead views Himself with love?
You bend o'er the most marvelous of Your creations
And beaming shines Your splendor back to You.
The pure beauty of all beings
United in the lovely form of
The virgin, Your flawless bride:
     Holy Spirit—
       Creator of the World.

VII

Are You the sweet song of love, and of holy awe,
Resounding ever round God's throne triune,
Which unifies the pure tone of all beings,
Within itself?
The harmony which fits the limbs to the head,
So that each blissfully finds the secret meaning
Of His being,
And exudes it with gladness freely dissolved
In Your streams:
     Holy Spirit—
       Eternal jubilation.

                              (*SW*)

XXIII

Blessed Titus Brandsma

(1881–1942)

Blessed Titus was born in 1881 and baptized Anno Sjoerd, but he took his father's name on entering Carmel. He was from Frisia in the heart of the Netherlands. His family was "country aristocracy", and his roots can be traced to the 1400s. He had a Franciscan brother and three sisters who became religious. His family was truly Catholic and filled with zeal for the faith, even though they lived in a land where they were in the minority. The Catholic faith was prohibited there at that time. Blessed Titus was a journalist who used the media for good. He even went against the Nazis to proclaim the truth. He was a well-loved professor at Nijmegen. When he was teaching mysticism it was felt that he was speaking from the fruits of his own devout prayer life. For Blessed Titus, community life was very important, and he was present at all the exercises. He was very interested in the theology of the Cross. This seemed to prepare him for what would come. He even forgave his captors, following in the steps of Jesus. He was considered a most dangerous adversary to the Nazis and was imprisoned in several camps. He was martyred at Dachau by injection of carbolic acid on July 6, 1942.

Canonization picture of Blessed Titus Brandsma

PRAYERS

Before a Picture of Jesus in My Cell

A new awareness of Thy love
Encompasses my heart:
Sweet Jesus, I in Thee and Thou
In me shall never part.

No grief shall fall my way but I
Shall see Thy grief-filled eyes;
The lonely way that Thou once walked
Has made me sorrow-wise.

All trouble is a white-lit joy
That lights my darkest day;
Thy love has turned to brightest light
This night-like way.
If I have Thee alone,
The hours will bless
With still, cold hands of love
My utter loneliness.
Stay with me, Jesus, only stay;
I shall not fear—
If, reaching out my hand,
I feel Thee near.

(CP)

Dear Lord, when looking up to Thee,
I see Thy loving eyes on me;
Love overflows my humble heart,
Knowing what a faithful friend Thou art.

A cup of sorrow I foresee,
Which I accept for love of Thee,
Thy painful way I wish to go;
The only way to God I know.

My soul is full of peace and light;
Although in pain, this light shines bright.
For here Thou keepest to Thy breast
My longing heart to find there rest.

Leave me here freely all alone,
In cell where never sunlight shone.
Should no one ever speak to me,
This golden silence makes me free!

For though alone, I have no fear;
Never wert Thou, O Lord, so near.
Sweet Jesus, please, abide with me!
My deepest peace I find in Thee.

(PLC)

THE STATIONS OF THE CROSS

First Station: Jesus is condemned and taken away

O God, it is thus that I must contemplate You. What has happened during this night; what have You done to Your people that they mistreat You in this way? Not only mistreated, but betrayed to be crucified. Certainly, You did foretell that during the night the shepherd would be struck and the sheep would be scattered. I can still hear Your warning: "Watch and pray that you not fall into temptation."

But I've already fallen asleep. At that moment You became unrecognizable for me. I feel icy cold as I ask myself whether, for You, O Christ, this Passion was a duty or a free choice. Besides, You pronounced the words: "During this night all of you will be scandalized in me." Unfortunately it's true, all of us are scandalized in You; we don't even have the courage to contemplate the Passion. And we caused it! While You cry out: "Look and see if there is a sorrow equal to mine," we think we are not capable of looking at it. Our soul rebels when it sees You unclothed, beaten and bruised, broken into bits to the extent that there is nothing in Your body that might be called "healthy."

As on a threshing-floor the flail of sin winnowed out the Sacred Wheat, and broke the straw. Your Blood flowed in torrents and is still issuing from Your wounds. We've not yet reached the last drop. Your body already reveals the pallor of death, but in Your eyes I still note the ardor of the flame of love, which burns like a fever and which consumes You until all is fulfilled. On this night, that gaze led Peter to repentance. I read there a silent reproof, insofar as I do not wish to recognize You. . . . Your powerlessness irritates me; I am ashamed of Your humiliation. You willed that they treat You like the worst of criminals, while I would like to see You like a king, who triumphantly places the cross on Calvary.

O God, free me from my scandal. I know, Your answer is, "Watch and pray." While the two executioners drag You away in a rough, unfeeling way, in order to crucify You, I again hear: "Watch and pray that you not fall into temptation." God, I will pray. I wish to see Your Passion, I wish to study the depths of Your love, as I gaze at the depths of Your humiliation.

Second Station: Jesus takes up His cross

My God, that heavy cross, to which they wish to nail You, You have to carry it? My God, You cannot. You've already suffered too much. The terrible loss of blood has already drained You of Your remaining strength. Still, Your executioners believe that You will succeed and will reach the top still alive. Still, it will be terrifying. That cross which You embrace will later bear Your tormented body, pinned there by nails. Just the thought of it should make You tremble before that cross, and even if Your strength allowed You to do so, that thought would prevent You from carrying it to Calvary. Couldn't they grant You a moment of rest before they started on a new series of tortures? Wouldn't they spare You at least the cruel torture of carrying it alone to the spot of execution? You, who already are drained of strength to make Your way even without the cross! Sin knows no rest. Desire of sin is never satisfied. Without pause the force of the executioner pushes the victim on. Like a lamb You let Yourself be led to slaughter. No complaint is heard on Your lips.

No, while Your body gives in and is not equal to the heavy load of the cross, Your eyes shine with a holy flame, as they gaze on the throne of the King, which is not of this world and from which they wish to remove You with four clumsy nails. For an instant it seems that You regain Your strength, as You embrace the tree of the cross. They thought they would have to force You, yet You carry the weight until the bitter end, even though it becomes even heavier because of our sins, which we do not wish to bear. There is no one to help You. Your eyes look for someone disposed to carry the cross, but there is no one. The winepress which squeezes out the last drop of blood from Your body, You must leave it to do its job. O cross, O sacred wood, in the hands of my God; certainly it is heavy, but carried by Him with His last remaining strength, I would like to take it on myself now that I see that my Jesus goes before me and thus makes it easy on my shoulders. O God, I will not only *follow* the Way of the Cross. I take up the cross with You, my cross which You pass on to me. Bearing my cross I shall accompany You to the holy mount.

Third Station: Jesus falls the first time

The Omnipotent in a state of powerlessness. Our strong God is not up to what is asked of Him, He is not up to His confrontation with His executioners. He has run out of strength. My Savior continues, wavering, and suddenly He stumbles and falls. Look at You, O God. Couldn't they crucify You here? Their aim is Your death. They don't see that You cannot continue. You must continue, this is the will of Your executioners, for whom Your powerlessness represents a new irritation. For them Your strength has not run out. They leave You alone for an instant, then they have You lifted up and prod You on to continue. They think they can stimulate Your remaining strength by kicking and beating You. They do not realize that You wish to carry the cross with a ready heart and that You wish to show us that this demanded Your remaining strength. O holy Exemplar, I now see that when we sink beneath the cross and can go no farther, our powerlessness finds comfort in Your fall. Our cross, when compared to Yours, is light, so long as we are not threatened with sinking beneath it. Knowing, O my God, that my sins made Your Cross so heavy that You had to sink beneath it, this makes me even more convinced that I must carry my cross together with You and that I should not shy away from it, even if I should sink beneath its weight. In Your weakness You overcame the world. Let me be weak with You and be bent low beneath the weight of life. Let me appear insignificant and trifling in the eyes of the world, as I get up with You, ready to take on new sufferings, until death represents the crown of my sacrifice.

Allow me to fix my gaze on You, as You fall under the cross like a worm on which one tramples, while You accept kicks and blows from those to whom You wish to give a blessing. Don't let me always think of You as strong and mighty, carrying the trunk of the cross with pride, head held high. Christ who was bent over, who had to fall, who had to sink beneath the cross, thus entering His glory. His sacred humanity had to be destroyed. So cruelly was He mistreated that no human form would be left. Here already we see that His strength has abandoned Him. My God, let me often reflect on Your humiliation at the hands of Your heartless executioners, and through that let me learn to suffer, so that people don't think me capable of doing what I wish to do.

(CIW, 1985)

Seventh Station: Jesus falls under His cross the second time
(composed in the prison of Scheveningen)

O Jesus, You did not think it enough to succumb under Your cross just once, so that Your enemies could gloat over Your powerlessness. Once again, while You are being helped to carry the cross, we see You collapse to show us that, notwithstanding the assistance, the burden on Your shoulders was still so heavy, that You allowed it to overcome You.

O Mary, what grief about the insufficient help given to Your dear Son; you must have looked around if someone would not completely take the heavy load off His shoulders, and you must have begged Simon to take over the full load of the cross.

O St. Boniface, the example of Jesus who fell under His cross for the second time must have strengthened you anew in moments when you shrank away from the suffering inflicted upon you. May that example constantly encourage us also in moments of weakness and flight from suffering.

O Jesus, gentle, etc.

Eighth Station: Jesus consoles the weeping women

O Jesus, You spoke to the women who sympathized with You along Your way of the cross and through them You told me too: "Do not weep for Me, but for your selves and your children, for if the green wood is treated thus, what then is to happen to the dead wood?" I remember Your other words: "Not they who cry Lord, Lord, will enter into the Kingdom of Heaven, but whoever does the will of My Father, who is in heaven." It is not enough, that I show pity with Your holy suffering, but I must shape my will along Yours and with a generous heart accept out of Your hand the grief and trials You send me and bear them united with You. You are the vine, we are the branches which, if they don't remain joined to You, wither and are thrown away.

O Mary, you did not only show compassion but you went the way of the cross with your Son; take me along with you.

St. Boniface, you stopped along the way of the cross, but united with your Savior and Model, you accepted from His hand suffering and death. Make me strong by your example.

O Jesus, gentle, etc.

Ninth Station: Jesus falls the third time under the cross

O Jesus, You wanted to expiate the threefold denial of Your apostle who considered himself so strong and our repeated falling into sin by Your threefold fall under the cross, and You wished to show us that You expended Your last energies in order to reach the top of the hill of suffering. You teach us in the cross and suffering which You send us, to use all our strength in order to carry out the task laid upon our shoulders by Your Providence and to look to Your falls under the cross, when we lose heart and feel weak, for the strength that we need.

O Mary, you witnessed your Son's final exertion of His energy with admiration and motherly compassion; help me to remember this with you when the carrying out of my task becomes too heavy for me.

O St. Boniface, in the threefold fall of your divine Model lay for you the strength to remain steadfast until the end, to overcome all fear and hesitation before death and to meet your attackers. May your example help us accept and carry out our task in life as steadfastly.

O Jesus, gentle, etc.

*Tenth Station: Jesus is stripped of His garments and
given gall and vinegar to drink*

O Jesus, You wanted to drink the cup of suffering to the bottom by allowing Yourself to be nailed to the hard wood of the cross naked and unshielded and by refusing the narcotic drink they tried to give You to ease Your pains.

O Mary, your heart must have been filled with new power of compassion when you saw your Son, stripped of all that covered Him, refuse the drink which was meant to ease His sensitivity for the pain and His example fortified you to be strong with Him in His trials.

O St. Boniface, the example of your Jesus, stripped and refusing any alleviation, must have strengthened you to willingly have everything taken away from you and, proudly and without fear to meet your enemies with no other cover than the Holy Bible, which even at that was pierced by their swords. Teach me to be courageous in accepting all suffering sent to me by God.

O Jesus, gentle, etc.

Eleventh Station: Jesus is nailed to the cross

O Jesus, how terrible it must have been for You to be nailed to the two cross bars by coarse nails and hanging from those wounds, to die slowly from pain and exhaustion.

O Mary, the sword of sorrows foretold by Simeon must have pierced your heart especially when you heard the cruel hammer blows with which the executioners pierced the hands and feet of your divine Son and nailed Him to the cross.

O St. Boniface, you must, from the memory of the crucifixion of your divine Example, have drawn the strength to persevere, with courage and readiness for sacrifice, when the Frisian pagans pierced your companions with swords and spears and finally drove their weapons also into your body, mortally wounding you. Obtain for me that I receive and bear the trials God sends me with equal courage and readiness for sacrifice.

O Jesus, gentle etc.

Twelfth Station: Jesus dies on the cross

O Jesus, it is for us an incomprehensible mystery how You finally did want to die for us, did wish to enter the realm of death as if Your whole mission had failed, as if all Your life had been useless: an apparent victory for Your enemies.

O Mary, it must have been terrible for you to see this end to your divine Son's mission, to see Him die before Your eyes the most cruel and shameful death, even though your faith told you that precisely thus, He wanted to return life to us.

O St. Boniface, your death resembled that of your divine Model; your third and last effort to convert Frisia and bring her to God seemed to have failed when they made you and your companions undergo the cruelest death and destroyed all your work. Teach us to mirror ourselves with you in our divine Model, mindful how only suffering leads to victory.

O Jesus, gentle, etc.

Thirteenth Station: The Body of Jesus is laid
in the lap of His mother

O Jesus, what an example You gave Your holy mother after Your death by allowing Your dead body to be laid in her lap. It did increase her sorrows and caused her even more intensely to identify with your pains and suffering but at the same time You must have filled her with Your strength in order, in this way, to crown her as Queen of Martyrs.

O Mary, Mother of Sorrows, the Church, when contemplating you with Jesus' Body in your lap, puts these words in your mouth: *"O you, who pass by here, see if there is any sorrow like unto mine?"* Teach me to contemplate with you the Body of your divine Son in order to bear all suffering with you.

O St. Boniface, how often you must have contemplated with Mary the wounds of your dead Savior and during the sacrifice of the Mass have pondered the memory of Jesus' death on the cross, in order to be strong in suffering and in death.

O Jesus, gentle, etc.

Fourteenth Station: Jesus is laid in a new sepulchre
(Left unfinished; he was writing in prison, and he was taken
to be executed before finishing)

O Jesus, when I look on You,
My love for You starts up anew,
And tells me that Your heart loves me,
And You my special Friend would be.

More courage I will need for sure,
But any pain I will endure,
Because it makes me like to You
And leads unto Your kingdom too.

In sorrow I do find my bliss,
For sorrow now no more is this:
Rather the path that must be trod,
That makes me one with You, my God.

Oh, leave me here alone and still,
And all around, the cold and chill,
To enter here I will have none;
I weary not when I'm alone,

For, Jesus, You are at my side;
Never so close did we abide.
Stay with me, Jesus, my delight,
Your presence near makes all things right.

(*CIW*, 1986)

XXIV

Servant of God Père Jacques de Jésus Bunel

(1900–1945)

On January 20, 1900, Lucien Bunel was born into a working-class French family at Barentin. He had a normal childhood, with five brothers and a sister to share laughter and chores. Lucien was an excellent student and was esteemed by all. He is described as gentle, fun-loving, and generous.

In 1912 Lucien entered the junior seminary at Rouen. His studies were interrupted by military service, but he was ordained in 1925. He was a teacher, a headmaster, spiritual director to scout troops, and an outstanding preacher, and he was invited on many occasions to speak at solemn events.

Father Lucien had a serious bout with typhoid fever, and during that time realized he needed to address a burning desire for the monastic life. At first he wanted to be a Trappist, but he had read many Carmelite works and met Carmelite nuns who influenced his thinking. In July 1927 Lucien received his call to Carmel in the parlor conversing with a Carmelite nun. Later he met Father Marie-Eugène, heard him speak of the Carmelite ideal, and knew that was what he desired. He was forced to wait two years after this to enter Carmel, since his archbishop refused to release him. Finally he entered in August 1931. It was all he had hoped to find: peace, solitude, and prayer. Upon reception of his habit he was given the name Père Jacques of Jésus. His prior declared that "his holiness overflows the cloister." In September 1932 he made his profession of temporary vows. Soon after he was sent to Avon to be the founder of the junior seminary (Petit College) and its headmaster.

The following summer he returned to his former Carmel and prepared to take his final vows the next year. Back at Petit College he resumed his busy schedule, finding brief interludes in which to escape to the woods for his much loved and needed contemplation. The school became famous for its excellent faculty and deep concern for the dignity of each student.

In 1938, however, Master Sgt. Bunel was drafted for service following the Czech crisis. Again he ministered to the troops and made lasting friendships. Once more he returned to Avon with the threat of war looming over his head. As a result Père Jacques returned to service. In the defeat of the French army he became a prisoner of war of the Germans for five months. Here his spirituality deepened, and he was able to exercise his priestly duties as chaplain. When released he found that the school at Avon had been used as a German military barracks and had to be restored. There he served again until his arrest for being an active member of the Resistance and for harboring Jews at the school.

He was held in four prisons, and wherever he went he brought hope and God's love. He said Mass surreptitiously and administered the sacraments. He gave away any extra food given him, and even gave away the meager amount allotted to him. This caused his health to fail, but he carried on. When the French were liberated, he would have been given food and received care first, but he chose to wait until others were aided. The war had taken its toll on Père Jacques, and he died very peacefully June 2, 1945. He is buried in a Carmelite cemetery at Avon.

PRAYERS

In the name of the Father and of the Son and of the Holy Spirit, in the presence of the Most Holy Virgin Mary, of Saint Joseph, the angels, and of all the saints, particularly of my patron saints, Louis, Lucien, Steven, Bernard, and Benoit, I the undersigned, Lucien-Louis Bunel, give myself today, joyously and irrevocably, to the Most Holy and Most August Trinity through the intercession of our Lord Jesus Christ.

Fully conscious of what I am doing, and after having thoroughly examined the obligations that may result from making this act, I consecrate myself for eternity in the service of the good God. I give Him my body with all my strength, without the least reservation of myself. I give Him my soul with all its power and faculties. In a word I give my entire being, desiring only one thing: that my life may be from now on incense perpetually rising toward God in order to please Him.

But I am fully conscious also of my weakness. Alone, I am able only to sin. I await, therefore, the mercy of the good God. I give myself to Him, that He Himself may work in me and transform me as He wills and carry me in His thought until eternity.

O my God, these are the darts of flame that are necessary to translate on this paper the fire of my sentiments. You see and You know with what ardor I desire You, with what passion I aspire to possess You, to know You, to embrace You! O my God, You Yourself act in me, consume me in Your infinite love, captivating me and absorbing me in You.

May this blessed day of Saturday, July 12, 1924, be truly a step in my life of union with You!

Lucien Bunel

—Prayer before diaconate ordination.
Major Seminary of Rouen, July 11, 1924.
(Supplied by the Vice Postulator for the cause
of Père Jacques at Avon and by Philippe Hugelé.)

O my Christ,
Communion,
is the mystery of Your love,
is life for souls,
is the sure salvation for those who
understand and receive It.
Therefore place in my mind
Fervent and clear thoughts,
put on my lips ardent and enlightening words,
that I may illumine all these souls,
That I may enkindle in them
Love for Your divine Sacrament;
And that in them, Your work
Of transformation may be fulfilled.

—Abbé Lucien Bunel, 1929, Eucharistic Congress of Havre.
(Supplied by Sister Christiane, O.C.D.,
archivist at the Carmel of Luxembourg.)

I thank Thee, O my God, for all the graces Thou hast granted me. . . . Especially for having tried me in the crucible of suffering. . . .

I do not wish to store up merits for heaven, I want to work for Thy Love alone, with the single goal of pleasing Thee, of bringing consolation to Thy Sacred Heart and of saving souls whom Thou wilt love eternally.   (PJ)

In the twilight of this life, I shall appear before Thee with empty hands, for I do not ask Thee, Lord, to compare my works. All our justices are tainted in Thine eyes. Hence I wish to wear the cloak of Thy justice and receive from Thy love eternal possession of Thyself. I wish no other crown or throne but Thee, my Beloved. (PJ)

Thou canst in an instant prepare me to appear before Thee. (PJ)

May this martyrdom, after having prepared me to appear before Thee, at last let me die and may my soul, without delay, soar to the eternal embrace of Thy merciful love. . . .

I wish, O my Beloved, with each beat of my heart to renew this offering an infinite number of times. . . .

Until the shadows have vanished. . . .

May I declare my love over and over, face to face, eternally. (PJ)

Canonization picture of Saint Teresa of Jesus of the Andes

XXV

Saint Teresa of Jesus of the Andes

(1900–1920)

Juana Enriqueta Josafina de los Sacrados Corazones was born in Santiago, Chile, July 13, 1900. Her parents were wealthy and aristocratic and had six children. Juana was the fourth and was affectionately called Juanita by her family. From the age of five, Juana never tired of listening to people talk about God or other religious subjects. She loved and excelled in horseback riding and was a real beauty. This led to vanity, which she worked very hard to overcome, along with other faults. From the time she was six she attended daily Mass and said that "Jesus took her heart to be His own." She yearned to receive Holy Communion, but was restricted because of her age. This was a time of purification for her. The night before her First Communion she went to the members of her family and begged forgiveness for any time she might have hurt them. She says that her First Communion was "truly a fusion between Jesus and her soul". This was at the age of ten. Each time she received Communion Juana records that "Jesus spoke with her for a long time." She had a deep devotion to the Blessed Mother and daily prayed the Rosary. Juana kept an intimate diary from the age of fifteen until she died. She suffered frequent and serious illnesses, but joyfully lived her faith even more seriously. Her diary reveals that Juanita saw her life as composed of suffering and love. Her scholastic achievements were very notable, but she was most proud of being a "Child of Mary". This gifted one was also a musician, playing the piano and the harmonium and singing beautifully. She made a vow of virginity at the age of fifteen and determined to enter Carmel. She loved parties and dancing, but she also had the desire to care for the poor. She prepared for her entrance to Carmel by corresponding with the prioress, opening her soul for guidance. The big day arrived on May 7, 1919, at Los Andes. She wrote to her family eight days later, "It is eight days since I have been in Carmel, eight days of heaven." This heaven was marked with serious illness, and during Holy Week of 1920 it reached its peak. Juanita, now Sister Teresa of Jesus, had contracted typhus. After receiving the last sacraments, she was permitted to make her religious vows in the Carmelite Order. On April 12, 1920, she went to sleep in the arms of her Lord. She had recorded earlier, "To die is to be eternally immersed in Love."

PRAYERS

My Jesus, pardon me. I am so proud that I do not know how to accept with humility the slightest humiliation. Dear Jesus, teach me humility and send me humiliations, even though I am unworthy of them. Dear Jesus, I want to be poor, humble, obedient, pure, as was my Mother and like You, Jesus. Make Your little house a palace, a heaven. I long to live adoring You as the angels do. I feel my nothingness in Your presence. I am so imperfect. I want to be poor as You were, and, since I cannot be this, I ask not to love riches in any way. (GJ)

Dear Jesus, may Your will be done and not mine. Tomorrow I will go to Communion. I obtained permission. Oh, what happiness: tomorrow I will have Heaven in my heart! Oh, I love You, Jesus. I adore You! I thank You and my Mother for this favor. I am all Yours . . . only You . . . no other creature.   (GJ)

My Jesus, You are my Life. Without You I will die; without You I languish.   (GJ)

Each day I feel worse. I have no courage for anything; but finally, it is the will of God. May this be done as He desires. My Mother, I place all this in your hands. Why have you abandoned me? Bring it about that I know my lessons very well and my compositions. My Mother, may I do "very well" in my compositions. Show that you are my Mother and give me everything, but above all humility. Dear Jesus, give me sufferings. Suffering is no bother because thus You love me.
                                                                    (GJ)

I am dying, I feel I am dying. My Jesus, I give myself to You. I offer You my life for my sins and for sinners. My Mother, offer me as a victim. Truly, yesterday I could not stand the pain in my chest. I was choking. I couldn't breathe and the pain was causing me fatigue. I offer all this to Jesus for my sins and for sinners.   (GJ)

Tomorrow I will go to Communion. How I long for this, my Jesus. I am so bad. I need You to be good. Come, Love, come quickly and I will give You my heart, my soul and all I possess. My Mother, prepare my heart to receive my Jesus.
                                                                    (GJ)

Juana Enriqueta Josafina de los Sacrados Corazones

My Jesus, I love You. I am totally Yours. I give myself completely to Your divine will. Jesus, give me the cross, but give me the strength to carry it. It matters not whether You give me the abandonment of Calvary or the joys of Nazareth. I only want to see You contented. It doesn't bother me to be unable to feel, to be insensible as a rock, because I know, my sweet Jesus, that You know I love You. Give me the cross. I want to suffer for You; but teach me to suffer by loving, with joy and with humility.

Lord, if it please You that the darkness of my soul become deeper, that I not see You, it will not bother me because I want to fulfill Your will. I want to spend my life suffering to make reparation for my sins and those of sinners and so priests will be sanctified. I do not want to be happy, but for You to be happy. I want to be like a soldier so that at every moment You can dispose of my will and preferences. I want to be courageous, strong and generous in serving You, Lord. You are the Spouse of my soul. *(GJ)*

Dear Jesus, what do You say about this soldier who is so cowardly and imperfect? Pardon me. The next time I will be better. I will throw myself into that immense ocean of the love of Your Heart, to lose myself in It like a drop of water in the ocean and to abase my littleness in the greatness of Your mercy. I notice that I am more proud, but, thanks be to God who has illumined me with His grace, from today on I want to be humble. I want to forget myself entirely. *(GJ)*

O my dear Jesus! I believe he (her father) is not going to want to let me go. I see so much hostility against the Carmelite nuns. My Jesus, I trust in You. You are all-powerful. Come steal me away and do it quickly, very quickly and forever. *(GJ)*

Jesus, I thank You for the cross. Make my cross heavier, but give me strength and love. Jesus I know that I am unworthy to suffer with You. Pardon my lack of gratitude. Have pity on sinners. Sanctify priests.   (GJ)

I live in a state of confusion. I have a constant headache that makes me see everything in different colors. My God, Thy Will be done and not mine. I offer You my sufferings for my sins, for sinners and for the sanctification of priests.   (GJ)

My dear Jesus, every time I feel bad, I feel homesick for You and for that Heaven in which I will never more offend You, where I will be inebriated with Your love, Jesus, where I will be one with You, since I must have my being in You and move in You.   (GJ)

O Jesus, when will I be able to live in You! May Your will be accomplished and not mine!   (GJ)

My Mother, I know you are my mother. Remember that I gave myself to you in your Immaculate heart, keep me pure, a virgin. May it be my refuge, my hope, my consolation, my solitude. I place myself in your maternal arms, so you may put me in the arms of Jesus. I abandon myself to Him. May His holy will be done.

Thank you, my Mother. For having freed me from all dangers and for having made me spend my vacation well. Thanks, my Mother. My Mother, I would tell you many things. But my language is so poor that it trembles in just telling you that I love you. My Mother, at your virginal feet I would love to sing your praises, but my voice is so weak that

I can only formulate a prayer. I have pain because, despite having asked and at the same time having mortified myself, I have not obtained my request that my father, Miguel and Luis make a retreat. But may God's will be done. (GJ)

Lord, I only ask that You grant me suffering. It will bring me to You. (GJ)

My Jesus, have pity on me. You know that I love You. My Mother, help me in darkness. . . . Nothingness. Jesus is not in my soul. The Virgin does not answer me. Jesus, have pity on Your unfaithful spouse. Yes, I love You. Do not abandon me. Oh, thanks! With Your word, Jesus, You can completely dissipate the storm. (GJ)

Why, my Jesus, are You placing this coldness around my poor heart? Ah! It is because You love me. You want to encircle me only with Your love so I will not be attached to any creature. This helps me see that love does not exist on earth, but only in God; because if favored, chosen and holy souls forget or are indifferent, what will other people be like? You, Jesus, are the only One capable of inspiring me to fall in love. My Jesus, be the Jesus of Bethany for me. (GJ)

Who are You, my God, and who am I? I am a creature formed by Your hands, a creature taken from nothingness, formed from clay, but with a soul that is like unto God, a soul that is intelligent and free, destined to give You the glory of the invisible world. My God, we are so miserable that we rebel against You, our Creator. Pardon me! For instead of loving You, we offend You. There is only one commandment

You have imposed on us and we do not fulfill that one. What does it profit us to gain the whole world if we lose our soul? What do riches, honors, glory, human affections matter, for they pass away and end? How do they compare with my soul, which is immortal and has been made worthy by the Blood of Jesus Christ, my God? How precious must a soul be since the devil will be watching out to destroy it. Either I am going to save my soul or I am going to condemn it forever. That is why I am resolved to save it.   (GJ)

Oh, what horror, my God! (I would) rather die a thousand times than offend You even slightly, since You are my Father, my Friend, my adored Spouse. You frequently punished Sarah, Moses, David, etc., for one venial sin, and yet You are not punishing me for having offended You thousands of times. Grant me pardon!   (GJ)

Oh, my Jesus and my Mother, may I belong to Him forever. May nothing on earth claim my attention but the tabernacle. Preserve me pure for Yourself so that when I die I can say: how happy I am now that at last I can lose myself in the infinite Ocean of the Heart of Jesus, my adored Spouse.

(GJ)

There are three things we will be judged on: Your blessings to us, our sins and our deeds, according to what our intention was. Oh, my God, I am not a saint even though You filled me with blessings! Pardon me so I may be a saint from now on. My Mother, make me become a saint!   (GJ)

My Jesus, there is something here that moved me so much:

Your love, O Jesus, for so ungrateful a creature. I prostrate myself at your feet, and then, filled with confusion, I beg pardon. Yes, my Jesus. From now on I want to live always by Your side. O love, consume this miserable creature!   (GJ)

My Jesus, I annihilate myself before Your love! You, God of Heaven and earth, of the seas, of the mountains, of the star-studded firmament; You, Lord, who are adored by the angels, in an ecstasy of love; You, Jesus, in Your humanity; You, the living bread! Oh, to be annihilated, all this would be so little! If they had a relic of You it would be a token of love worthy of our veneration; but You Yourself remain, knowing that You would be the object of profanations, sacrileges, ungratefulness, abandonment. Lord, are You mad with love? You are not in one place on earth for us but in all the tabernacles throughout the world. Oh, Lord, how good You are, how great is Your love that You make it appear to be nothing. What is more, You disappear by letting them see a creature, a criminal nothingness.   (GJ)

Jesus, I am happy because I suffer. I desire to suffer more, but I do not ask You for any other thing than that Your divine will be accomplished in me.   (GJ)

Today I felt annihilated, but I held my crucifix tightly and I only told Him: "I love You."   (GJ)

I offered myself as victim so that He would manifest His infinite love to souls.   (GJ)

You who created me, save me. Since I am unworthy to pronounce Your most sweet name, because it would bring me consolation, I dare, being annihilated, to implore Your infinite mercy. Yes; I am ungrateful. I acknowledge this. I am a rebellious bit of dust. I am a criminal nothingness. But are You not the Good Shepherd? Are You not the One who came in search of the Samaritan woman to give her eternal life? Are You not the One who defended the adulterous woman and the One who wiped away the tears of Mary the sinner? It is true that they knew how to respond to Your tender looks. They recognized Your words of life. And I— how many times have I not felt Your Heart beating within my own by listening to Your melodious accent!—yet still I do not love You. But pardon me. Remember that I am still a criminal nothingness, that I am only capable of sin. Oh, my adored Jesus, by Your divine Heart, forget my ungratefulness and take me entirely to Yourself. Free me from all that is happening around me. May I live by always contemplating You. May I live submerged in Your love, so it will consume my miserable being and transform me into You.   (GJ)

BIBLIOGRAPHY

Bardi, Joseph. *Sister Theresa Margaret*. Derby, N.Y.: Daughters of Saint Paul, 1939.

Batzdorff, Susanne. *An Edith Stein Daybook*. Springfield, Ill.: Templegate Publishers, 1994.

————. *Aunt Edith. The Jewish Heritage of a Catholic Saint*. Springfield, Ill.: Templegate Publishers, 1998.

Benedictine of Stanbrook. *Just for Today*. Springfield, Ill.: Templegate Publishers. 1988.

Brunot, Amedee, S.C.J. *Mariam the Little Arab: Sr. Mary of Jesus Crucified*. Eugene, Ore.: Carmel of Maria Regina, 1984.

Bush, William. *To Quell the Terror*. Washington, D.C.: ICS Publications, 1999.

Buzy, D., S.C.I. *The Thoughts of Sister Mary of Jesus Crucified*. Jerusalem, 1974.

Carmel of Flemington. *God Alone and I*. Flemington, N.J.: Carmel of Flemington, 1965.

Carmelite Missionaries. *The Solitary Life: Fr. Francisco Palau y Quer*. Rome: Carmelite Missionaries, 1988.

————. *Francisco Palau*. Rome: Carmelite Missionaries, General House, 1988.

Carmelite Nuns of Salford, England. *Del Carmela al Calvario: The Three Martyred Carmelites of Guadalahara*. Rome, General Postulation, O.C.D., 1986.

Carrouges, Michel. *Père Jacques*. New York: McMillan, 1961.

De Beaurepaire de Louvagny, La Comtesse D. *Saint Albert de Messine de l'Ordre des Carmes*. Paris: Ancienne Maison Ch. Douniol, 1895.

Discalced Carmelite Nuns of Milwaukee. *Carmelite Devotions*. Milwaukee, Wis.: Carmelite Nuns, 1956.

Doran, Hilary, O.C.D. *Living in Christ Jesus: Blessed Mary of Jesus Crucified, O.C.D.* Darlington, Eng.: Carmel of Darlington.

Elizabeth of the Trinity. *Complete Works of Elizabeth of the Trinity.* Edited by Conrad de Meester, O.C.D. Vol. 1. Translated by Sr. Aletheia Kane, O.C.D. Washington, D.C.: ICS Publications, 1984. Vol. 2. Translated by Anne Englund Nash. Washington, D.C.: ICS Publications, 1995.

———. *Light, Love, Life.* Edited by Conrad de Meester, O.C.D. Washington, D.C.: ICS Publications, 1987.

———. *Reflections.* Darlington, Eng.: Carmel of Darlington.

Evaristo, Carlos. "Nuno Alvarez Pereira: The Saint for Our Time". *Carmel in the World* 36, no. 3 (1998).

Gabriel of St. Mary Magdalen, O.C.D. *Divine Intimacy*. 4 vols. San Francisco: Ignatius Press, 1987.

———. *From the Sacred Heart to the Trinity.* Kansas City, Mo.: Chapel of St. Theresa Margaret Discalced Carmelite Nuns, 1965.

Gil, Czeslaus, O.C.D. *Father Raphael Kalinowski.* Krakow: Karmel/TowBosych, 1978.

Giordano, Silvano, O.C.D. *Carmel in the Holy Land.* Arenzano, Italy: Messagero di Jesus Bambino di Praga, 1995.

Gonzalez, Marcelo, D.D. *The Power of the Priesthood.* San Antonio, Texas: Society of St. Teresa of Jesus, 1971.

Griffin, Michael, O.C.D. *God the Joy of My Life: Blessed Teresa of the Andes.* Washington, D.C.: Teresian Charism Press, 1989.

———. *Letters of Saint Teresa of Jesus of the Andes.* Hubertus, Wisc.: Teresian Charism Press, 1994.

Institutum Carmelitanum. *Proper of the Liturgy of the Hours.* Rome: Carmelite Institute, International Center, 1993.

John of the Cross. *The Collected Works of St. John of the Cross.* Translated by Otilio Rodriguez, O.C.D., and Kieran Kavanaugh, O.C.D. Washington, D.C.: ICS Publications, 1979.

La Vierge, Victor de, O.C.D. *The Spiritual Realism of St. Thérèse of Lisieux.* Milwaukee, Wis.: Bruce Publishing Company, 1961.

Lawrence, Brother. *The Practice of the Presence of God with Spiritual Maxims.* Westwood, N.J.: Fleming Revell Company, 1967.

Mary Magdalen de' Pazzi. *The Complete Works of Saint Mary Magdalen de' Pazzi.* Translated by Gabriel Pausback, O.Carm. Darien, Ill.: Carmelite Province of the Most Pure Heart of Mary, 1969–1975.

Member of the Order of Mercy, A. *A Year with the Saints.* Rockford, Ill.: Tan Books and Publishers, 1988.

Minima, Mary, O.Carm. *Seraph among Angels.* N.p.: Carmelite Press, 1958.

Murphy, Francis. *Père Jacques: Resplendent in Victory.* Washington, D.C.: ICS Publications, 1998.

O'Donnell, Christopher. *Love in the Heart of the Church.* Dublin: Veritas, 1997.

Office Central de Lisieux. *The Photo Album of St. Thérèse of Lisieux.* Commentary by François de Sainte-Marie, O.C.D. Translated by Peter-Thomas Rohrbach, O.C.D. Allen, Texas: Christian Classics, 1995.

Praskiewicz, Szczepan, O.C.D. *Saint Raphael Kalinowski: An Introduction to His Life and Spirituality.* Washington, D.C.: ICS Publications, 1998.

Rodriguez, Gloria, S.T.J., and Silvia Casado, S.T.J. *Experiencia espiritual de Enrique de Osso.* Barcelona: Ediciones STJ, 1995.

Sciadini, Patricio, O.C.D. *Francisco Palau Profeta Da Esperanca.* São Paulo: Edicoes Loyola, 1990.

Teresa Benedicta of the Cross. *Edith Stein: Selected Writings.* Edited by Susanne Batzdorff. Springfield, Ill.: Templegate Publishers, 1990.

──────. *Reflections.* Darlington, Eng.: Carmel of Darlington, Eng.

Teresa Margaret, D.C. *God Is Love: St. Teresa Margaret—Her Life.* Milwaukee, Wis.: Spiritual Life Press, 1964.

Teresa of Jesus. *The Collected Works of St. Teresa of Avila.* Translated by Otilio Rodriguez, O.C.D., and Kieran Kavanaugh, O.C.D. 3 vols. Washington, D.D.: ICS Publications, 1976–1985.

Thérèse of Lisieux. *General Correspondence.* Translated by Donald Kinney, O.C.D. Washington, D.C.: ICS Publications, 1996.

──────. *Her Last Conversations.* Translated by John Clarke, O.C.D. Washington, D.C.: ICS Publications, 1977.

──────. *Poetry of St. Thérèse of Lisieux.* Translated by Donald Kinney, O.C.D. Washington, D.C.: ICS Publications, 1996.

──────. *The Prayers of St. Thérèse of Lisieux.* Translated by Aletheia Kane, O.C.D. Washington, D.C.: ICS Publications, 1973.

──────. *Story of a Soul.* Translated by John Clarke, O.C.D. Washington, D.C.: ICS Publications, 1976.

Valabek, Redemptus, O.Carm. *The Beatification of Father Titus Brandsma.* Rome: Carmelite Institute, International Center, 1986.

──────. *Mary, Mother of Carmel.* 2 vols. Rome: Carmel in the World Paperbacks. Carmelite Institute, International Center, 1988.

──────. *Prayer Life in Carmel.* Rome: Carmelite Institute, International Center, 1982.

Wermers, M. *Prof. Dott. Tito Brandsma.* Fatima: Edicoes Carmelitanas, 1959.

ILLUSTRATIONS

Mount Carmel priory. An anonymous seventeenth-century portrait of Saint Teresa of Avila. From Silvano Giordano, O.C.D., *Carmel in the Holy Land* (Arenzano, Italy: Messagero di Jesus Bambino di Praga, 1995).

122 Saint John of the Cross. Loano. Mount Carmel priory. An anonymous seventeenth-century portrait. From Silvano Giordano, O.C.D., *Carmel in the Holy Land* (Arenzano, Italy: Messagero di Jesus Bambino di Praga, 1995).

131 Christ Crucified. A drawing by Saint John of the Cross. From *The Collected Works of St. John of the Cross,* translated by Otilio Rodriguez, O.C.D., and Kieran Kavanaugh, O.C.D. (Washington, D.C.: ICS Publications, 1979).

150 Saint Mary Magdalen de'Pazzi. 1566–1607. Carmelite Mystic. From *A Year with the Saints,* by a member of the Order of Mercy (Rockford, Ill.: Tan Books, 1988).

162 Father Cyril of the Mother of God. From *The Infant Jesus of Prague*, revised by Ludvik Nemec (New York: Catholic Book Publishing, 1986).

166 Adoration Chapel. Blessed Katherine Drexel Hall. St. Patrick's Church, Carlisle, Penn. Henry Treffinger.

168 Ascending Mount Carmel. Cover of *A Commentary on the Rule of Life. OCDS.* Drawn by Peggy Wilkinson, O.C.D.S. Washington, D.C.

172 God is Love. Saint Teresa Margaret. From *God Is Love: St. Teresa Margaret—Her Life,* by Sister Teresa Margaret, D.C. (Milwaukee, Wis.: Spiritual Life Press, 1964). Permission granted by the Institute of Carmelite Studies, Washington, D.C.

182 The sixteen martyrs of Compiègne. On a prayer leaflet encouraging prayer for the canonization of the martyrs. Vice-postulator for the cause of canonization of the

Blessed Carmelite Martyrs, Carmel of Compiègne (Carmel of Compiègne, France).

185   Statue kissed by the martyrs of Compiègne before dying on the scaffold. From *To Quell the Terror,* by William Bush (Washington, D.C.: ICS Publications, 1999).

188   Francisco Palau. From *Francisco Palau* (Rome: Carmelite Missionaries, 1988).

190   Saint Raphael Kalinowski. From *Saint Raphael Kalinowski: An Introduction to His Life and Spirituality,* by Szczepan Praskiewicz, O.C.D. (Washington, D.C.: ICS Publications, 1998).

194   Saint Henry de Osso. From *The Power of the Priesthood: A Life of Father Henry de Osso,* by Marcelo Gonzalez, D.D., Archbishop of Barcelona (San Antonio, Texas: Society of St. Teresa of Jesus, 1971).

198   Sister Mary of Jesus Crucified. Mariam "The Little Arab". Carmel in the Holy Land. Photo by Messagero di Jesus Bambino di Praga, © 1995.

230   Saint Thérèse of the Child Jesus and the Holy Face. In the courtyard of the Lourdes Grotto between September 14, 1894, and February 5, 1895. From *The Photo Album of St. Thérèse of Lisieux,* with commentary by François of Sainte-Marie, O.C.D. (Allen, Texas: Christian Classics, 1995). Illustration © Office Central de Lisieux.

288   Blessed Elizabeth of the Trinity. After her veiling. About January or February 1903, in the garden of the monastery. From *Light, Love, Life,* edited by Conrad de Meester, O.C.D. (Washington, D.C.: ICS Publications, 1987).

302   The three martyred Carmelites of Guadalajara. From *Del Carmelo al Calvario: The Three Martyred Carmelites of Guadalahara,* by the Carmelite Nuns of Salford, England (Rome: General Postulation, 1986).

306   Sister Teresa Benedicta of the Cross. 1938. Passport
      photo taken before she left for Holland. From *Aunt
      Edith: The Jewish Heritage of a Catholic Saint,* by Susanne
      Batzdorff (Springfield, Ill.: Templegate Publishers,
      1998).

313   Edith Stein. 1926. From *Aunt Edith: The Jewish Heritage
      of a Catholic Saint,* by Susanne Batzdorff (Springfield,
      Ill.: Templegate Publishers, 1998).

324   Blessed Titus Brandsma. A painting by the artist
      Stephen Andrew Titra in the 1980s. It was blessed by
      Pope John Paul II and displayed at many of the events
      for the beatification of Blessed Titus. From *The Beati-
      fication of Father Titus Brandsma, Carmelite,* by Redemp-
      tus Valabek, O.Carm. (Rome: Carmelite Institute,
      International Center, 1986).

336   Père Jacques de Jésus Bunel. Shown with his students at
      Avon. From *Père Jacques: Resplendent in Victory,* by
      Francis Murphy (Washington, D.C.: ICS Publications,
      1998).

342   Saint Teresa of Jesus of the Andes. The official canoni-
      zation picture by the Chilean artist Gonzalo Correa.
      From *Letters of Saint Teresa of Jesus of the Andes,* by
      Michael Griffin, O.C.D. (Washington, D.C.: ICS Pub-
      lications, 1994).

346   Saint Teresa of Jesus of the Andes as a young woman.
      From *Letters of Saint Teresa of Jesus of the Andes,* by
      Michael Griffin, O.C.D. (Washington, D.C.: ICS Pub-
      lications, 1994).

INDEX OF CARMELITES